God's Solution
for
Depression, Guilt
and
Mental Illness

by
Colin D. Standish
and
Russell R. Standish

Published and Distributed
by
Hartland Publications
Box 1
Rapidan, Virginia, U.S.A.

Hartland Publications
A Divison of Hartland Institute
Box 1, Rapidan, Virginia 22733-0001, USA

Previously entitled Family Crisis—God's Solution
First printing, December 1984
Second Edition, June 1994
Third Edition, August 2002

ISBN 0-923309-22-7

God's Solution
for
Depression, Guilt
and
Mental Illness

by
Colin D. Standish
and
Russell R. Standish

Contents

Section 1 -- Spiritual Issues

1 From Secular to Christian Psychology / 7
2 Mental Health and Spiritual Growth / 14
3 Mental Health and Character / 20
4 Personality and Individual Differences / 26
5 Love and Mental Health / 31
6 Law and Love / 38
7 The Problem of Guilt / 44
8 Negative Emotions / 51
9 Conflict and Frustration / 59

Section 2 -- Therapy

10 Encounter and Sensitivity Groups and Christianity / 69
11 Mind Control and Hypnosis / 74
12 The Perils of Counseling / 80
13 Christian Therapy / 86
14 Success and Failure / 91
15 Motivation / 102
16 Habituation / 109

Section 3 -- Physical Factors

17 The Senses / 118
18 Diet / 124
19 Mental Health and Legal Drugs / 130
20 Physical Factors in Mental Health / 136

Section 4 -- Developmental Factors

21   The Prenate and the Infant / 145
22   Childhood / 150
23   Adolescence and Independence / 158
24   Adolescence and Decision Making / 163

Section 5 -- Marital Issues

25   Morality and Sex / 169
26   Homosexuality / 179
27   Preparation for Marriage / 186
28   Marriage and the Family / 194

Conclusion / 201

Appendixes -- Theoretical Issues

A   The Nature of Man / 203
B   Choice and the Will / 211
C   Mental Health and Creation / 217
D   Theories of Personality and Individual Differences / 224

Glossary / 6
Scriptural Index / 226
General Index / 229

Glossary

ambiversion	having characteristics of both extroversion and introversion
aversive	painful or uncomfortable
counselee	one who is receiving counseling
hyperbolizing	exaggerating or greatly emphasizing, using hyperbole
maladaption	poor or inadequate adaptation
monism	the view that there is only one kind of ultimate explanation of a truth
narcotic	a soothing or numbing agent (does not coincide with the legal definition of narcotic drugs in U.S.A.)
neonate	a newborn babe to the age of one or two months
noninhibitory	counseling which sets no restraints on the one counseled
Ockham's razor	(also Occam's Razor) A rule stating that entities should not be multiplied needlessly, meaning that the simplest of two or more competing theories is preferable and that the unknown should be first explained in terms of the known.
parsimony	using the briefest, most economical explanation of things, events or phenomena, see Ockham's razor
prenate	a human being from comception to the time of birth
valence	the ability to unite, or combine with, in an acceptable way
ultimacy	an idea carried to its logical conclusion

1

From Secular to Christian Psychology

IT seems only proper that authors dealing with what is potentially a controversial field should give some explanation of where they are coming from, in an attempt to orient the reader to the philosophic bases they espouse. Our intrusion into the field of mental health was certainly less than orthodox. There has never been a time when we have had an overwhelming fascination for the study of psychology, and our direction toward a psychological emphasis evolved slowly. Indeed it would be fair to say that our own heritage was such that we would not have anticipated moving into it as a university program.

We were born in the Australian city of Newcastle, which at the time was without a university. Our parents were deeply committed Christians, but no members of our family on either side had ever completed high school.[1] However, it was our parents' deep Christian commitment that first gave us an interest in human behavior and its relationship to conversion and salvation.

After completing a two-year teacher training course at Avondale College in Australia, and teaching elementary school for three years, we proceeded to the University of Sydney. At that point our great interest was in history. Our main desire was to obtain a major in history with a purpose of teaching history at the high school level. Because of financial limitations we undertook our degrees as evening students and found that the

---

1. In the 1930s in Australia, only one percent of Australians received more than nine grades of education. Following the British system of education, the Australian educational system is based on the concept that only superior students are entitled to 12 grades of education. Thus even today the majority of students receive no more than 10 grades of schooling. In the economic depression of the 1930s even bright children were deprived of a full high school education.

only way we could fit in three subjects toward the Bachelor of Arts degree was to study history, English, and either psychology or philosophy.

Because we had received a smattering of psychology during our teacher training education at Avondale College, we elected psychology as our third subject. Ironically, we both did considerably better in psychology than we did in history. This success, we believe, was not due to any special aptitude in psychology, but rather to the system undertaken at the University of Sydney, where much more class work was required for psychology than for history. Thus, in the press of our being evening students, history had to be put aside for the more demanding requirements of psychology.[2] Both of us were invited to join the honors class in psychology. Within the provisions of the University of Sydney, only those invited because of their first-year performance in a particular subject could join the honors class in that subject. It meant quite a different approach for both of us, because in Australian tertiary (higher) education only those fulfilling a special honors course were eligible to graduate with honors.

This requirement entailed greatly increased academic work over and above that taken for a pass major—in the second year probably fifty percent more than for a major, and maybe seventy-five percent in the third year, and an additional final year dedicated to the major (in the case of psychology this year included two sizeable theses: one empirical and the other theoretical).

While we were able to complete our history major, Colin's direction was set toward the field of psychology by the fact that, at the University of Sydney, a student is required to be an honors graduate or have an honors equivalent before proceeding into a doctoral program. Now, with a vision fired with doctoral aspirations, he continued in the direction of psychology, eventually completing his Ph.D. in 1964. Russell developed an interest through the study of psychology and went on to complete his medical degree, also in 1964.

However, it must be emphasized that Colin's doctorate was not in the field of clinical psychology, but in experimental psychology. Since he was trained in the precise, tough-minded tradition of men such as Clark

---

2. A second factor involved is that, curiously, we both misread a major essay question in the final history examination paper. Since the year's result was based entirely upon that single examination, it was a minor miracle that we passed it at all, since 50–67 percent of students were failed in each course of B.A. degrees at the first-year level.

Hall and Kenneth Spence, the emphasis was never upon practical applications, but more upon the contributions to theory building. It was obvious that the stimulus-response emphasis with its deterministic underpinnings[3] was at considerable conflict with our own Christian heritage built upon free choice. This conflict was increasingly resolved on the side of free will rather than for determinism.

During Colin's six years in pursuing graduate work at the University of Sydney, he taught in the Department of Psychology, but subsequently his teaching of psychology has been somewhat fitful. Accepting appointment back to his alma mater, Avondale College, and becoming chairman of the Education Department there, he undertook a program which involved the teaching of both psychology and education. When in 1970 he moved to Jamaica, West Indies, he taught very little psychology, becoming president of West Indies College for three years before moving to the United States in 1973 where he had been appointed chairman of the Psychology Department of Columbia Union College in Washington, D.C.

It was while home in Australia in 1973 that Colin very seriously reevaluated his own psychological bases. It seemed to him that he should first seek his own answers within the paradigm of Scripture and then, perhaps, make some comparison with the writings of other authors.

While in Australia he had the opportunity to talk with two Australian psychiatrist friends. One was home briefly from the United States where he had been conducting a strong community mental health program in the New England area. The other was a psychiatrist in Sydney. Colin, with these two friends, spent the morning dealing with the community mental health program of the psychiatrist who was revisiting Australia from the United States. This man was explaining to them the rather traditional program he was directing, built upon the principles of L.A.W.—*Love*, *Acceptance*, and *Worthwhileness*—and the use of community and family resources to help the patient. The longer they listened, the more the Sydney-based psychiatrist and Colin were convinced that something was dramatically wrong with the program, and this feeling was at least somewhat confirmed by the indication that results being achieved in the program were not commensurate with the effort and moneys expended.

---

3. See appendix entitled "Choice and the Will."

The program, which will be discussed later in this book,[4] seemed very logically built upon the assumption that mental illness is the result of the inadequacy of love and security in infancy and early childhood. Thus there is a need to establish love and security in the lives of these maladjusted people. Yet they were puzzled and not a little concerned about its failure to offer strong evidence of success. Their friend from the United States left the same afternoon, and they discussed further the implications of what they had heard.

Related to this question were the conclusions drawn from the time spent at the psychiatric hospital where the Sydney based psychiatrist had given eight years of service. After participating in large and small group therapy and individual interviews, Colin concluded that the programs were at best minimally productive. In the subsequent discussions, the Sydney psychiatrist and Colin came to the conclusion that the program was counterproductive in many cases. Rather than helping to formulate life patterns consistent with normally accepted behavior systems, the program indeed sometimes reinforced the unacceptable behavior of the patients.

In the latter part of 1973, as Colin traveled to the United States to take up his new appointment, he was unprepared for the cultural shock of being a psychologist in the United States. The dependency syndrome that he has come to recognize as a significant part of the way of life in a large segment of the American population was foreign to someone brought up in the Australian tradition. It appeared that the mental health of American youth and adults was tragically fragile.

He recognized that even among sections of Christians there was a major dependence upon fellow humans for psychological support. It seemed that many students were very insecure in spite of, or maybe because of, the freedom and non-inhibitory approaches to child and youth training, and that somehow the present generation of Americans had among the lowest level of security and individual self-esteem of any communities in the world. He was overwhelmed by the way in which he was inundated not only by students, but also by members of the community, seeking psychological counseling. It seemed to make no difference to them that his training and background were not in a clinical or counseling field.

---

4. See chapter entitled "Christian Therapy."

This situation led him to the examination of the home experiences that might lead to such large-scale group neuroses.

Although eight months after arriving at Columbia Union College he became president of the college, his interest and concern in this area were not lessened, and as subsequently he has accepted the challenge of pioneering the college programs at Weimar Institute and Hartland Health and Education Institute, he has continued broadening his understanding of God's plan in mental health. He has written a number of articles and has lectured widely in the area, and his contribution to this book arises out of the convictions that have developed especially during the last five years.

The second author, Russell, upon completion of his medical course soon discovered that a not inconsiderable segment of his practice involved dealing with the personal problems of his patients. While his medical training gave virtually no assistance in coping with such matters, patients nevertheless have considerable faith that their medical practitioners can assist them in finding solutions in these areas. Many situations encountered were very tragic indeed, and it became obvious that more than human wisdom was required in order to provide assistance. Russell's Psychiatry course undertaken during his medical training and the Psychology degree he had completed prior to his study of Medicine were of minimal assistance. Many patients had sought standard psychiatric assistance, without the least amelioration of their problems. This experience naturally resulted in further frustration and despair.

When, in 1967, Russell was appointed to Malaysia, he found that the tensions of modern living were equally as severe there as in Australia. True, some of the problems were caused by different social customs, but their bases were identical. Clinical experience subsequently in the United Kingdom and Thailand has confirmed the universality of human discontent and misery. Indeed it became apparent that a major portion of the people in this world live an existence totally bathed in unhappiness. With untold millions, this condition is unrelated to physical deprivations.

Faced with the urgent needs of his patients, Russell was compelled to restudy God's plan for mental health. It was obvious that His plan differed substantially from the secular solutions which have been offered. Russell discovered that suicide rates, for example, have increased since the discovery of antidepressant drugs. Sedatives and tranquilizers have played quite a minor role in assisting unhappy people, and in some cases have added to the person's burdens in a way not too dissimilar from the use of alcohol. It was only in God's Word that Russell found the formula for the peace "which passeth all understanding." (Philippians 4:7)

The whole premise of this book is that God is interested in every phase of man's life. Not only is He interested in the spiritual bases of man's life, but also in his physical and emotional health, and thus, within the Holy Scripture must be found those principles which above all else will lead to a healthy emotional state and consequent happiness. God created the mind and established its functions based upon immutable laws governing man's intellectual, emotional and behavioral development. It must therefore be confidently assumed that in His Word are revealed to man those laws by which true happiness, contentment, and peace of mind may be achieved. It is further assumed that Satan has a counterfeit to God's simple mental health principles. This counterfeit is based upon premises that are at least in part incompatible with biblical principles. The Bible labels it "science falsely so called." (1 Timothy 6:20)

It is obvious that those who suffer from deep mental disturbances cannot adequately fulfill their spiritual commitments. The simple trust, the peace that alone comes from a unique relationship with Jesus Christ cannot be achieved by the fearful, the anxious, nor the deeply disturbed. But God's Word gives hope for such persons. The prophet Malachi assures us that to those who fear the name of God "shall the Sun of righteousness arise with healing in his wings. (Malachi 4:2)

And so this book is offered as a preliminary investigation by one psychologist, and one internist, to those who are sincerely seeking God's answers to mental health.

The state of uncertainty in psychiatric care can be gauged by the fact that currently there may be as many as two hundred identifiable forms of psychiatric therapy, all vying for acceptance. Further, there is a rapid intrusion of the occult, and eastern mysticism, into the area of psychiatric healing. Surely the time has come for Christianity to declare what it offers for both the prevention and the cure of emotional illness. That modern psychiatry has been amazingly inept in coping with the international mental health dilemma is clear from the increase in mental illness and the high rate of re-institutionalization of those supposedly cured in psychiatric hospital wards. In the United States, where there are presently close to thirty thousand psychiatrists, pastoral counselors, educators, clergymen, physicians, and others attempting to confront the massive spread of psychosis and neurosis, the much-muted voice of Christianity needs to be heard declaring what the Word of God has to say that will reestablish an emotionally balanced society. The opinion of half a century ago, that man could soon solve the mental illness problem, has all but vanished. It is therefore time to give God the opportunity to show what emotional strengths can be achieved by following the principles of His Word.

The Christian certainly has a basic concept of mental health, and this volume unashamedly searches for God's answers independent of most current theorizing. It is not likely that non-Christian psychologists and psychiatrists will agree with many of the concepts enunciated here, yet it is believed that considerable advances in the field of mental health could be achieved if these very same principles were employed even by the secularist. However, the complete evaluation of their success can come only when both counselor and counselee seek earnestly to implement them in the power of Christ..

2

Mental Health and
Spiritual Growth

VERY few things are more important or more highly valued than mental health. The implications of mental health upon the total experience of life is such that none can escape its relevance to his own life-style. A human being, though always a unified whole, is manifested through the physical, the intellectual and the spiritual facets of his being. Chronologically in the history of human life we develop first physically, then intellectually and finally spiritually. At conception we begin our physical pilgrimage, capable of growth and development at a very rapid rate through cell multiplication. Long before birth, man becomes an intellectual being—that is, a being capable of monitoring some of his environmental influences. However, the last development, the spiritual dimension, becomes apparent only in postnatal life.

It is quite obvious that without the physical there could not be the intellectual being, for the mental or intellectual capacities of man are dependent upon the physical growth of the organism and especially upon the development of the brain and the nervous system. Further, man cannot be a spiritual being until the intellectual capacities have developed significantly. These three, throughout life, become very strongly interdependent upon each other. It is not just a one-way reaction, but it is a multiphasic reaction in which each interacts with the other. Unless there is sound intellectual development and mental health, it is impossible to have the kind of spiritual life that God provides for humanity, just as it is impossible to have the fullest development of the other capacities without all three being uniformly developed.

Accepting that every worthwhile principle of right living is embodied in the Word of God, the Christian should recognize that a sound mind is a gift from God. Millions are facing the chronic problems of mental illness to the extent that the incidence of mental illness is greater in the present generation than it has ever been. In some way the complexities and structures of modern life, the pressures, the strains, the tensions, the stresses are resulting in larger numbers succumbing to the tragedy of mental breakdown. This stress is even evident within the ranks of Christians. Thus in honesty Christians must address themselves directly to the problem of mental breakdown and the increasing inability of many to function adequately in the home. This inadequacy in turn leads to marital problems and the breakdown of home relationships. The spectacle of mental health problems in the Christian church has led many to attempt to deny a relationship between a sound Christian life and sound mental health, but such attempts deny the unity of man and the provisions of God for man.

A sound mind does not necessarily mean the ability to be academically outstanding. Yet there is no question that Christians have an obligation to individually determine truth from error and to be careful students of God's Word. But a sound mind is more than this. It is a clear and tranquil mind, able, by the power of God, to comprehend and face even the sternest pressures. The question is not so much the kind of tensions, or tension-inducing problems that are faced, because frequently there is little control over these. For example, the wife who has a drunkard for a husband often finds it very difficult to control that aspect of her life, but she nevertheless has the opportunity, by divine power, to control the kind of reaction and relationship she has to the pressure and tension-inducing situation with which she is constantly confronted. Those who have succumbed to mental breakdown or who experience numerous neurotic incidents are frequently under little more pressure in their lives than a great number who are living well-adapted lives. Sometimes the pressures to which they have yielded are even less than those surrounding well-adjusted persons.

Of course we are confronted with two basic problems here. Biologically, some people are born with predispositions to greater or lesser tolerances to strain and stress. Second, the environmental circumstances of others, especially during their infancy, childhood and adolescence also play a key role in the kind of ability that they have to face stress-inducing situations in later life. Nevertheless, the Lord has promised that there is no temptation (trial) that will be experienced for which He will not give the strength to surmount.

> There hath no temptation taken you but such as is common to man:
> but God is faithful, who will not suffer you to be tempted above that
> ye are able; but will with the temptation also make a way to escape,
> that ye may be able to bear it. 1 Corinthians 10:13

This promise can be accepted by every committed Christian both for spiritual and emotional tests. It is perhaps one of the greatest promises in all of Scripture, for though humanly it is probable that all have breaking points, God here promises that it is impossible to be placed under tension and stress that cannot be handled when one is strengthened and secured by Him. This promise does not deny that there is great variation in tolerance to stressful situations, but it does offer the assurance that either Christ strengthens man's weakness or that He will preserve us from those situations which are beyond our capacity to handle. Perhaps this assurance is encompassed in Paul's declaration:

> But we have the mind of Christ. 1 Corinthians 2:16

Much of the issue of functional mental illness depends upon who is in control of the mind. If not Christ, then Satan is in control, and he seeks in many ways to precipitate emotional breakdown and take possession of the minds of men and women. This control successfully limits God's restoration in human lives. Thus total submission to Christ spiritually is the surest security against emotional breakdown. God has a plan for the spiritual health of humanity which is also invigorating to man's mental and physical health.

The mental health of every Christian is bound up individually with his spiritual growth. God's true children will have sound minds and will be emotionally able to cope with every condition in the strength of Christ.

The mind requires discipline if it is to reach its full potential. Such discipline requires a confrontation with inherent human tendencies. As the human mind breaks from the shackles of the confinement of its inborn self-centeredness through communion with God, there is an expansion of the mental perceptions of man. As the mind is disciplined, the will is brought into unity with the will of God so that the image of God is more perfectly reflected in man. Such maturing processes reduce the fluctuation in moods so that there is less dependence upon amusements for excitement as a response to difficulties or depression. As man, through a responsive study of God's Word, recognizes the infinite price paid for his salvation, he cannot devalue himself. A right response to Christ is the basis of self-respect and is a most successful antidepressant.

The problem of sin is at the root of emotional instability. The basis of sin is both inherent and environmentally learned, and through no other means than the power of the Holy Spirit in the life can temptation be successfully overcome. Obedience to God is freedom from the tyranny of sin. This obedience is possible only with divine power. Any attempt to overcome the emotional results of sin by human support is destined to be inadequate, or at best of transitory value. A pure and holy life is best suited to the development of sound emotional health. Modern trends to ignore sin or excuse it have had devastating emotional repercussions. Part of the basis for the denial of sin is the desire to avoid the guilt implied in recognition of sin. But for the converted Christian, the recognition of sin is accompanied by the recognition of Christ as Savior, the One able to remove guilt from the repentant sinner. Christ does not ask man to overcome in his own strength, but offers His infinite strength and victorious life as the basis of man's confidence for success. As man accepts the power of Christ, Satan has no power.

The role of prayer is vital in the resistance to sin. Each morning there must be a recognition of one's inability to live a successful life free from sin; one must call upon Christ to appropriate His power for victorious living. Neglect of prayer leads to reliance upon one's self or other fallible humans, which in turn leads inevitably to failure. Too often those who do not respond to their conscience feel a compulsion to trample upon the conscience of others. Or alternatively, in justification of gross moral aberrations, they look for evil in others, a futile means of self-absolution.

Faith, the support of the true Christian, is developed only by the constant studying of God's Word and exercising a positive response to the love of God. Faith accepts at face value the promises of God, which leads to obedience to God's laws. Faith rests the future with God, allowing Him to lead in ways that reject anxiety or uncertainty. Paul declared:

The just shall live by faith.   Romans 1:17

Perhaps there is no greater expression of the essence of faith than that of beleaguered Job:

Though he slay me, yet will I trust in him.   Job 13:15

Job surely demonstrated that faith does not depend upon feelings nor circumstances. Faith develops with each successful conflict with doubt. The fuller and more secure the relationship with Jesus, the more enduring will be the trust. It was as a consequence of such a relationship that Paul could affirm,

> I know whom I have believed. 2 Timothy 1:12

Trust in God is the basis of the fullest development of Man. Paul declared:

> Ye are complete in him. Colossians 2:10

Christ Himself gave a gracious invitation:

> Come unto me, all ye that labour and are heavy laden, and I will give you rest. Matthew 11:28

God encourages dependence upon Him, man's only true security, while Satan encourages dependence upon man. While it is good to fellowship and counsel together, it is unwise for man to be dependent upon, or controlled by, other human beings, and indeed such dependence is counterproductive to consistent human development. Self-esteem, independence, and worthwhile pursuits are established upon a selfless relationship between God and man. The well-balanced person has neither a too-high nor too-low estimate of himself, and is so secure in his relationship to God and his fellow human beings that his own self worth is not a conscious matter of concern.

The greater percentage of disease has its basis in wrong thinking. It includes neurotic and many psychotic responses to environmental stress, the simple tension headaches, as well as much of the more serious digestive tract diseases such as ulcers, and potentially fatal conditions such as heart disease and strokes. But it extends far beyond this category to diseases that are life-style related—to poor dietary habits, lack of physical exercise and poor rest patterns. Each of these can be changed first by an intelligent understanding of profitable habit patterns and then by a choice to follow what is best. By far the best prevention, and often best cure for such diseases, is related to reversion to a simple life style.[1] But health extends beyond this. There are physical and emotional conditions that can be cured only by trust in God. For many, the gospel of Christ is the only creative agency for their broken minds and bodies. God is the source of happiness and joy. Thus true happiness can come only to those who have an irrevocable relationship with Him.

---

1. See chapters 18, 20 entitled "Diet" and "Physical Factors in Mental Health."

INTERRELATIONSHIP OF THE
VARIOUS FACETS OF MAN

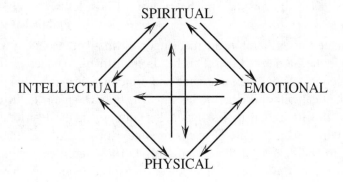

3

Mental Health
and Character

WHEN man was created, he was created perfect, yet all his capacities were capable of development. Man was created to share the divine mind, and this goal is still Christ's object for man.

> Let this mind be in you, which was also in Christ Jesus.
>
> Philippians 2:5

The same claims therefore are made upon the mind of man today as were made in the Garden of Eden. This fact is not difficult to understand when one recognizes that the same aims and principles of man's total growth are identical with those before his fall. The only change is in the conditions—the limited capacities of man, his failures, and the deterioration of his environment. In spite of man's limitations, God provides emotional strength and health for those who seek it. These are attainable in their fullest degree only when divine power transforms the limited capacities of man. Such power is necessary for all who seek God's blessing.

> Be ye transformed by the renewing of your mind, that ye may prove what is that good, and acceptable, and perfect, will of God.
>
> Romans 12:2

It will be noted that true spiritual growth and transformation of character start in the mind. "Be ye transformed by the renewing of your mind." One common approach to human needs, affecting education, prison reform, treatment of the mentally ill, and almost all facets of life, is based upon the previously discussed principles of behavior modification.[1] Here the whole basis of behavioral change is built around the restructuring of the

---

1. See appendix A entitled "The Nature of Man."

responses of the person according to the kind of values the counselor considers to be good, as opposed to those considered to be unproductive or bad. Yet this approach seems inconsistent with God's program of restoration. True restoration does not result from a simple restructuring of behavior, but can be effected only by the transforming power of the Divine. The Bible refers to this transformation as the new birth.

> Jesus answered and said unto him, Verily, verily, I say unto thee, Except a man be born again, he cannot see the kingdom of God. Nicodemus saith unto him, How can a man be born when he is old? can he enter the second time into his mother's womb, and be born? Jesus answered, Verily, verily, I say unto thee, Except a man be born of water and of the Spirit, he cannot enter into the kingdom of God. That which is born of the flesh is flesh; and that which is born of the Spirit is spirit.   John 3:3–6.

When the mind is transformed to do the will of God, there is a concomitant transformation in behavior patterns.

Character is more than reputation. This truth is certainly evidenced in the life of Christ. Jesus' low reputation with the Jewish leadership[2] contrasted with the only unspotted character in the history of the world. Character details the thoughts, the feelings and the motives, as well as the behavior of man. Only God can truly evaluate character. Reputation is man's subjective evaluation of the behavior of fellow humans. Motives and thoughts may be judged, but they can never be ascertained accurately.

The development of character is a lifelong challenge and can be validated and evaluated only by the perfect standard that God has outlined in His moral law, and thus is normally independent of reputation. There is frequently great conflict when good reputation rather than good character becomes the motive for human action. The seeking of human approbation results inevitably in compromise and in wrong actions, even should the source of the approbation be good men. Should the behavior be even "good," the motivation which seeks human approval is egocentric and therefore inconsistent with the pure motives of God. When one seeks to please God and man at the same time, the resultant conflict can be very severe. If the choice made is to follow God contrary to the expectations of

---

2.   See John 18:29–30.

man, the resulting criticism often causes great mental anguish. However, should a wrong course be chosen to placate human demands, emotionally destroying guilt follows. The Christian must realize that he will be criticized for doing right and he will be criticized for doing wrong. If he has committed his life fully to Christ, he will determine that any criticism he receives will be only for doing right, recognizing that such vocal and vehement criticism comes from those who themselves are uncommitted to divine principles.

True character cannot be developed independent of a total commitment of the life to God and His way, irrespective of the consequences. It cannot be achieved by human effort alone, though this must be exerted, but results from the power that Christ alone can impart. The emotional security resulting from such a singular following of God's leading has its basis in a self-image that supersedes human approbation.

The response to conscience is central to the development of character. While the conscience is the guiding force for life, it is not necessarily an infallible guide. Paul clarifies this thought when he refers to having a conscience void of offense:

> And herein do I exercise myself, to have always a conscience void of offence toward God, and toward men. Acts 24:16

He further refers to other types of impaired consciences:

> Howbeit there is not in every man that knowledge: for some with conscience of the idol unto this hour eat it as a thing offered unto an idol; and their conscience being weak is defiled. 1 Corinthians 8:7

> Speaking lies in hypocrisy; having their conscience seared with a hot iron. 1 Timothy 4:2

Paul also recognized the presence of a pure conscience:

> Now the end of the commandment is charity out of a pure heart, and of a good conscience, and of faith unfeigned. 1 Timothy 1:5

> Holding the mystery of faith in a pure conscience 1 Timothy 3:9

It must be accepted that a good conscience is one educated by the Word of God and under the enlightening influence of the Holy Spirit. Such a conscience is a trustworthy guide, the Holy Spirit faithfully monitoring the environmental influences according to the paradigm of the law of God. Once established, a reliable conscience warns of impending moral danger and temptation, with its threat of concomitant spiritual and emotional loss. Yet one's own conscience must never be used as a basis for judging others.

True character is not inherited. It results from a choice to accept a growing relationship with Christ. After the fall of man, such a choice would have been impossible, had it not been that God Himself had extended His grace to man, enabling him to choose to resist Satan.

> And I will put enmity between thee and the woman, and between thy seed and her seed; it shall bruise thy head, and thou shalt bruise his heel. Genesis 3:15

As the character involves the totality of man's being, including actions, words, thoughts, feelings and motives, it cannot be developed by a process of conditioning nor by the imposition of another's will. It requires an overt choice to permit divine power to transform the life. If that choice is not made, the life remains in bondage to Satan. Man can never give himself to God, but he can invite God to take his life and do for him what he cannot do for himself.

Man, unlike the animals, is governed by God's moral law. God has created man's mind with the capacity to discriminate between right and wrong, and His law to define right and wrong. The power of choice must be constantly exercised for right, if emotional strength is to be developed. For just as there is an unbreakable connection between sin and emotional difficulties, so there is an indivisible link between emotional strength and moral purity. Mankind, weighed down with the burden of sin, can find relief from anxiety only when Christ's positive principles of living actuate the life. A disregard of God's law is the primary basis of human misery in the world. An unregenerate life leads to distrust of self which is evidenced by distrust of God and distrust of others. Such is the basis of much anguish to oneself, as well as to others.

As has been stressed earlier, motivation is the true basis of character. Paul defines the three primary motives of the converted Christian as faith, hope, and love, with love having primacy in this trio.

> And now abideth faith, hope, charity, these three; but the greatest of these is charity. 1 Corinthians 13:13

Love is the motivation that determines the heavenly value of an act. This love is of heavenly origin, and can be the principle of human motivation only when Christ has been permitted to plant that love in the life. A truly fruitful character is one in which the love of Christ is the basis of all behavioral activity. This love was defined by Christ when He prayed—

That ye love one another; as I have loved you.   John 13:34

In the delivery of the sermon on the mount, Christ exposed a further facet of this love in what is now referred to as the golden rule:

Whatsoever ye would that men should do to you, do ye even so to them.   Matthew 7:12

As the Holy Spirit effects a new life within, one's motivation becomes less self-centered and more responsive to the needs of others. There is, associated with this growth, an increase of contentment and happiness which cannot result from following natural inclinations. True Christians are happy above all others on earth; and no matter what one professes, unhappiness, restlessness and anxiety reveal a lack of commitment of the life and a motivation which is untransformed. The converted person has allowed his natural independence to be replaced by a childlike submissiveness and a teachable spirit. The sign of true selfless submission is expressed in the words of Saul of Tarsus at his conversion:

Lord, what wilt thou have me to do?   Acts 9:6

Christ, Himself, demonstrated the same selfless dependence upon His Father when He exclaimed,

Not as I will, but as thou wilt.   Matthew 26:39

Christ came to the earth to demonstrate that such surrender is the basis, not only of perfection of character, but of peace and happiness.

Moral character cannot be developed to its finest level without careful attention to physical and mental laws. Carelessness in physical habits results in carelessness in moral character. Without a careful monitoring of the physical laws, including diet, exercise and rest, the moral forces automatically subserve the self-indulgence of the natural man.[3] The results are similar if the mind is not carefully monitored from dwelling upon that which is trivial or morally polluting.[4] The strong person is one who restrains passion and controls every facet of his life. Uncontrolled passion and temper are the result of undiscipline, and are indicative of character weakness.

---

3. See chapters 18, 20 entitled "Diet" and "Physical Factors in Mental Health."
4. See chapter 17 entitled "The Senses."

Character development may be equated with the biblical principle of sanctification. It centers around the conquest of self. This growth in holiness is a lifelong battle. It rests upon a daily submission of the will to Christ. At no time can man continue in holiness without this daily commitment. Jesus sanctifies, that man might rise above the failure of yielding to temptation. He has promised,

> A new heart also will I give you, and a new spirit will I put within you; and I will take away the stony heart out of your flesh, and I will give you an heart of flesh.   Ezekiel 36:26

Yet this new heart can be retained only by a daily fellowship with Jesus. Each victory over temptation strengthens right principles[5] and makes further right choices easier. The emotional satisfaction resulting from each temptation resisted is of inestimable value to the mental health of the person. Thus character development not only is necessarily prerequisite to salvation, but it also provides the greatest fulfillment in our present life.

---

5. See chapter 16 entitled "Habituation."

4

Personality and
Individual Differences

IT becomes clear that while there is a definite interrelationship between personality and character, personality is not character and character is not personality.[1] Personality can best be defined in terms of the totality of the characteristic behavior patterns of a person including his thoughts, emotions, behavioral responses, temperament, his appearance and any other distinctive patterns which distinguish him as a unique individual. On the other hand, character deals with the response to God's immutable law, involving the motives, thoughts, words and actions. It is very possible for a man to have a pleasing personality, while his character is yet greatly defective. For example, many confidence tricksters have had winning and very persuasive personalities which have, at least to a large measure, effectively masked their characters.

Yet we must not overlook the fact that some personality characteristics are more consistent with character development than are others. For example, the temperament of a person has much to do with determining both the personality and the character. An anxious, reactive person has obvious character defects needing to be transformed by the grace of God. The response to the talents and gifts that each one has, while also partly determining the personality, greatly affects the development of the character.

It is almost axiomatic to say that there is a wide range of different personalities among fully committed Christians. In the twelve apostles, different personalities are portrayed. Obviously John was a man of great love and compassion, having developed especially the softer graces, though

---

1. See Appendix D entitled "Theories of Personality and Individual Differences."

at times he had been volatile. On the other hand, Peter was aggressive, impetuous to the point of rashness, and very quick to verbalize his convictions and beliefs. After their conversion many of these characteristics remained, but under the transforming power of Christ these positive characteristics were directed toward the challenge of spreading the gospel commission to the ancient world. This transformation can be seen even more clearly in the personality of the apostle Paul. Prior to his conversion, Paul (or Saul, as he was then known) was an aggressive leader, strongly committed to the cause he espoused, fearless of the consequences of his actions.

> As for Saul, he made havock of the church, entering into every house, and haling men and women committed them to prison.   Acts 8:3

> And Saul, yet breathing out threatenings and slaughter against the disciples of the Lord, went unto the high priest, and desired of him letters to Damascus to the synagogues, that if he found any of this way, whether they were men or women, he might bring them bound unto Jerusalem.   Acts 9:1–2

The same Paul, after his conversion, retained the same aggressive leadership personality characteristics, but now they were directed toward extending the kingdom of Christ rather than destroying it.

> And straightway he preached Christ in the synagogues, that he is the Son of God. . . . But Saul increased more in strength, and confounded the Jews which dwelt at Damascus, proving that this is very Christ. . . . But Barnabas took him, and brought him to the apostles, and declared unto them how he had seen the Lord in the way, and that he had spoken to him, and how he had preached boldly at Damascus in the name of Jesus.   Acts 9:20, 22, 27

Extremes in personality need to be addressed when there is a response to the claims of Christ upon the life. The extremely shy, withdrawn, unsociable person, while perhaps never becoming a leader, realizes that he needs a redirection of his personality, so that he may more effectively and more frequently witness to the faith he now espouses. Thus it is not surprising to recognize major changes in the intersocial relationships of some who allow the power of the Holy Spirit to transform their lives. Similarly, for those who have extreme personality characteristics in the opposite direction (whose extroversion may be exhibited in roughness of personality, crudeness, insensitivity to others' feelings), there will be a seeking for the modifying power of the Holy Spirit so that they may be an offense to none as they share their new-found faith.

In the fullest sense of our understanding of individual differences, we cannot accept the dictum, "All men are created equal," for there are vast differences acknowledged in the Word of God between the number of talents men have, and the quality of each of those talents. In the parable of the talents[2] Christ explained that different men were given different talents. But it is also important to note that the discrimination in terms of the value of each of these individuals was not in terms of the number of talents that each had. The man with five talents was commended for doubling them, with the words:

Well done, thou good and faithful servant.   Matthew 25:21

The same words were also used to commend the man with two talents who had doubled his talents. The man with one talent was rejected, not because he was inferior in ability to the other two men, but because he did not use his single talent. This parable gives a clue to the sense in which all men are created equal. Though they vary in intelligence and in aptitudes and later in achievements, their acceptance and equality before God depend upon their response to the opportunities that He places before them. This fact is seen when we understand that in God's reckoning of man He takes into account the totality of his background. Man is judged, not according to his absolute performance, but according to his response to the opportunities that have been laid before him. David pointed out that God in His reckoning of man takes into account where he was born.

The LORD shall count, when he writeth up the people, that this man was born there.   Psalm 87:6

Further, he points out that God knows the frame of His people and makes allowance for the fact that they are but dust.

For he knoweth our frame; he remembereth that we are dust.
          Psalm 103:14

A just and all-knowing God will reward every man according to every opportunity to which he has responded.

The individual talents that God has given, while allowing for a wide range of personal fulfillment, are given so that man may be able to live as

---

2. See Matthew 25:14–30.

a complement to his fellow man. The diversity of personalities and gifts allows for a unique interdependence of every member of the human family upon each other member. It allows for the opportunity for all to serve others. It allows the strengthening of one another and confirms that no man can live adequately unto himself. Thus the great bond of Christian cooperation is endowed with the diversity of talents and gifts that God has provided. But for these gifts to be a blessing, they must be used for the benefit of others.

> As every man hath received the gift, even so minister the same one to another, as good stewards of the manifold grace of God.
>
> 1 Peter 4:10

Every purpose of God can be fulfilled as man cooperates with man, motivated by the Holy Spirit, to fulfill His purpose. Surely this is the demonstration that the Christian church makes to the world; this demonstration in which, as a corporate body, the unity of purpose and the fruitfulness of cooperative extension of God-given talents, results in a miniature preview of the unbroken cooperation of God's children subsequent to their redemption. Paul particularly defines the diversity of gifts:

> And he gave some, apostles; and some, prophets; and some, evangelists; and some, pastors and teachers; for the perfecting of the saints, for the work of the ministry, for the edifying of the body of Christ: till we all come in the unity of the faith, and of the knowledge of the Son of God, unto a perfect man, unto the measure of the stature of the fulness of Christ. Ephesians 4:11–13

> But the manifestation of the Spirit is given to every man to profit withal. For to one is given by the Spirit the word of wisdom; to another the word of knowledge by the same Spirit; to another faith by the same Spirit; to another the gifts of healing by the same Spirit; to another the working of miracles; to another prophecy; to another discerning of spirits; to another divers kinds of tongues; to another the interpretation of tongues: but all these worketh that one and the self-same Spirit, dividing to every man severally as he will. For as the body is one, and hath many members, and all the members of that one body, being many, are one body: so also is Christ.
>
> 1 Corinthians 12:7–12

In so doing, he emphasizes that the diversity of these gifts is given—

for the perfecting of the saints, for the work of the ministry, for the edifying of the body of Christ: till we all come in the unity of the faith, and of the knowledge of the Son of God, unto a perfect man, unto the measure of the stature of the fulness of Christ.

Ephesians 4:12–13

But there are two ways in which these gifts to man may be perverted. The first is by failing to employ them, thus allowing the gift to atrophy. The second is by developing and using them for self-seeking purposes. It is not difficult to see how the gift of oratory, of administration, of music, of healings, of teaching, or any other of the gifts, could be perverted to self-centered and therefore Satan-controlled purposes. Only when these gifts are under the guidance of the Holy Spirit, do we see the result of their use in the fruit of the Spirit:

Love, joy, peace, longsuffering, gentleness, goodness, faith, meekness, temperance.   Galatians 5:22–23

Individual differences may be seen to represent the graciousness of God as, on the one hand, He gives talents that we may be able to show our appreciation to Him by serving our fellow man; and on the other, to help in the realization that none of us has been provided with such an array of talents that we are not dependent upon others for the supplementation, complementation and enhancing of our own lives.

Paul summarizes it beautifully in the love chapter:

Though I speak with the tongues of men and of angels, and have not charity, I am become as sounding brass, or a tinkling cymbal. And though I have the gift of prophecy, and understand all mysteries, and all knowledge; and though I have all faith, so that I could remove mountains, and have not charity, I am nothing. And though I bestow all my goods to feed the poor, and though I give my body to be burned, and have not charity, it profiteth me nothing. 1 Corinthians 13:1–3

Here is the total basis for the development and extension of the distinctiveness that God has given to each one of us. As this distinctiveness is shared in love, it blesses both the sharer and the receiver beneficiary.

5

Love and
Mental Health

LOVE enters into almost every facet of human life. All want to be loved, but few appear to be sure that they are loved. Generally the more frustrated one has been in the past, the more frustrated he is in the present. Do all have a right to be loved? And if so, how can one really be sure whether the love is genuine?

These and many more questions are running through the minds of a large segment of society. Some of the best answers are provided in the following basic facts:

1. All are born with a tendency to sin.

> In sin did my mother conceive me. Psalm 51:5

Thus all have a basic disposition to walk in pathways that alienate from God.[1] The natural unconverted tendency of all mankind is to develop a pattern of living inconsistent with eternal life.

2. This alienation is due to egocentricity, or selfishness, and is demonstrated in the self-centered acts of the infant, who, as soon as he is able to coordinate his actions, tries to grab everything to himself, often failing to perceive those things that might be harmful.

3. Because selfishness is at the base of all human motives, self-love dominates, and true love for others is relatively rare. To many this realization is disconcerting.

4. Selfishness provides the basis for most emotional problems, and is at the base of functional mental breakdown—that is, mental breakdown

---

1. See appendix A entitled "The Nature of Man."

not due to a physical cause. For example, many schizophrenics, unwilling or unable to relate to the real world, turn inward, living in the world of their own make-believe. The paranoid is concerned that people are out to "get" him. This is the classical persecution complex. The megalomaniac has an insane lust for power. The masochist injures himself, often in a way which draws attention and possibly sympathy to himself. The hypochondriac becomes physically ill because of his inward turning. Even those suffering depression are often overly concerned with what others, especially members of their own families, have done to them. Perhaps there is no more self-centered act than suicide, where a person, believing that his life has been meaningless, or that he has been mistreated or rejected, decides to end his own life. There seems rarely to be any thought on the part of the suicide that he has been created to address the needs of others.

Typical of the situation is the patient whom one of the authors treated at the Prince of Wales Hospital in Sydney. He was brought in, struggling and screaming, by two large policemen. He had deep cuts to both wrists and it was the author's duty to suture these while the two policemen only partially succeeded in restraining his violent movements. This patient continually screamed out, "She doesn't love *me*!" His emphasis was continually upon the last word of the sentence.

5. No one can force another to love him. Many attempt to gain love by force, but often the greater the attempt to force the love of another, the less it is reciprocated.

6. Nowhere does the Bible ever suggest that men should expect to be the recipient of the love of others.

7. Many times in the Word of God there is the exhortation to love others; it occurs at least twelve times in the New Testament alone. Instances include Matthew 22:39; Romans 13:9; Galatians 5:14; James 2:8.

8. This love for others involves both love to God and to fellow human beings.

Perhaps here is the first principle of being loved. To be loved by others we must show ourselves loving. Wanting to be loved is natural. Wanting *to* love is not natural. Thus many find it very difficult to love others. Yet true Christian love is the best prevention against mental illness, frustration and despondency. The person who is concerned about whether others love him is egocentric and therefore unhappy. It is true that in later life this passion to be loved often has something to do with early childhood experiences, for those who come from homes where love has not been demonstrated nor experienced tend to crave love much more in their adolescence and in later life. Often this craving is like a bottomless pit—there is no way to satiate it.

By far the most productive approach to the "unloved" is to help them learn how to love others. It is not easy, for, as previously stated, the natural inclinations of man are against it. For the "unloved" there have often been many years of habituation in a direction of self-will, toward self-gratification and self-love. Very often associated with self-love is self-pity. This feeling is one of the most dangerous expressions of self-love, for it offers an excuse and basis for maladaptive behavior. It is inevitably self-destructive.

As explained later,[2] the Word of God sees fear as an opposite of love. Fear comes from feelings of inadequacy, feelings of not being wanted, and feelings of insecurity. But the one who moves out in love for others, lightening their burdens, sharing their concerns, less and less will remain in the morass of his own introspective problems. It is virtually impossible to extend oneself in love without its being reciprocated by at least some of the recipients of that love.

Perhaps the two least effective ways of dealing with discouragement and despondency are to brood over problems in some place of isolation, or to recount the problems to others. The first "solution" only accentuates the isolation, the loneliness and the self-pity experienced by the depressed one, without offering a constructive solution for the problem. This turning inward leads to physical, intellectual and spiritual weakness. The second tends to reinforce the feelings of frustration, often validating them and exaggerating them with each sympathetic hearing. By centering on self we feel much worse than we really are.

The two most effective ways of dealing with despondency and discouragement involve praising God, and moving out to others, thus avoiding the results of introspective isolation on the one hand and the reinforcing effects of the constant recounting of one's own problems on the other.

---

2. See chapter 6 entitled "Law and Love."

The first involves a relationship with God. By recounting God's blessing, by literally lifting one's voice in praise to Him, a power otherwise unknown to man is available to him. In this way, recognizing the matchless love and concern of God for us, our own problems seem to diminish rather than to escalate. The second involves outreach to someone who is in greater need than we ourselves are, beginning to extend ourselves to that person in such a way that he or she will be helped. Soon the despondency and discouragement will be lifted. It is often not easy for one to change into this pattern, for the discouraged person finds it most difficult to move out of himself. It will take perseverance, but the results will be tremendously rewarding.

Love in its truest sense is also at the root of self-image. In the highly competitive society in which we live it is very difficult to seek that selfless outreach for others. We are trained to compete with people, excel over others, rejoice at our virtues and successes. But the Bible says:

> It is more blessed to give than to receive.   Acts 20:35

If self-image depends upon strength, speed, skills, academic achievements, career advancements, and similar values, the vast majority would be losers; and in this world no one wants to be a loser. Love, on the other hand, makes us deaf to criticism and insults, and blind to the weaknesses of others, as well as accepting of our own limitations.

Psychologists and psychiatrists spend much time trying to establish the self-image, especially of the adolescent, but also of many of those in older life. Often this is done by trying to establish in the mind of the one counseled his areas of success and of worthwhile achievement. But such an attempt is doomed to failure, for the human ego is insatiable. The Word of God has the only effective remedy—dying to self. At first this thought seems contrary to the whole theme of self-image. How can a dead self produce self-esteem? Paul put it this way:

> I die daily.   1 Corinthians 15:31

But on further investigation it will be seen to be the only possible way of gaining self-image.

Is it any wonder that there is such low self-esteem when modern society is teaching the constant defense of self-image? It is easy to be bitterly hurt by every criticism, by everyone who outperforms us or does better than we, by those who do not like our ideas, by those who are more popular than we, or by those who are promoted over us. Thus our love and emotional security can become invincible only when we crucify self and follow the humble pathway of Jesus. Then, and only then, is it impossible to be hurt. Sharing the love of Jesus, knowing that He loves us and that we are children of God and joint-heirs with Christ, establishes the only firm and secure self-image a human being can have.

> The Spirit itself beareth witness with our spirit, that we are the children of God: and if children, then heirs; heirs of God, and joint-heirs with Christ; if so be that we suffer with him, that we may be also glorified together. Romans 8:16–17

It is impossible to be hurt emotionally when we are dead to self.

The death of self is rarely an attractive alternative; but it is the foundation of peace and contentment. It is the basis of Paul's counsel to esteem others better than ourselves:

> Let nothing be done through strife or vainglory; but in lowliness of mind let each esteem other better than themselves. Look not every man on his own things, but every man also on the things of others.
> Philippians 2:3–4

But man is not left to battle self alone. Christ is man's ever-constant Helper, and His selfless life, when contemplated daily, is a firm basis for turning the mind from self-gratification. As faith in Christ develops, it works by love to purify the soul of all selfishness.

> For in Jesus Christ neither circumcision availeth anything, nor uncircumcision; but faith which worketh by love. Galatians 5:6

Pride, selfishness and covetousness are not only self-destructive; they are also an offense to God. With Christ's help man may be led step by step to look away from self to reflect the laws of love which contain the very principles of God's kingdom. Those who have the least thought for self are closest to the kingdom of God. This self-renunciation surely underpins the counsel of Christ:

> If any man will come after me, let him deny himself, and take up his cross, and follow me. Matthew 16:24

It is in the light of these principles that much concerning trade unions and civil rights movements is destructive. Such movements tend to center upon self-seeking, and though directed at redressing social evils and injustices, they frequently generate hatred, mistrust and physical violence.

It is often better to suffer physically than to suffer the spiritual losses that negative emotions generate.

Yet the true Christian will not be unmoved by the oppression of the underprivileged of society. It is his responsibility to do all in his power to relieve the oppressed and to seek the redress of social ills. But the motivation to help others is productive of Christian growth, whereas self-seeking is counterproductive. Love for others eradicates strife and division.

Love cannot long exist without expression, whereas fear holds back expression. Love is manifested by kind words and actions, whereas fear is afraid of rejection and therefore recoils from positive extension to others. The rewards of loving others are reinforcing, benefiting not only the recipient but also the giver. Real happiness comes from doing good and being good.

Human love is always a reflection of God's love. John expresses it in relationship to man:

> Behold, what manner of love the Father hath bestowed upon us, that we should be called the sons of God.   1 John 3:1

> Herein is love, not that we loved God, but that he loved us, and sent his Son to be the propitiation for our sins.   1 John 4:10

Jesus came to settle once and for all the verity of God's infinite love and to disprove beyond any doubt the falsity of Satan's claim that God is selfish. In doing so, He provided for us an example in selfless love for others.

RELATIONSHIP OF FUNCTIONAL MENTAL ILLNESS TO EGOCENTRICITY

CAUSE

FUNCTIONAL MENTAL ILLNESS

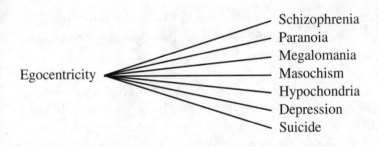

Egocentricity
- Schizophrenia
- Paranoia
- Megalomania
- Masochism
- Hypochondria
- Depression
- Suicide

MENTAL HEALTH

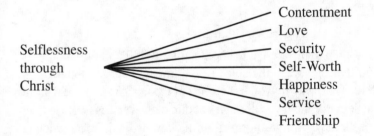

Selflessness through Christ
- Contentment
- Love
- Security
- Self-Worth
- Happiness
- Service
- Friendship

6

Law and Love

IN the ways of God, law and love are inseparable Siamese twins. To separate one from the other inevitably destroys both. The legalists have tried to separate them, but in so doing they destroyed the very essence of the law, which is love. The antinomians have tried to separate them, but love outside the context of the law is meaningless. Love without law is like a ship with a rudder, just as law without love is like a rudder without a ship.

There is no way we can love our parents and be persistently disobedient to them, any more than we can love our country without keeping inviolate its laws. Neither can we love God without keeping His commandments.

If ye love me, keep my commandments   John 14:15

In justifying their indifference to the details of God's commandments, many claim that they keep the spirit of the law without the letter of the law. But there is no way in which the spirit of the law can be kept without keeping the letter of the law, although of course it is very possible to keep the letter of the law without the spirit of the law, as Paul meant when he said,

Who also hath made us able ministers of the new testament; not of the letter, but of the spirit: for the letter killeth, but the spirit giveth life.   2 Corinthians 3:6

However, to pretend to keep the spirit of the law while breaking the law is, in effect, to make the law of no consequence. In 1951, students attending Avondale College were permitted to leave the college campus to go to the village one mile away only on certain days. The purpose of this rule was to ensure that young men and young women could not meet outside of the college campus, since men and women were allocated separate days. On one occasion the authors took the liberty of going to the village to transact some business on the women's day. When duly summoned before the discipline committee for this breach of college laws, we weakly attempted to defend ourselves on the ground that we kept the spirit of the law (since we met no young women during our visit) while breaking the letter. The discipline committee rather resolutely rejected our "defense," as was proper. Is it possible to disobey our parents and still keep the spirit of the fifth commandment? to kill and keep the spirit of the sixth commandment? to commit adultery and keep the spirit of the seventh commandment? or to steal and keep the spirit of the eight commandment? to break the Sabbath and yet keep the spirit of the fourth commandment, or to blaspheme the name of God and keep the spirit of the third commandment? Thus it is imperative to keep God's holy law to the letter. The keeping of the spirit of the law automatically assures that the law is kept precisely.

It was in the context of a broken law that God demonstrated His love to man:

> Where sin abounded, grace did much more abound.   Romans 5:20

The infinite love of God the Father and the condescension of His Son, leading to the Incarnation; the life and ministry of Jesus, the great sacrifice of Christ, and His redemption of mankind, demonstrated to all beings throughout all ages that indeed not only is the law an expression of the character of God, but that His character is also exemplified in love. Thus it is not surprising that all the commandments are based upon two great principles: love to God, and love to man.

> Jesus said unto him, Thou shalt love the Lord thy God with all thy heart, and with all thy soul, and with all thy mind. This is the first and great commandment. And the second is like unto it, Thou shalt love thy neighbour as thyself. On these two commandments hang all the law and the prophets.   Matthew 22:37–40

In the Garden of Eden a broken commandment brought fear to the fallen couple. Their feeble attempts to hide from God indicated that no longer did they have a trust and faith relationship with Him. To break the commandments of God is to break the love relationship with Him. John has very plainly put it this way:

There is no fear in love; but perfect love casteth out fear: because fear
hath torment. He that feareth is not made perfect in love.1 John 4:18

Paul also perceived this relationship:

For God hath not given us the spirit of fear; but of power, and of love,
and of a sound mind.   2 Timothy 1:7

A lack of love for God leads to the breaking of His commandments; a
failure to recognize the purity of the character of God leads to carelessness and indifference and to the justification of wrong acts. Too often
such justification leads to continued sin which inhibits the fruitful development of the person and often maintains the conflicting situation which
is destructive to mental health.

For all those who love God, there is a simple faith and trust in Him.
Just as the little infant expresses his love for his parents by an abiding
faith and trust in them, so those who love God express it by constantly
following His leading. Thus it is not surprising that the breaking of this
faith relationship inevitably leads to sin. It is in this light that the definitions of sin by Paul and John are rightly understood:

Sin is the transgression of the law.   1 John 3:4

Whatsoever is not of faith is sin.   Romans 14:23

If we do not keep the commandments of God it is because we do not have
a faith relationship with Him, and, conversely, if we do not have a faith
relationship with Him, it is impossible for man to keep the commandments of God.

Jesus Himself always taught love in association with keeping the letter of the law. In condemning the Pharisees as hypocrites He said,

For ye pay tithe of mint and anise and cummin, and have omitted the
weightier matters of the law, judgment, mercy, and faith: these ought
ye to have done, and not to leave the other undone. Matthew 23:23

Because the law is the foundation of God's government, the happiness of
mankind is dependent upon perfect accord with it. To many the law of
God is viewed as restrictive, but a recognition that these laws flow from a
God of infinite love will lead to a recognition that only in keeping these
laws can man have true emotional freedom. Thus an understanding of the
relationship of the unchanging law of God to true love is, perhaps, at the
basis of an understanding of Christian mental health principles.

Each desecration of God's commandments has its basis in egocentricity destructive of emotional health. Bearing false witness against a fellow human is motivated by avarice, desire for approval, personal ambition, self justification, or some other self-centered drive. Covetousness is clearly egocentric, as is stealing. It is also self-gratification and uncontrolled passion which lead to adultery; and murder is incited by such motives as hate, avarice and ambition for power. Parents are dishonored by self-willed children; and the Sabbath is secularized by those who have little time for God. Perhaps there is no more egocentric act than using the name of God blasphemously. It is also self-centeredness that leads to the placing of other "gods" before the God of heaven or "creating" gods to take the place of the great Creator of the Universe.

It is impossible to be happy and contented and to achieve fulfillment while love for self reigns supreme. This great psychological problem faces society today. It is not surprising then that eminent men have recognized this distortion. In his book, *Whatever Became of Sin?*[1] Karl Menninger, the renowned psychiatrist, quotes the famous late British historian, Arnold Toynbee:[2] "Science has never superseded religion. . . . Science has (also) begun to find out how to cure psychic sickness. So far, however, science has shown no signs that it is going to be able to cope with man's most serious problems. It has not been able to do anything to cure man of his sinfulness and his sense of insecurity, or to avert the painfulness of failure and the dread of death. Above all, it has not helped him to break out of the prison of his inborn self-centeredness into communion or union with some reality that is greater, more important, more valuable, and more lasting than the individual himself. . . . I am convinced, myself, that man's fundamental problem is his egocentricity. He dreams of making the universe a desirable place for himself, with plenty of free time, relaxation, security, and good health and with no hunger or poverty" (K. Menninger, *Whatever Became of Sin?*, p. 226). In commenting upon this analysis, Menninger says:

> Egocentricity is one name for it. Selfishness, narcissism, pride, and other terms have also been used. But neither the clergy nor the behavioral scientists, including psychiatrists, have made it an issue. The

---

1. Reprinted by permission of Hawthorn Books Inc.
2. Reprinted by permission of the Oxford University Press.

popular leaning is away from notions of guilt and morality. Some politicians, groping for a word, have chanced on the silly misnomer, permissiveness. Their thinking is muddy, but their meaning is clear. Disease and treatment have been the watchwords of the day and little is said about selfishness or guilt or the "morality gap." And certainly no one talks about sin. . . . Clergymen have a golden opportunity to prevent some of the accumulated misapprehensions, guilt, aggressive action, and other roots of later mental suffering and mental disease.

How? Preach! Tell it like it is. Say it from the pulpit. Cry it from the housetops.

What shall we cry?

Cry comfort, cry repentance, cry hope. Because recognition of our part in the world's transgression is the only remaining hope.

Ibid. pp. 226–227

In many ways this psychiatrist has summed up the challenge to Christianity today. The challenge is to recognize any attempt to separate law and love as destructive to human emotional and psychological development.

Now the end of the commandment is charity out of a pure heart, and of a good conscience, and of faith unfeigned.   1 Timothy 1:5

Christ's condemnation of the Pharisees came because they kept the letter of the law without the spirit of the law. The love that should have been demonstrated in judgment, mercy and faith was lacking in their ministry, but Jesus did not fail to indicate that they were right in paying a careful tithe. "These ought ye to have done," He said, "and not to leave the other undone." Thus it is the keeping of the *letter* of the law in the *spirit* of Christ that is essential. This principle is further demonstrated in the relationship between Jesus and the adulterous Mary Magdalene.

Neither do I condemn thee: go, and sin no more.   John 8:11

Here Jesus shows His love and compassion while also upholding the standards of His law.

John, the great apostle of love, puts it this way:

And this commandment have we from him, That he who loveth God love his brother also.   1 John 4:21

This verse, of course, is a restatement of the two great commandments, for the commandments and love are inseparably joined. There is no way in which we can claim to keep God's commandments and not love others. It is well to note that this verse is put in the positive sense. It is not sufficient not to hate, but in the positive, full sense of the word, we must love all God's children.

Adam and Eve demonstrated the flaw in their love by disobedience. There is a great need for parents to carefully train their children in obedience if they are looking for children who will have a loving, respectful relationship with God and man. A lack of love for others is the supreme sin.

He that loveth not his brother abideth in death.   1 John 3:14

Putting it another way, self-love is the supreme sin, for it is the antithesis of *agape* love. It is the supreme barrier preventing our love for others.

When love becomes a motivating principle of action, it transforms the character, controls behavior and influences interpersonal relationships.

7

The Problem of Guilt

MANY mental problems result from reluctance to accept as immutable, the commandments of God. The very close link suggested by Menninger[1] between values spiritual and moral on the one hand, and mental and emotional on the other, is a great challenge to the Christian community. When so many of the clergy have begun to see their role as counseling and caring for the social needs of the community, it may be that a cry like Menninger's is necessary to reorient the Christian ministry to its most important role, that of caring for the spiritual needs of the flock in a manner which, in turn, will have vital implications for the mental and emotional health of the community.

One of the most important areas reviewed by psychologists in recent times has been the area of guilt. For many years psychologists have inclined strongly away from the classical Christian view that guilt results from sin and the breaking of God's moral law, which in turn results in separation from communion with God. There have been many attempts to ignore guilt, to rationalize, it, to encourage a view of the guilt-inducing behavior which in turn will lead to a reduction, if not the elimination, of guilt. But the fact remains that if man had not sinned, he would not have experienced guilt and its resultant fear.

Perhaps no one has done more than Sigmund Freud to develop a notion of guilt differing from the traditional Bible view. He asserted, "The sense of guilt is, at bottom, nothing else but a topographical variety of anxiety, in its later phases it coincides completely with fear of the super-ego." (Freud, Sigmund, *Complete Works*, ed. Strachey, vol. 21, p. 135)

---

1. See chapter 6 entitrled "Law and Love."

It is therefore refreshing to read the kind of appeal that Menninger has made, in which he rediscovers the rightful role of the church in the handling of guilt. The Bible asserts that guilt has its source in sin, which is the breaking of God's commandments. In fact, within the commandments themselves is a clear indication of this fact, for in the third commandment we are told the consequences of violation of this precept:

> Thou shalt not take the name of the LORD thy God in vain; for the LORD will not hold him guiltless that taketh his name in vain.
>
> Exodus 20:7

Both the Old and the New Testaments further confirm that sin and the breaking of God's law result in the guilt of the lawbreaker.

> Then it shall be, because he hath sinned, and is guilty, that he shall restore that which he took violently away, or the thing which he hath deceitfully gotten, or that which was delivered him to keep, or the lost thing which he found.   Leviticus 6:4

> For whosoever shall keep the whole law, and yet offend in one point, he is guilty of all.   James 2:10

The burden of sin with its restlessness and unsatisfied desires is the primary basis of guilt. This burden can never be lessened by excusing sin. While man continues in sin, it is impossible for him to come back from condemnation and despair. Only when sin is confessed and forsaken does he have true peace and happiness.

No amount of effort to ignore or to rationalize can in any way eradicate the experience of guilt. So it is that many who have sought to do just that have failed. In fact, it is certain that the Christian has the only valid way to eliminate guilt, by the submission of his life to the love of Jesus. The Word of God assures us:

> If we confess our sins, he is faithful and just to forgive us our sins, and to cleanse us from all unrighteousness.   1 John 1:9

Here is the real answer to the eradication of guilt from the life. This fact is reaffirmed in the Old Testament, where we are assured that our sins will be cast into the depth of the sea and are promised that as far as the east is from the west, so has He removed our transgressions from us.[2] Coming to Jesus leads to a new relationship in which guilt can no longer have do-

---

2. See Micah 7:19 and Psalm 103:12.

minion in the life. Paul confirms that victory in Christ results in the elimination of guilt.

There is therefore now no condemnation to them which are in Christ
Jesus, who walk not after the flesh, but after the Spirit. Romans 8:1

It seems that the Christian behavioral scientist has a vital role to play in lending his influence toward the recognition that the only way in which guilt and its effects can be eradicated is through an acceptance of the merits of the saving grace of Jesus.

Too often guilt has been viewed as counterproductive to sound human development. But there is a vital role for guilt in the experience of every human being. Guilt is more frequently the internalized reaction resulting from doing that which separates from God. Such feelings should lead to God and to the Source of true forgiveness, and hence the elimination of those guilt feelings. Here alone is the real answer to the massive psychological problems faced by those whose lives are guilt-ridden.

Christians, above all others, have opportunity to help men and women to understand the best way to handle guilt and to deal with the emotional results of inadequate responses to guilt. Further, as they refer their acquaintances to the basis of right and wrong, they will provide a foundation for them to discriminate between guilt which is the direct result of sin against the law of God on the one hand, and those guilt-inducing behavior patterns which have nothing more than home or societal bases. Also they have the opportunity to precisely define between temptations and sin so that the temptation is not equated with the yielding to temptation.

It seems likely that in Freud's effort to reduce what he saw as the undesirable effects of the inhibitory process of society, and to handle repressed fear, he in fact has succeeded in leading many to stifle conscience and repress guilt feelings. Thus many are less able to handle their guilt than ever before, which in turn is making dramatic inroads into the mental health of the community. Inherent within the message of Christ is the basis of true mental health. Paul's counsel, "For God hath not given us the spirit of fear; but of power, and of love, and of a sound mind" (2 Timothy 1:7) is relevant here. It is certain that the religion of Christ is the first basis for emotional adjustment, for only as man comes into a meaningful relationship with God can he develop his emotional and mental powers according to the divine purpose.

The problem of guilt is another area closely allied to problems of self-image. Many feel a lack of self-worth, a lack of identity and a lack of awareness of their specific role in life, and therefore the tendency is to suffer considerably from emotional conflict. Christ again has the basic answers to low self-esteem and low self-worth. While it is true that the Bible stresses—

For all have sinned, and come short of the glory of God

Romans 3:23,

As it is written, There is none righteous, no, not one. Romans 3:10,

All our righteousnesses are as filthy rags Isaiah 64:6,

For without me ye can do nothing John 15:5,

—yet the whole purpose of Christianity is to develop self-worth of mankind. When man was created, he was created in the image of God, but when sin engulfed the whole world, the image of God was well nigh obliterated. The purpose of the ministry of Christ and of the Holy Spirit for mankind is the restoration of the image of God in man.

As we come to Christ, we develop a new concept of self-worth. As the penitent believer recognizes that all heaven was paid in the sacrifice of Christ, that he might have eternal life, he begins, at least in part, to recognize the great worth that God has placed upon him. The fact that we are called to be sons and daughters of God and joint-heirs with Christ leaves no place in the thinking of the Christian for low self-esteem.[3]

A feeling of worthlessness should not be confused with pride, for pride has its roots in human self-exaltation and achievements based upon the person's own performance. But the true worth of the Christian is a recognition, not of what the person is, but of what Christ has done for him. Thus Christ, not self, is the center. It is essential that the emphasis be upon the great worth that God has placed upon every soul. The fact is that in every human being, Jesus saw unlimited potentialities.

This recognition will not bring complacency, but will bring a challenge as men and women seek to reflect in its fullness the beauty of the image of Jesus. Such a man or woman can no longer be tormented with feelings of self-worthlessness and uselessness, for such a one has an undimmed vision of the magnitude of what Christ has wrought for his life

---

3. See chapter 5 entitled "Love and Mental Health."

and what can be further accomplished through Him. He appropriates the promises of Jesus:

> My peace I give unto you: not as the world giveth, give I unto you.
> Let not your heart be troubled, neither let it be afraid.   John 14:27

The mature Christian has a peace which can be achieved by no other relationship than with Christ. The Lord promised that He will—

> bless his people with peace.   Psalm 29:11

This peace of mind is achieved when that unique relationship between man and God is attained, so that self is completely subjected and Christ is allowed to reign supreme in the life.

> Thou wilt keep him in perfect peace, whose mind is stayed on thee:
> because he trusteth in thee.   Isaiah 26:3

Thus when all selfishness and all self-defensiveness is done away, restful peace results.

This relationship comes to those who have surrendered and submitted their life and their will to the Lord. It comes as man realizes the freedom gained through obeying the law of God.

> Great peace have they which love thy law: and nothing shall offend
> them.   Psalm 119:165

This is the peace that all humans seek today.

All guilt should be laid at the cross of Christ. The erring, discouraged person can find pardon as he accepts the One who has promised to—

> save them to the uttermost that come unto God by him, seeing he ever
> liveth to make intercession for them.   Hebrews 7:25

Christ never disappoints the one who comes to Him. He gives pardon full and free. As man humbles himself, acknowledging his sin before God, true relief from guilt is obtained. But such confession of wrong requires the making right of disputes or injustices involving others.

> Therefore if thou bring thy gift to the altar, and there rememberest
> that thy brother hath ought against thee; leave there thy gift before
> the altar, and go thy way; first be reconciled to thy brother, and then
> come and offer thy gift.   Matthew 5:23–24

Obeying such counsel results in a freedom of human relationships that is richly rewarding.

At this critical time in history, when there is a breakdown of both moral and emotional structure within the community, the Christian church has to reassert its role and its true pulpit function, providing the masses a clearer understanding of the basis of true spiritual, mental, and emotional strength, which can come only through the power of Jesus. There has been a strong tendency for the preacher to move into the field of pastoral counseling. Basic to most techniques of counseling is an avoidance of any response which might impute wrong or moral judgment upon the individual being counseled. This attitude has frequently been translated into the pulpit presentation of the preacher. No longer are right and wrong clearly defined, and congregations are left to their uncertainty and sin. It is the preacher's God-ordained responsibility to present the word of truth so clearly that none will be in doubt as to the purpose of God in his life. True repentance is effected only when wrong is recognized. It is the minister's role to set before the people—

life and good, and death and evil   Deuteronomy 30:15

The Christian counselor has a similar responsibility.

Yet while seeking God's forgiveness of sin, the objective of Christian living is the resistance of temptation. Right doing is a wonderful medicine for a disturbed mind. Pure hearts, good health and sound minds are positively correlated. To continue to indulge in sins leads to the loss of self-respect, and to the perversion of principle and judgment. There is a great need to develop fruitful activities to preserve the purity of life. Aimlessness and idleness destroy self-respect and lead to great guilt. In the parable of Joshua the High Priest, the removal of the filthy garments prior to their replacement with the pure white robe is symbolic of the removal of sin from those who walk in newness of life.

And he shewed me Joshua the high priest standing before the angel of the LORD, and Satan standing at his right hand to resist him. And the LORD said unto Satan, The LORD rebuke thee, O Satan; even the LORD that hath chosen Jerusalem rebuke thee: is not this a brand plucked out of the fire? Now Joshua was clothed with filthy garments, and stood before the angel. And he answered and spake unto those that stood before him, saying, Take away the filthy garments from him. And unto him he said, Behold, I have caused thy iniquity to pass from thee, and I will clothe thee with change of raiment.

Zechariah 3:1–4

Thus the solution to the problem of guilt is the honest confession of sin, seeking the promised forgiveness of God and, by the power of Christ, forsaking the ways of sin.

Some argue that when the Christian sins he is not cast from God's family. God, like a human father, does not send His child away when he sins. Nevertheless, the fact is that sin is an indication that we have separated *ourselves* from the family of God.

Your iniquities have separated between you and your God.

Isaiah 59:2

Only a faithful God, through the sacrificial provisions of His Son, can restore that family relationship through forgiveness and power to overcome.

8

Negative Emotions

EMOTIONS and feelings, the affective dimensions of man, play a central role in human life, revealing and often dominating intellectual and cognitive forces. While it is not desirable that emotions supersede reason in decision making, neither is it beneficial when decisions are made on the basis of cold, calculating intellectualism. Emotions offer a fundamentally unique response to environmental stimuli while in turn they are largely the result of past environmental influences. Reason must therefore be aware of, and responsive to, emotional reactions, while yet never permitting itself to subserve emotions.

Emotions are educable. They can be directed either to foster a growing fulfillment in life or to cast heavy shadows of negative reactions upon life. Emotions themselves are neither good nor bad. Even positive emotions such as elation can have negative consequences, while at times some negative emotions, such as sorrow, can have beneficial outcomes. It is not physically advantageous to be in a state of heightened emotionality for extended periods of time, for both positive and negative emotions drain the body's resources. On the other hand, sorrow and grief, especially when resulting from one's own wrong actions or from abusive personal relationships, have a useful role in securing repentance and restoration.

Generally a state of contentment and serenity does not exhibit strong emotive responses. The well adjusted person does not experience frequent nor prolonged states of emotional excitability, negative or positive. Constant emotional turmoil has strong adverse results affecting both the physical and the spiritual dimensions of man. The relationship between strong emotionality and cardiovascular disease is well established. Many hyperemotive states result in sympathetic nervous system reactions, including the secretion of adrenalin, increased heart rate, increased breathing rate, sweating and the inhibition of digestive processes. Such constant stress reactions are highly productive of degenerative disease.

The effects of modern urban living tend to produce emotional stress, militating against the simple life most protective to human health. There is much therapy in uncomplicated country living, free from much of the excitement-inducing features of modern life. The entertainment media must take considerable blame for initiating and maintaining excessive heightened emotionality. To spend hours each day in the contrived environment of television drama must inevitably have a cumulative effect upon the emotional resources.

Further, the development of a highly competitive society has resulted in serious emotional tensions, competitiveness, and appeals to pride, anger, selfish ambition, bitterness and rivalry. Competitiveness dominates a wide range of life from schooling to sports to business pursuits, imposing an environmental hazard for most of life. Much can be achieved by developing the Christian attribute of cooperation, seeking those achievements which do not lead to loss to others, or to their hurt. Each has an influence upon the other. Cooperative attitudes and activities are helpful to all cooperating parties. Right thoughts and feelings are generated when we see our fellow humans as partners, not as rivals or enemies. Perhaps there is more than a little truth in the dialogue attributed to the British playwright, A. A. Milne—a noted pacifist. When asked if he did not agree that the wars of England were won on the playing fields of Eton and Harrow (two famous schools of England), he is said to have replied, "They were not only won there; they were started there."

The authors are well aware of the intense emotions which these "playing fields" can engender. Both were avid and successful sportsmen in their youth. Both captained the Sydney University Table Tennis Team in matches against other Australian universities and, indeed, after he had won the Combined Australian Universities' singles championship, Colin captained the Australian Universities' Table Tennis Team in its first international match against the Combined New Zealand Universities' team. We know full well that rather than being beneficial exercises, these matches became matters of great tension. We fully recall our bitter disappointment when we narrowly lost the Sydney University doubles championship final, and our heightened elation when on subsequent occasions we succeeded in winning this event and many others. But a more mature evaluation of that period leads us to admit that such activities did not bring us closer to Christ and to our fellow man. We are content that those days are now far behind.

While heightened constant positive emotions can at times have long-term adverse effects, such effects inevitably result when negative emotions persist. Most positive emotions such as courage, hope, faith, love, sympathy, and joy tend to strengthen the life forces, but they are usually dissipated by the negative emotions of grief, anxiety, fear, depression, hatred, jealousy, distress, enmity, and guilt. Negative emotions, by their debilitating consequences, affect the strength and reduce life's effectiveness. These results become more apparent in middle and later life.

Yet many negative emotions have positive connotations in a limited sense. Paul admonishes:

> Be ye angry, and sin not; let not the sun go down upon your wrath.
>
> Ephesians 4:26

Solomon says there is—

> a time to hate. Ecclesiastes 3:8

James indicates that we should be at enmity with the world:

> Know ye not that the friendship of the world is enmity with God? whosoever therefore will be a friend of the world is the enemy of God. James 4:4

And Paul counsels that we should—

> covet earnestly the best gifts. 1 Corinthians 12:31

Yet we can understand these negative emotions in a positive sense only as we recognize that each of these admonitions deals with the expression of such emotions outside the context of egocentricity. The anger referred to by Paul must represent a righteous indignation as when God's sacred name or institutions are being desecrated. Jesus expressed such anger when He cleansed the Temple.

> And Jesus went into the temple of God, and cast out all them that sold and bought in the temple, and overthrew the tables of the money-changers, and the seats of them that sold doves, and said unto them, It is written, My house shall be called the house of prayer; but ye have made it a den of thieves. Matthew 21:12–13

When Moses witnessed the children of Israel worshiping the golden calf, he expressed anger:

> And it came to pass, as soon as he came nigh unto the camp, that he saw the calf, and the dancing: and Moses' anger waxed hot, and he cast the tables out of his hands, and brake them beneath the mount.
>
> Exodus 32:19

Anger generated when injustice and cruelty are perpetrated upon fellow humans or animals may also constitute a proper expression of that emotion.

The hatred and enmity referred to by Solomon and James cannot be hatred for other human beings, for we are told to love even our enemies.

> But I say unto you, Love your enemies, bless them that curse you, do good to them that hate you, and pray for them which despitefully use you, and persecute you.
>
> Matthew 5:44

There is hatred that the Christian must develop for transgression of God's law. Peter writes in this sense when he directs,

> Let him eschew evil, and do good; let him seek peace, and ensue it.
>
> 1 Peter 3:11

In the context in which Paul is writing, coveting the best gifts refers to spiritual gifts to be possessed so that the greatest possible work can be accomplished in spreading the gospel of Jesus. In such a sense coveting has nothing to do with personal possessions or prosperity, but with a desire to better fulfill the purposes of God in the life.

However, it must always be admitted that the expression of most negative emotions emanates from selfish motives, and herein lies the danger both physically and spiritually. Those who are pure in heart are free from anger, jealousy and hatred toward their fellow men, and also are free from restlessness, discontent, uncertainty and boredom. It is almost inevitable that self-centered negative emotions lead eventually to depression and discouragement. Often vital and far-reaching decisions are made in this state of despondency. Such decisions must inevitably be poor choices, for Satan is the author of discouragement and every decision made in discouragement will be his decision. Because discouragement has its source in self-centered emotion, it is wise to withhold decision-making until a closer walk with Christ is secured, and the discouragement has been lifted.

Anger and hatred in their various manifestations are perhaps the most destructive emotions. The indulgence of anger opens the mind to Satan, allowing us to be partakers in sin. So serious is this emotion that John equated it with murder.

> Whosoever hateth his brother is a murderer: and ye know that no murderer hath eternal life abiding in him. 1 John 3:15

Jesus expressed serious eternal consequences for those who exhibit anger:

> But I say unto you, That whosoever is angry with his brother without a cause shall be in danger of the judgment: and whosoever shall say to his brother, Raca, shall be in danger of the council: but whosoever shall say, Thou fool, shall be in danger of hell fire. Matthew 5:22

Solomon wisely counsels that—

> A soft answer turneth away wrath. Proverbs 15:1

Hatred and revenge began with Satan, and were so strong that he did not stop short of taking the life of the Son of God.

> Then entered Satan into Judas surnamed Iscariot, being of the number of the twelve. And he went his way, and communed with the chief priests and captains, how he might betray him unto them.
> Luke 22:3–4

It was enmity born of pride which led Cain to murder his brother Abel,[1] and led King Saul to seek the life of David.[2] Malice frequently bears fruit unto death. No matter what might have stimulated the hatred, the expression or even the cherishing of hate places the hater under severe condemnation of guilt. Often hate and anger have their source in false or malicious accusation, and the hate is established in self defense. How much easier, wiser and more fruitful it is to leave our reputation to God! Rebuttal does not live down false accusations and may indeed fan them. It is far wiser to be silent when falsely accused than to suffer the negative consequences that are experienced by reprisals. In following our Pattern, Jesus, we can gain great spiritual and emotional benefit by silence.

> He was oppressed, and he was afflicted, yet he opened not his mouth: he is brought as a lamb to the slaughter, and as a sheep before her shearers is dumb, so he openeth not his mouth. Isaiah 53:7

---

1. See Genesis 4:3–8.
2. See 1 Samuel 18:6–11.

Fear and doubt are also successful weapons used by Satan to destroy man. Like all emotions, fear may be expressed in thoughts, words and actions. Fear has many potential causes, but there are few more likely causes than unbelief and sin. Doubt and skepticism normally result from a love and practice of sin. Those who express doubts concerning the existence of God, the love of God, or the saving grace of God in respect to their own lives, are almost always prisoners of sin. The dissatisfaction and discouragement of a sinful life inevitably lead to fear. Fear dominated Adam and Eve when they tried to hide from God after their sin.

> And the LORD God called unto Adam, and said unto him, Where art thou? And he said, I heard thy voice in the garden, and I was afraid, because I was naked; and I hid myself.   Genesis 3:9–10

Unbelief was the basis of the disciples' fear during the storm on the sea of Galilee.[3] That is why Paul declares,

> Whatsoever is not of faith is sin.   Romans 14:23

When doubt and fear are resisted, despondency is lifted and faith is strengthened.

There is no greater antidote for despondency than implicit faith and trust in God. Even for the hesitant and the doubting, a faltering trust can be strengthened. This fact is beautifully illustrated in the response to Christ of the father of the dumb son. Christ told him all things were possible to those who believe. With tears in his eyes the father cried out,

> Lord, I believe; help thou mine unbelief.   Mark 9:24

Christ was able to take this faltering faith and heal the son. Faith is strengthened by speaking often of the goodness and the power of God, especially recounting His blessings to us individually. It is particularly important never to speak doubt and gloom to others. Irrespective of feelings of hesitancy we must form the habit of thinking and acting as if our faith cannot fail. It was just such a faith which motivated Paul and Silas to pray and sing praises to God in prison at midnight after being severely beaten.[4] Worry and anxiety result from faithlessness, and both are emotional and physical destroyers. To have faith in Christ is to accept His invitation to cast our burdens upon Him.

---

3. See Mark 4:37–41.
4. See Acts 16:23–25.

Casting all your care upon him; for he careth for you.   1 Peter 5:7

Come unto me, all ye that labour and are heavy laden, and I will give you rest. Take my yoke upon you, and learn of me; for I am meek and lowly in heart: and ye shall find rest unto your souls.

Matthew 11:28–29

Trust in God must be maintained independent of feelings. God can never be blamed for distress and adversity. In fact, in response to conflict and trial, one's spiritual and emotional life can be strengthened as the faith principle becomes more and more meaningful.

Faith also offers the only true fortress against sin, because faith takes God at His word and follows it implicitly. This faith is in contrast to presumption which, knowing the same promises, ignores God's plans and ways, and attempts to fulfill them in men's way. In the life of Abraham both faith and presumption are clearly illustrated. Abraham demonstrated complete trust in God when God called him to leave the security of the affluent society of the city of Ur to travel to an unknown land.[5] On the other hand, Abraham tried to accomplish God's promise of a son and heir by taking his handmaiden Hagar as a second wife to bear him that son.[6] This course of action was presumption. True faith believes that God's word cannot fail, and though tested and tried, all may bask in the assurances of God's love and the certainty—

that all things work together for good to them that love God.

Romans 8:28

Man may not always perceive God's workings, but an unshakable faith in God's goodness and personal concern can uphold us in our times of greatest difficulties. The more we talk of God's love and the less we center on our trials, the greater will be our strength. Every day we are surrounded by the bounties of God's love, and a recognition of this loving care should dispel all doubts and fears. Rather than attempting to remove all difficulties, by turning to Jesus we are assured of the strength to overcome them. Often those who have been through the greatest trials and difficulties are able to bring the greatest comfort to those in need, and to offer the fullest assurances of God's love. And in so doing the comforter lifts any despondency he himself might have.

---

5. See Hebrews 11:8–9.
6. See Genesis 16:1–4.

Those who have surrendered their lives to the dominance of the love of God will be freed from the enslavement of self-centered emotions, with all their destructive side effects. Increasingly the dominant emotion will be love generated from a pure heart. The shadows will be lifted and the spirit brightened. The assurance of God's ever-present guidance will be the total basis for confidence to face the challenges of every day, no matter what their difficulty might appear to be.

9

Conflict and Frustration

THERE is almost no limit to the situations that can frustrate man, and, as if there were not enough real situations to frustrate him, he is often capable of devising imaginary situations motivated by fears, apprehensions, and anxieties, to accentuate his frustration. Frustration results when any circumstance, real or imagined, presents a barrier to our hopes, motives, ambitions, the satiation of our physical needs, social needs, or personal desires. Frustration normally results in negative and unpleasant feelings which assume many manifestations, and the debilitation of human potentialities consequently follows. These barriers may be broadly defined in three areas:

1. **Personal barriers.** Such barriers result from physical and personal limitations, including physical handicaps such as deafness and blindness; and barriers resulting from certain limitations: intellectual, educational, or measured by our abilities.

2. **Interpersonal barriers.** These barriers result from our social or interpersonal relationships. Such frustrations result when someone else is successful in obtaining the job we had wanted, or in marrying the young woman we were desirous of marrying, or from poor social relationships either at peer-group, subordinate, or superordinate level, or all of these.

3. **Physical barriers.** These factors result from environmentally produced barriers. For example, the farmer may receive too little rain at the right time or perhaps too much. Other illustrations include the frustration caused by a traffic snarl, or perhaps by a snowstorm when one is anxious to meet an appointment.

Experiments have shown that the causes of frustration are usually relative. For example, children tend to be happy with makeshift toys until they see the real ones. Adults in previous generations were pleased with a good wick lamp or a hot-coal iron or a good washing tub and scrubbing board or a large ice chest, but today few in Western society would be satisfied with any of these. This relativism is often determined by the society or subsocial group in which we live. The "keeping up with the Joneses" syndrome is a real and constant source of frustration to the majority of people. Often the pressure of frustration does not result from barriers in some overwhelmingly aversive situation, but rather from the buildup of pressures from little and frequent inconsequential happenings. Frustration is especially strong when we give in to self-pity, developing the "all the world is against me" attitude. There is a vast difference between human abilities to handle stressful and strain-inducing situations. Some have low tolerance to stress, others have high tolerance; but probably all human beings have a breaking point. Some with moderate tolerance to stressful situations may, during their lifetime, develop psychotic conditions because of the high degree and intensity of stressful situations to which they are subjected, while others with much lower basic resistance to stress may nevertheless proceed through life without any such psychotic incidences because they have not been subjected to constant and severe stressful situations.

Often frustration is defined in terms of conflicting situations which are divided into a number of different types:

1. **Approach-Approach Conflicts.** This type of conflict results when we are faced with a situation involving two or more mutually exclusive acts, both of which are expected to result in positive consequences. In everyday human experience this conflict could involve such incidences as, on a beautiful summer day wanting to go swimming at the beach or alternately driving into the cool of the mountains, or wanting to finish a special project while also desiring to visit and fellowship with friends.

In the Scriptures we see this approach-approach conflict in the tragic experience of the rich young ruler. He wanted to have eternal life, but also wanted to continue to love his riches. Thus both eternal life and a love for his riches had positive valences for him, and tragically he chose the latter.[1] On the other hand, two other men faced with choices similar to that of the rich young ruler, chose the road of eternal life. Abram chose to follow the leading and the direction of God to a land not even defined to him. And in so doing, he had to leave the positive valences of the comfort of his home in Ur of the Chaldees and the fellowship of his family and friends.[2] Also, Moses, when confronted with the positive valence of enjoying the pleasures of Egypt during his lifetime, chose rather the fellowship of God and His people.[3]

Usually approach-approach conflicts are readily resolved, yet they are significant not only in the ordinary pursuits of life, but also may have dramatic eternal consequences. Unquestionably the choices of Abram and of Moses led to a fulfillment the rich young ruler could never have achieved.

2. **Approach-Avoidance Conflicts.** These conflicts result when we face a decision, the result of which will have both positive and negative consequences. Thus, while reaching the goal will have desired results, there will also be undesirable results associated with it. This conflict can readily be exemplified in our physical activities. Perhaps we want the benefit derived from a cold shower but also want to avoid the negative sensation of coldness. Or we want the benefits of vigorous exercise, but want to avoid the pain of aching legs and heaving lungs.

In our spiritual life we also often face approach-avoidance conflicts. A typical example is recorded in the experience of the prophet Balaam. Balaam was offered huge wealth by King Balak if he would disobey God and curse the children of Israel. Balaam was moved by his avaricious desire to obtain the wealth, yet in so doing he faced the negative consequences of disobedience to God. Unhappily, Balaam was more strongly attracted by the wealth offered by King Balak.[4] Perhaps no better and more vivid example of approach-avoidance conflict can be discovered than in the experience of Jesus in the Garden of Gethsemane, when He prayed,

---

1. See Matthew 19:16–22.
2. See Genesis 12:1–4.
3. See Hebrews 11:24–27.
4. See Numbers, chapters 22, 23.

> O my Father, if this cup may not pass away from me, except I drink it, thy will be done.
> Matthew 26:42

Here Christ faced the awesome agony of bearing the sins of the whole world, dying the death of a lost man, and in so doing following the will of His Father, or alternatively turning away from such infinite responsibility and avoiding the trauma associated with His sacrifice. To the eternal gratitude of all God's children, Jesus chose to follow the will of His Father.

In most situations, approach-avoidance conflicts are more difficult to resolve and therefore are more likely to cause frustration, indecision and despondency, than are approach-approach conflicts.

3. **Avoidance-Avoidance Conflicts.** These conflicts result when we are faced with a decision that cannot be avoided, when either choice results in negative and painful consequences. This conflict is by far the most difficult to resolve. It is well exemplified in the experience of the child who is unhappy at home and is subject to frequent mistreatment. He has a choice of either running away—a consequence of uncertainty that he wants to avoid on the one hand, and yet staying at home means receiving severe and continual punishment. It can also be confronted in the decision faced in certain physical conditions where, perhaps because of serious cardiac problems, the life expectancy of a man is most uncertain, yet where the proposed operation is hazardous. This conflict is better understood in the experience of the Israelites fleeing from the land of Egypt. As they came to the Red Sea, they perceived the armies of the Egyptians in hot pursuit. Now they were faced with two consequences—both of which seemed negative. On the one hand was the impassable Red Sea in which they would surely drown, and on the other the Egyptians who would either destroy them or take them back into slavery. Humanly there was no possible way through this dilemma.[5] And thus it is with many avoidance-avoidance situations. There seem to be no suitable resolutions of the conflict. This impasse results in most intense frustration, which in turn often leads to many other negative manifestations such as aggression, anger, hatred, jealousy, depression, fantasy, vacillation, regression, and serious emotional breakdown. The avoidance-avoidance conflict is thus by far the most difficult to resolve. Of course there are many conflicts

---

5. See Exodus 14:10.

which have both double positive and negative valences which add to the complexity of human decision making.

The avoidance-avoidance conflict becomes even more critical in situations in which two evils are involved. The situational ethics philosophy has proposed many such choices in an effort to indicate that it is not possible for even a Christian to hold absolute moral values. Some of the classic examples given are as follows:

1. A passenger boat sinks. There are insufficient lifeboats to save all the passengers. Quickly a lifeboat is filled to safe capacity, yet many others in their desperate efforts to save their lives attempt to come aboard. But if they were allowed to do so, all would be lost, for the boat would not be able to support them. Therefore, it is "good" to choose the lesser evil of stopping others climbing aboard so that some of the sunken ship might be saved.

2. It would be good to tell a lie if that were necessary to prevent someone from being killed.

3. It would be good to commit adultery if in so doing, one could save one's own life or the lives of others.

On February 11, 1971, at San Diego State College, Professor Joseph Fletcher debated Dr. John Warwick Montgomery on the issue of situational ethics.[6] Fletcher supported the situational ethics postulate. After defining **legalists** as those who were bound by unchanging principles which would include the law of God, and **antinomians** as those who lived without principle, he proposed what he inferred was an in-between posture— **situationism** in which he claimed that there are typically right things to do. However, he refused to accept an absolute standard of right, claiming that the only first-order value is agape love. Thus adultery can sometimes be better than chastity, lying than truthfulness, stealing than respecting private property. In all decisions, the end justifies the means, for in situationism there are no normative moral principles.

On the other side, Montgomery argued for absolute values, demonstrating some of the dangers to be faced in situationism. However, Montgomery stopped short of denying that sometimes we are forced to do a

---

6. J. Fletcher and J. W. Montgomery, *Situational Ethics*, Bethany Fellowship Inc., 1972.

lesser evil to avoid a greater evil. But unlike Fletcher, who argued that such action would be good because it was the best thing that could have done under the circumstances, Montgomery argued that should such wrong be performed, it was indeed still wrong and needed the forgiveness of God.

Neither Fletcher nor Montgomery has a complete answer for Christians confronted with difficult moral decisions. It is true that the non-Christian may not infrequently find himself in those circumstances in which he may have to choose between two evils, but is that true of the Christian?

While it is possible that sometimes Christians are faced with situations where both consequences are wholly undesirable,[7] and that would be examples of avoidance-avoidance conflict, it is inconceivable that God would allow His children to be placed in a conflict which would demand that they break God's commandment or do evil. While He allows His children to be severely tested, never will it be beyond the capacity of such a one, in the power and strength of Christ, to overcome the temptation to violate God's law.

> There hath no temptation taken you but such as is common to man: but God is faithful, who will not suffer you to be tempted above that ye are able; but will with the temptation also make a way to escape, that ye may be able to bear it. 1 Corinthians 10:13

This promise emphasizes that no one who is a child of God will be allowed to face trials beyond his tolerance level. Further it indicates that God will provide a means by which the apparent irresolvable conflict can be handled by those who in faith turn to Him. This promise is consistent with the salutation of Jude:

> Now unto him that is able to keep you from falling, and to present you faultless before the presence of his glory with exceeding joy Jude 24

Not only is it inconceivable that God would allow His children to be placed in a conflict demanding an evil consequence, but it is also totally

---

7. David was given his choice of three punishments for his sin, 2 Samuel 24:12, and the people of Judah were given the choice to surrender to Babylonian captivity, or to die in Jerusalem, Jeremiah 38:2.

inconsistent that, while He would allow His children to be severely tested, never will it be beyond the capacity of such a one in the power and strength of Christ to bear the temptation. Thus we may return to the earlier comment that probably all human beings have a breaking point. This assertion is true only to the extent that man does not link his life indivisibly with that of God. For the Christian, no matter what his breaking point might have been, God has promised strength to overcome and to sustain in all difficulties.

For Fletcher to say that love is the only absolute, is to deny that love is expressed in the keeping of God's law.[8] Both the individual and society suffer greatly when immutable restraints are "removed." Without the security of absolutes, man wanders in a maze of uncertainty which produces further frustration and failure. Toward the end of the last century, there was the beginning of a shift away from belief in the immutable law of God, to reliance upon social mores. Even at this level, there was a tendency for society to remain reasonably intact and for morality to be retained. But in the latter part of the twentieth century the dominant mores have been existential ones, in which each person becomes his own measure of right and wrong, of truth and error. These existential mores are exemplified by catch phrases such as "Do your own thing," "Be yourself," "Have fun," but such advice leaves man like a boat without a rudder in a storm-tossed sea. The situationist, though perhaps denying existentialist mores, in the final analysis has to leave the decision of "right" response to the individual judgment.

If, as it is said, the end justifies the means, we have the dilemma of whether or not we can always know what the end will be before pursuing a course of action. And in a situation where the end is not clear, the situationist faces the dilemma of not knowing what action would be best in the circumstances. Often our reactions have to be made so suddenly and so spontaneously, that we do not have time to consider what might be the consequence of the action—only those who have habituated a pattern of life upon immutable principles of God, will in such circumstances, in almost reflex action, respond in a manner consistent with the moral code of God. If there are times when the best good is served by deception, we

---

8. See John 14:15, 21.

face the dilemma of not being able to believe or trust the situationist. John assures us that God is love.

> And we have known and believed the love that God hath to us. God is love, and he that dwelleth in love dwelleth in God, and God in him.
>
> 1 John 4:16

Thus if love is the very essence of the character of God, and He cannot change, how then can agape love be the only first-order value, the only absolute; for this love of God is embodied in the commandments of God. If the end justifies the means, who determines what is the best end or the least-evil end? Surely this dilemma ultimately leads to egocentricity, as man is predisposed to seek those ends which he perceives as best for him rather than for others.

Throughout the Scripture the answer to conflicting situations is an implicit trust in God. This principle is demonstrated in the previously used illustration of the children of Israel faced with the Red Sea on one hand and the Egyptian army on the other. Here was a problem insuperable and irresolvable in human terms. But God had an answer for His trusting people.

> By faith they passed through the Red sea as by dry land: which the Egyptians assaying to do were drowned. Hebrews 11:29

God had an answer to what seemed an irresolvable conflict. But let us look a little more closely at experiences in modern day. Let us take the lifeboat experience, discussed earlier. In the Second World War, three army chaplains, Catholic, Protestant, and Jewish, showed that they did not have to make a choice between two self-centered evils when faced with this very situation. The three gave up their seats in the lifeboat and were last seen holding hands as they followed the example of Jesus in the supreme selfless act of dying that others might live. This act was commemorated by a postage stamp, but its ultimate recognition will be eternal. The answer to barriers which might be seen as producing overwhelming frustration, is surely the development of complete trust in God to do for us what it is impossible for us to do for ourselves. Many times we are assured that God's people will live by faith.[9] This faith can be developed as we recognize how God has in the past removed insuperable barriers.

---

9. See Habbakuk 2:4; Romans 1:17; Galatians 3:11; Hebrews 10:38.

And what more shall I say? for the time would fail me to tell of Gedeon, and of Barak, and of Samson, and of Jephthae; of David also, and Samuel, and of the prophets: who through faith subdued kingdoms, wrought righteousness, obtained promises, stopped the mouths of lions. Hebrews 11:32–33

God's promise to Abraham that he should have a son seemed an impossible goal, for Sarah was well beyond the menopause, but God is able to do that which man cannot do. Faith is therefore an ever present characteristic of God's people.

He that leadeth into captivity shall go into captivity: he that killeth with the sword must be killed with the sword. Here is the patience and the faith of the saints. Revelation 13:10

Here is the patience of the saints: here are they that keep the commandments of God, and the faith of Jesus. Revelation 14:12

When it is fully recognized that there is no barrier too difficult for God and that each barrier presents yet another opportunity for us to exercise and grow in faith, we respond to His invitation,

casting all your care upon him; for he careth for you. 1 Peter 5:7

John assures us,

this is the victory that overcometh the world, even our faith.

1 John 5:4

This promise is surely the assurance that every barrier and conflicting circumstance faced can be solved as it is placed by faith in the hands of God. Perhaps nothing is more critical in responding to frustration-inducing situations than James' counsel,

Ask in faith, nothing wavering. James 1:6

CONFLICT SITUATIONS

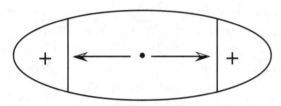

APPROACH - APPROACH CONFLICT

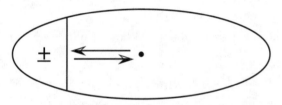

APPROACH - AVOIDANCE CONFLICT

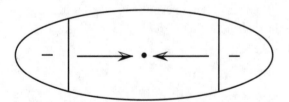

AVOIDANCE - AVOIDANCE CONFLICT

10

Encounter and Sensitivity
Groups and Christianity

IN a room devoid of furnishings other than carpet and pillows, a group of twelve persons is engaged in an Encounter workshop. The workshop continues for a few days with a number of two-hours sessions each day. The age of the participants varies from adolescence to the aged. For the duration of the session all participants live in the same residential setting. The program is unstructured. The group center their activities upon the discovery and the uninhibited expression of feelings, emotions and attitudes. The frankness of the group increases as the sessions pass by, and often the emotional expression intensifies. There are those whose emotional strength is brought to breaking point. Few restraints on what the group might do or say are evident, with perhaps the major limitation prohibiting that which might involve physical violence. There is an increased emphasis upon noninhibitive forms of expression, and not uncommonly, in some of the more extreme Encounter and Sensitivity sessions the group is encouraged to interact in a state of nakedness. It commences when the leader of the group indicates that he or she feels "far more comfortable without the inhibition of clothing."

It is confidently asserted by the proponents of Encounter groups that in this free, uninhibited environment, great psychologically therapeutic advantage is gained. However, increasingly there have been serious questions raised about the productive efforts of Encounter groups. Perhaps nothing did more to focus questions on the effectiveness of Sensitivity and Encounter training than the research done by Diana Hartley, Howard Roback, and Steven I. Abramowitz from Vanderbilt University.[1] Here the

---

1.   Diana Hartley, H. B. Roback, S. I. Abramowitz, "Deteriorative Effects in Encounter Groups," *American Psychology*, vol. 31, March 1976, pp. 247–255.

authors presented telling evidence which seriously questions the thera-peutic value of Encounter groups and indicates many casualties in the program. Even dealing with some of the more conservative programs, such as the National Training Laboratory program initiated in 1947, or Carl Rogers' Basic Encounter Groups initiated in 1967, the authors indi-cate that there have been serious repercussions following the Encounter group program.

Perhaps one of the most vigorous and controversial experiments of the Encounter group method has been William C. Schutz in the Esalen program at Big Sur, California. In his book,[2] Schutz explains some of the basic principles of encounter and also produces a brief history of the de-velopment of the Encounter program. Because many Christian leaders are increasingly attracted to the methodology of the Encounter psycholo-gists, it is worthwhile to examine the problems of Encounter, its philo-sophical bases, and its concomitant effects.

Encounter is a method of human relating. It involves openness, hon-esty, self-awareness, self-responsibility, awareness of the body, attention to feeling, emphasis on the here and now. Schutz goes so far as to say, "Encounter is education and religion in that it attempts to create condi-tions leading to the most satisfying use of personal capacities" (W. G. Schutz, *Elements of Encounter*, p. 5). But lest we be confused by his reference to the religious experience, this statement ought to be placed beside a further statement, "The Encounter Group is a demythologized and secularized form or style of interpersonal encounter and community which is familiar to historians of Protestant pietism" (Ibid., p. 8). Schutz further makes the dangerous assumption, "One thread running through the history of Encounter is clearly religious. The assumption that God is within, or works from within you, that you are a vehicle for expressing God, is a common theme. As I gain experience with Encounter, it be-comes clearer that the Encounter goal of realizing one's potential is virtu-ally identical with the religious goal of finding the God within" (Ibid., p. 8). Encounter psychology has a base deeply entrenched in the mysticism of ancient and Eastern religions as well as philosophic mysticism such as yoga, the martial arts of the Chinese and Japanese, the Holiness and Pen-tecostal groups of Christianity, the Muslim Sufi mysticisms and psycho-

---

2.   William G. Schutz, *The Elements of Encounter*, 1973.

synthesis. And interestingly enough, Schutz declares, "The Encounter Culture follows the counterculture" (Ibid., p. 24).

Its link with dangerous philosophic and psychological principles becomes very apparent as one analyzes more fully the background of the movement. Many see Encounter as probably the first step in availing oneself of the energy of the universe—a step toward the fullest spiritual actualization of the individual, very much similar to that expressed in the Eastern religions. The emphasis is constantly upon the physical and upon feelings, and is placed in a natural progression from Socrates' emphasis upon intellectual encounter.

In modern times, group therapy had its origin more than five decades ago under the direction of the field psychologist, Kurt Lewin, who in 1947 established the first Training Groups (T groups). Since then the concept of group dynamics has mushroomed and has taken many different forms. But fundamentally the emphasis upon personal awareness, the emphasis upon self-expression, upon that which is physical and that which expresses the emotions, becomes dominant. Perhaps no one has given greater credence to the Encounter group movement than Carl Rogers, who has gone so far as to say that it is the most important social invention of the twentieth century.

A wide range of techniques is used in most of these Encounter sessions, such as nonverbal communication, psychodrama, fantasy, passage, meditation, yoga, and oriental martial arts and psychosynthesis (dealing with the whole person including the spirit). It is claimed that such uninhibited encounter removes the psychological blocks so that one may flow naturally. It is further claimed that society is based upon deception, the masking of feelings, and the disowning of the body. The emphasis is very much upon the here and now, the realization of the full potentialities of the present; and this emphasis has a persuasive impact upon the person who is facing emotional stress and psychological strain.

Unfortunately, many church leaders and pastors have rushed to establish Sensitivity groups, accepting uncritically the argument that they indeed have religious significance. But many dangerous fallacies lie within the Encounter-group philosophy.

For example, if all other members decided to remove all their clothes, the center of attention rests upon the one resisting or deciding not to follow the group. Under such circumstances the pressure of the group can be impelling, especially for an insecure person. When questions such as "What are your hang-ups?" "What are your inhibitions?" "Why are you ashamed of your own body?" begin to pierce the troubled mind of the nonconforming group member, it is indeed very rare for such a member to resist that kind of pressure. Thus the group establishes its own mores; and the nonconformist to those mores becomes, as it were, a social outcast; because in most cases, the members of the group themselves have been troubled by maladaptive behavior and by emotional problems. It is evident that the pressure to conformity within the group becomes almost overpowering. We call this pressure the tyranny of the group.

Encounter and Sensitivity groups are based upon a view of man consistent with the Greek pagan view of innate goodness: that somehow resident within man is the ability to find answers to his own problems; and if he is free enough, if the inhibiting social forces are destroyed, then man will have a full and complete life. The emphasis is upon doing that which is natural and that which is free. This emphasis is in contradistinction to the biblical teaching that man is born with a predisposition to move in pathways that alienate from God; that the natural man cannot be a complete being, and cannot be a fully developed personality. Only by the new-birth experience, as man is united with God, can one achieve his full potentialities.

There is no way an emotionally disturbed person can accept the frankness of other members of the group. Their expressed dislikes of him, their criticisms of the way he looks, the way he acts, the way he speaks, result in serious emotional implications. Such frankness, even under a cloak of helpfulness, is a misuse of truthfulness and is absolutely contrary to the love which ought to be extended to others. The Christian philosophy that we are to see the very best in others, that we are not to judge, neither are we to condemn, does not allow for such group interaction.

There is strong emphasis upon the expression of emotions, including the aggressive emotion of anger, which is inconsistent with the Christian love philosophy.

> He that is slow to anger is better than the mighty; and he that ruleth his spirit than he that taketh a city.   Proverbs 16:32

Encounter and Sensitivity theory places self at the center of the issue; one's own feelings, one's needs, one's body become the total pivot around which this therapy revolves. How inconsistent this philosophy is with the counsel of Scripture to crucify self and to die daily! There is no way that one who is actively egocentric can indeed have emotional security and peace, for with an active ego he becomes vulnerable to every criticism, to the successes of others, to those who disagree with him, and to those who are exalted above him. Therefore it is inevitable that there are many casualties where human beings, rather than being restored to stable emotional lives, have suffered temporary, and in some cases permanent, emotional breakdown.

The Encounter and Sensitivity group psychology encourages participants to express all the innermost feelings and situations of their lives. Of course there is no acknowledgment of sin, and so the great emphasis is upon the verbalization of all the most intimate sins of one's life. This frankness tends to address the guilt problem, which can be effectively eradicated only by the forgiveness that comes from confession and by the forsaking of sin through the power of Christ.

There is no question that the Christian church has an important function to fulfill in group dynamics of behavior. The Scripture encourages us not to forget the value of Christian fellowship.

> Not forsaking the assembling of ourselves together, as the manner of some is; but exhorting one another: and so much the more, as ye see the day approaching.   Hebrews 10:25

Much positive therapy comes from the fellowshiping together of Christian believers. There is emotional strength and courage that can be derived beyond the spiritual strengthening. This strength does not come from the dynamics of a program like Encounter therapy but comes through praying together and through helping others together. In Christian therapy the emphasis is not upon man himself, but upon Christ, the Redeemer. His matchless love and power provide strength and victory; they bring restoration and peace, and provide motivation for selfless outreach which offers to others hope and assurance for fullness of life here and hereafter.

11

Mind Control and Hypnosis

HYPNOSIS had its modern foundation in the research and writing of Anton Mesmer (1734–1815), the Austrian mystic and physician. After studying theology and medicine at the Universities of Ingolstadt and Vienna, Mesmer began to delve into the influence of the stars upon human health and behavior. Believing that this influence was exerted through the power of an invisible fluid, Mesmer became convinced that there was special healing in magnetism–a force permeating the whole universe. By the middle of the 1770s he had generated both great interest and opposition in Austria, and by 1778 was forced to leave Austria when fellow physicians accused him of practicing magic.

Mesmer continued his research, lecturing and writing in Paris, where even greater interest was exhibited in his research. However, in 1784 the French government appointed a commission of physicians and scientists (including Benjamin Franklin) to study what now had become known as mesmerism, after its founder. The report was most unfavorable, and while Mesmer lost much support as a result of the commission's findings, nevertheless mesmerism still continued to receive considerable popular support, and books on the topic multiplied rapidly. Mesmer believed that illness was due to a lack of magnetism, and that a strong, healthy person could heal by the rhythmical massaging of the sick person, allowing magnetic strength to be transferred to the patient.

It was largely from the work of Mesmer that modern hypnosis has developed, although there is much evidence that the trancelike state of hypnosis was well known to the world of antiquity. Hypnosis is usually defined as a trance or sleep-like state mediated by another person. Most researchers in the field relate it to suggestion, and see a direct relationship between one's suggestibility and the ease with which one can be hypnotized. A casual reflection will confirm that some humans are strong, independent persons while others tend to be dependent and in need of considerable human support. This difference of course is not a dichotomy, for a whole continuum exists between the two extremes. It is usually held that the more dependent one is, the more susceptible he is to hypnotic suggestion. Suggestion is common in all facets of life. It is used often by parents with their children. For example, a parent before retiring to bed will frequently use suggestion while his young child is in a state of sleep to produce urination in an attempt to forestall bed-wetting. As in hypnosis, the child may or may not have some recollection of the event, depending upon the degree of sleep maintained during the act of urination. Advertisers depend heavily upon suggestion, as do others representing a wide sphere of human activity.

Hypnosis is distinctive, however, in that it is a man-induced state designed to greatly increase the person's openness to suggestion and influence. While definitions of hypnosis vary, most include a view in which it is said to result from the functional suppression of the cortical (awareness) areas of the brain, important to inhibition, decision making, choice and control. This suppression permits the subcortical, or more basic functions of the brain, to dominate, and can lead to another person's controlling the behavior of the subject through processes of suggestion. The hypnotic state is usually induced by repetition, monotone suggestions or other forms of auditory stimulation alone. There is considerable debate as to the degree of control that a hypnotist has over his subject, but obviously much depends upon the depth achieved of the induced trancelike state. Some have claimed in the past that the subject will not respond to any suggestions that are contrary to his own moral code, but this claim or assertion is extremely doubtful because the inhibitory and decision-making centers of the brain appear to be depressed during hypnosis.

Autohypnosis, in which the hypnotic state is self-induced, is also receiving considerable attention. Autohypnosis results from a self-imposed slowing down of bodily functions, such as heart rate and breathing rate, initiated by the person concentrating upon certain audio and/or visual stimuli. As in hetero-hypnosis, described above, the subject becomes psychologically removed from reality, and probably his inhibitory and decision-making processes are also affected.

Both forms of hypnosis are widely practiced in pagan and Eastern religions. Hetero-hypnosis is widely practiced in the primitive cultures of Africa and the West Indies and probably is the basis of the death produced by bone-pointing, practiced by the Australian aborigines.

In Malaysia and Singapore, Hindu Indians celebrate Thaipusam annually. In this religious festival devotees have large rods, up to two and one-half centimeters (one inch) in diameter passed through their cheeks. Others have large hooks piercing their backs to which are attached ropes used to pull carts. Still others carry gaily colored constructions upon their heads and shoulders, called kavadis. From these kavadis numerous strings attach to small hooks about the side of large fish hooks. These are inserted into the devotee's chest and back. All this is done as penance or an act of gratitude to the goddess of mercy. The various metallic objects are all inserted in a particular temple where the participants are placed in a trance by the rhythmic chanting of the Hindu priests. From here they walk three miles, stopping frequently to dance before booths broadcasting Hindu religious music. The three-mile pilgrimage can take several hours in the hot tropical sun.

Autohypnosis has achieved perhaps its highest level of success among the yogis of India and may also be seen as basic to transcendental meditation. Hypnosis has also been thought by many to be a basis of acupuncture, in which the ancient Chinese sought to restore health by stimulation and pressure of peripheral nerve areas thought to have direct relationship with certain organs of the body. Like Mesmer, the Chinese acupuncturists saw an astrological relationship between the starry heavens and the microcosm of the human organism. The theory of the conjunction of opposites embedded in the Chinese concept of *yin* and *yang* also is deeply inherent within acupuncture practice. Surprisingly, like yoga, transcendental meditation and other forms of Eastern mysticism, acupuncture has been eagerly embraced by many in the Western world.

Since World War I hypnotism has generated widespread interest and acceptability, especially in medical and psychological circles. This interest has corresponded to the increased respectability of the study of parapsychology—the study of human behavior thought to be beyond the normal, with such mysticism as is involved in extrasensory perception, clairvoyancy, necromancy, spiritism, sorcery, Satanism, and predictions. This study has been fostered at many universities, including such prestigious institutions as Duke University. The use of hypnosis as an analgesic, or for other forms of therapy, received considerable respectability when many national medical associations, including the British and the American, accepted it as a valid therapeutic form in the 1950s and 1960s. Its use by both medical and dental surgeons is well known, with many claiming that its use is far less dangerous than traditional anesthetics. It has also become a popular medium of the psychologist and the psychiatrist, especially for determining deeper and earlier causal events leading to mental breakdown.

Associated with the increased interest in, and respectability of, hypnosis has been the development of mind-control programs. Such programs variously claim to increase the mental processes, expand the human intellectual potentialities and unlock brain capacities in such a way as to greatly enhance the life of the student. Not uncommonly such a program begins by explaining that humans during their lifetime use only a small percentage of their brain capacity and that the program is designed to open new dimensions and frontiers to them. The seeming reasonableness of such statements is designed to gain the acceptance of even the most skeptical student. But not uncommonly such programs quickly develop into the area of spiritism, where first the student is asked to imagine he has a counselor to whom he is to address questions of importance. Later this "imaginary" counselor becomes a real and critical part of the so-called mind expansion program. The student has soon become ensnared in a way of life that he had not previously considered. Often the programs develop toward such spiritualistic areas as astral projection (where the spirit supposedly leaves the body for a time—an act claimed to add a new and wonderful dimension to life). There are some frightening stories indeed in which spirits, having left the body, and then finding it impossible to find their body, produce a state of great panic. One of the most popular mind expansion programs is the Silva Mind Control Program, which has had sensational success in the United States and in some other parts of the world. The program was first initiated by an obscure Mexican, Jose Silva, and has enticed tens of thousands.

Whether it be hypnosis, mind control or some other form of parapsychological phenomena which have their traceable roots in ancient paganism, the Christian must be vigilant to perceive their spiritual and mental danger. Man was created with the powers to think, decide, and choose. It is those powers which God has given to man which most reflect the characteristics of God Himself. God does not design that any two people must think alike. Individuality is one of the most precious gifts God has entrusted to man, and every effort must be made to ensure that this gift is not destroyed or seriously impaired. Although it may be hoped that hypnosis or mind control might extend important vistas of life, the submission of the mind to another can but have serious implications. To put one's trust in other men's judgment is to put trust in imperfection and to turn away from the trust that should be placed only in God.

> Blessed is that man that maketh the LORD his trust, and respecteth not the proud, nor such as turn aside to lies.   Psalm 40:4

> It is better to trust in the LORD than to put confidence in man.
>   Psalm 118:8

> Thus saith the LORD: Cursed be the man that trusteth in man, and maketh flesh his arm, and whose heart departeth from the LORD.
>   Jeremiah 17:5

God's counsel is that we place our trust only in Him. Our minds are a gift from God to be wisely developed to fulfill His purposes and to expand in His grace. The apostle James gives this unequivocal counsel:

> If any of you lack wisdom, let him ask of God, that giveth to all men liberally, and upbraideth not; and it shall be given him. But let him ask in faith, nothing wavering. For he that wavereth is like a wave of the sea driven with the wind and tossed.   James 1:5–6

The mind of man is created for communion with God, and any human relationship which in any way limits this communion, no matter how inviting it may seem, leads to spiritual, intellectual and emotional loss. One of the great dangers in the use of hypnosis is the lack of understanding of what psychological processes take place in the one who submits his mind to another. Even for the so-called therapeutic purposes of medicine and psychiatry, its use will not be sought by the Christian. It is a law of habit that each behavior strengthens with usage, and the submission to hypnosis strengthens the habit of submitting to the mind of another and concomitantly weakens the independent powers of the person.

Satan is eagerly seeking to capture the minds of men. Though he does not have direct access to man's mind, nevertheless he uses every conceivable subtlety to weaken and distract men's intellectual capacities so that they cannot reflect the mind of Christ. It is his purpose that man's mind will be so destroyed that he no longer is capable of following God and choosing to do right. While Satan cannot control our mind without our consent, he can gain access when the human mind is given to subserve the purposes of another. Thus Satan's purposes are served by mind controlling practices.

The warnings of mind control are also relevant to parents. Because in the initial months of the child's life the parent tends to be mind for the child, there is a danger that parents will overly control the life of the child as he matures. However, one of the greatest responsibilities is to educate the child to independent thinking and wise decision making.[1]

While the damaging effects of hypnosis and mind control cannot be overstressed, there is a legitimate and valuable role for human counseling. Human encouragement is important in lifting the spirit of those discouraged. Counseling together is frequently advantageous, but should be clearly distinguished from the circumstances where one mind controls that of another. The admonition of Paul presents the best wisdom for those seeking the fullest potentiality of their intellectual capacities.

Let this mind be in you which was also in Christ Jesus.

Philippians 2:5

---

1. See chapter 22 entitled "Childhood."

12

The Perils of Counseling

OVER the past few decades, counseling has grown into a mammoth, multimillion-dollar industry, with increasing numbers assuming the role of counselors to the untold multitudes of men, women and children who are suffering from one or another of the various forms of emotional problems.

The Christian church has quickly taken up the role, especially as it has been seen that more and more people are seeking counsel from psychologists and psychiatrists and moving away from the clergy who have traditionally played this role. This trend has led many church pastors to seek more in-depth training in counseling and to develop counseling techniques effective in their pastoral work. Counseling is not a new art, for there are many examples in the Old and the New Testament where counsel was given. For example, in the ministry of Christ, men such as Nicodemus[1] and the rich young ruler[2] sought Him out for direct counsel to guide their personal lives. No doubt there is value in men and women counseling together to strengthen one another and to guide in pathways of righteousness. There are, however, also serious dangers in counseling, especially today when many ministers have tended to place the strength of their work in the counseling ministry. It is important to look at some of the dangers related to this work, both for the counselee and the counselor.

One essential role of every Christian is to learn complete dependence upon Christ and not upon man. God is the one to whom we must look for an understanding of individual duty. It is right that brethren should coun-

---

1. See John 3:1–21.
2. See Matthew 19:16–22.

sel together, but when one man arranges just what another should do, let him answer that he has chosen the Lord for his counselor.

There is a danger that men will receive the counsel of men, and by so doing discard the counsel of God. This danger is the first peril of counseling. Wittingly or unwittingly, the counselor may encourage his counselee to lean upon him rather than to lean upon God. Even the most dedicated counselor can never take the place of God, and there is an increasing tendency for men to look to men rather than to God. In many cases such dependence has become debilitating to the spiritual and emotional stability of the counselee, for he feels such a dependence upon the counselor that frequently, when separated from the counselor, he experiences a loss, an emptiness and a fear that come as a result of his total dependence upon man. This danger can be avoided as the counselor emphasizes that, while he is unable to solve any of the issues that are raised, he can direct the counselee to the true Counselor and to His written Word. Above everything else, the aim of the counselor in his counseling should be to turn the one counseled away from man to God, helping him to tell his troubles to the Lord rather than to man. Any indication that he is developing a human dependence must be quickly, though lovingly, met by the counselor in a way that will help the one seeking counsel to draw closer to God as his sure strength and trust.

All counseling should be given in the fear and knowledge of God. Every effort should be made to help the person to see Christ as the One in whom he can rest his problems. Unfortunately, today some men posing as Christian counselors are giving advice in direct opposition to the plainest words of Scripture. Thus some have advised husbands to divorce their wives in order to attain happiness. Such advice to break solemn vows made before God does not originate from our Creator. The consequences of the acceptance of such advice are further misery and emotional instability and, worse still, alienation from God.

Some difficulties can be experienced when one seeking advice is not oriented to Christianity and may even be antagonistic to the suggestion that Christ has any viable answers to his needs. In such a situation, wisdom dictates that the counselor not destroy his rapport with the patient by referring to the answers of Christianity. However, this tactic in no way prevents the counselor from referring to those principles that are Bible-based. These principles are still the best for mental health. Later, when the counselee has seen their value in his recovery, the counselor may be able to show that they are God's principles. From there the counselee may be helped to see the assurance of resting his concerns with Christ.

The second peril confronted by the counselor is that of egotism. It is easy to build egotism as more and more seek counsel and guidance from him. This peril represents a deep-seated threat to the soul of the counselor, for egotism, born of unconquered self, imperils his own Christian development. Any man taking to himself a role that God has never entrusted to him is in grave danger. We can certainly agree that God is greatly dishonored when men are placed in the position where God should be. God alone can give unerring counsel.

The counselor's egotism will lead him to foster a dependency relationship, and the more those seeking his counsel emphasize how much he is able to help them, the greater will be the risk that such flattery will lead into dangerously unproductive pathways.

The minister-counselor is confronted by a third dilemma. The more time he spends in this type of work, the less he has for active presentation of the gospel commission. The minister cannot turn aside from Christ's direct command to—

preach the gospel.   Mark 16:15

It is true that today there has been a broadening of the terms of the gospel and what is represented by it. But even here we may find an imperative need to redefine, so that the true meaning of that gospel commission is emphasized. Many ministers are so involved in the work of administration and of counseling that very little time is given to the direct proclamation of the gospel and the pushing forward of the frontiers of God's kingdom. It is essential that every man called to the gospel ministry recognize his primary work, the work of telling men and women of the love of Jesus and forwarding the frontiers of the kingdom of God. Too often a pastor is so inundated with counseling that it is impossible for him to do the work for which he has been primarily ordained. Also important is the call of Karl Menninger for ministers to rediscover their pulpit function as the most important avenue of emotional healing.[3]

Unfortunately, some gospel ministers have become convinced that counseling is their primary work and have left the work of the ministry

---

3. See chapter 6 entitled "Law and Love."

for full-time counseling. Is it possible that in many instances the motivation for this change is avarice, as it is realized that incomes well above that of the minister are available to the popular counselor? It is for the pastoral counselor to fully investigate his motives.[4] Other ministers drift into counseling, not for any monetary benefit, but because they perceive that it is their primary role in a given appointment. One such area of labor is the appointment as a hospital chaplain. Modern chaplaincy theory seems more concerned with making patients and their relatives feel more comfortable with imminent death, than it is with the vital role of preparing people to meet their God. Comforting the sick and dying is indeed a worthy activity, but the chaplain must never lose sight of his responsibility to point the patient and the sorrowing loved ones to the great Comforter.

The Austin Hospital in Melbourne commenced the first hospital chaplaincy training program in Australia. As each new class arrived, one of the authors took part in the orientation presentations. It was found that almost without exception these pastors, from all the larger Christian denominations, saw themselves in a changing role when entering the class. They felt that they had to assume a role akin to that of social workers. Since the Austin Hospital had a first-class Social Work Department, this role was entirely unnecessary. In this orientation presentation each pastor was challenged to recognize the dire spiritual needs of many of the patients, a great number of whom were hospitalized directly as a consequence of following paths alienated to God. All our patients need Jesus. They need not only to know *about* Him, they also need to know *Him*. The dominant task of the hospital chaplain must be to spread a saving knowledge of Jesus.

From this knowledge flow comfort and true strength in times of adversity. All attempts to meet human crises outside the love of Jesus are doomed to utter failure.

The fourth concern for the counselor relates to his own soul needs. While we sometimes fail to recognize it, the counselor himself needs to safeguard the avenues of the soul just as carefully as any of his counselees; maybe more so. In the type of counseling often employed today, the counselor very frequently is confronted with persons who will pour out the most vivid details of their lives of sin and immorality. It is in itself debili-

---

4. See chapter 6 entitled "Law and Love."

tating to the spiritual growth of the counselor to daily listen to such spiritually eroding talk, and his own eternal destiny can be held in peril as a
result of it. It is very easy to become a confessor to other humans. God
has never given this responsibility to man. At all costs it should be avoided
as patients are pointed to the Source of true forgiveness. Even if the counseling does not involve discussion of direct transgression, the talk of discouragement and despondency, of trials and difficulties, can rarely be
uplifting for either counselee or counselor, and rarely can the existing
problems be solved by such discussion.

Fifth, the desire for so much counseling especially among professing
Christians may be symptomatic of the faithlessness of the age. Men and
women, torn by the exigencies of life, lacking that peace which alone can
bring contentment, seek man's aid and man's direction in the formulation
of their lives. The Bible has the very surest remedy for a lack of faith, but
this remedy is decreasingly a part of the life of Christian believers.

Faith cometh by hearing, and hearing by the word of God.

Romans 10:17

The greatest efforts need to be made by the ministry to bring congregations to a consistent study of the Word of God by which the true basis of
Christian life and Christian development can be laid. If there is one lack,
it is the lack of faith, which in turn leads to disillusionment and to a life-
style independent of Christ, and to spiritual declension. The more faith
and trust are talked and practiced, the more they enhance the life.

The role of counseling often conflicts with the essential need to present
the straight testimony of God's Word. The counselor is confronted with
the dilemma of a biblical training which leads him to seek to love the
sinner but to point out the sin, while on the other hand having a counseling training to accept both the counselee *and* his behavior, seeking to help
the one counseled to be comfortable with his behavior. Unfortunately often, the conflict is resolved on the side of the latter. This solution too
frequently leads to a loss of one of the most essential ministries, the ministry of reproof. The membership suffers from a ministry which fails to
clearly define between—

life and good, and death and evil.   Deuteronomy 30:15

Those of us who are ordained ministers need to be reminded of the solemn ordination charge presented to us on our day of ordination:

So thou, O son of man, I have set thee a watchman unto the house of Israel; therefore thou shalt hear the word at my mouth, and warn them from me. When I say unto the wicked, O wicked man, thou shalt surely die; if thou dost not speak to warn the wicked from his way, that wicked man shall die in his iniquity; but his blood will I require at thine hand. Nevertheless, if thou warn the wicked of his way to turn from it; if he do not turn from his way, he shall die in his iniquity; but thou hast delivered thy soul. Therefore, O thou son of man, speak unto the house of Israel; Thus ye speak, saying, If our transgressions and our sins be upon us, and we pine away in them, how should we then live? Say unto them, As I live, saith the Lord GOD, I have no pleasure in the death of the wicked; but that the wicked turn from his way and live: turn ye, turn ye from your evil ways; for why will ye die, O house of Israel?   Ezekiel 33:7–11

Another real danger occurs when counselors agree to give counsel, particularly upon marital issues, to members of the opposite sex. Numerous are those who have found themselves in compromising circumstances during such counseling sessions. Such a counseling situation has cost many pastors their ministerial credentials. So perilous are such circumstances that pastors should be themselves counseled to avoid them entirely. If marriage advice is required, then it should be given in the fear of the Lord with both marriage partners present. If this arrangement is not possible, the counselor's spouse should be present.

The real answer to social, emotional and spiritual problems cannot be found within man himself, nor within his fellow man, but within Christ. But frequently in counseling, attempts are made to find answers within the person himself. There is a real need to reevaluate the role of the counselor, his effectiveness, and his limitations, so that counseling which is truly Christ-centered may achieve its maximal value in the lives of needy men and women.

Perhaps the most productive efforts of the counselor are to encourage the counselee to think and talk positively, avoiding verbalization of discouragement and despondence, and to avoid hyperbolizing trials and problems which can only increase and reinforce negative emotions. The more the counselor can lead the counselee to exercise faith and trust in God, the more thorough will be the solution to his problems, and the greater will be his ability to move in productive channels.

13

Christian Therapy

MANY theories have been postulated as to the basic principles of sound mental health. Paul's comment to Timothy is certainly relevant. He declares that God has given us power, love and a sound mind.

> For God hath not given us the spirit of fear; but of power, and of love,
> and of a sound mind.   2 Timothy 1:7

However, some translations (e.g. T.E.V.) use the term *self-control* rather than "a sound mind." These two, i.e. a sound mind and self-control, are closely interrelated, for the basis of a sound mind is self-control. Mental illness is on the increase. Home breakup is also increasing, as are child and adolescent problems. But God is willing to help men and women find the way through the issues of mental breakdown. These men and women will be the ones who take hold of His promise of a sound mind, who will be secure in God, knowing that He will do in them the work of full spiritual and emotional regeneration. This belief holds that the Word of God to man has all the principles and guidelines for his mental health.

This promise becomes most controversial in a world where the Bible is very frequently put aside as a sourcebook for the discovering of mental health principles as well as curative principles for mental illness. In fact, many psychologists and psychiatrists hold that one of the great problems faced by men and women is the problem of a spurious kind of life-style due to the crutch of religion. There is often an attempt to undermine faith and trust in the Word of God and the pursuance of a Christlike life, proclaiming these virtues to be the cause of mental illness. Many hold that the most common cause of mental breakdown is the inhibiting effect of religion. But does this religious relationship to mental illness result from true Christianity? The Scripture is replete with assurances of peace that comes to the truly converted person.

The LORD lift up his countenance upon thee, and give thee peace.
Numbers 6:26

The LORD will give strength unto his people; the LORD will bless his people with peace.
Psalm 29:11

And the work of righteousness shall be peace; and the effect of righteousness quietness and assurance for ever.
Isaiah 32:17

These things have I spoken unto you, that in me ye might have peace. In the world ye shall have tribulation: but be of good cheer; I have overcome the world.
John 16:33

It is true that the one who is struggling in the area of indecision between a life-style contrary to God and the challenges of Christ in his life may suffer mental breakdown, and certainly is in a state of terrible conflict.[1] Only when a firm, full and daily commitment is made to Jesus Christ can we have the security promised in God's Word. Thus the negative effects of frustration resulting from the battle for mastery of the life and frequently producing continual upheaval, are often erroneously thought to be the result of Christian commitment. In fact they result from the evidence of commitments not yet made. Those who have irrevocably turned away from God will often exhibit less conflict than the one who, though still open to Christ's claims upon his life, is not yet prepared to surrender his will fully to Christ. Thus the Christian counselor will center his efforts not so much upon the unsettled behavior of the one seeking counsel but upon how he might submit his life to Christ. It is certain that until this submission is accomplished he will not have a fulfilled life, and he will be tormented by emotional insecurity.

The Word of God is not made the center of life and experience as it once was. The study of God's Word is losing its power because human beings are neglecting it. It is thus far more likely that there is a form of godliness without a deeper commitment. Work programs, societies and clubs, recreation, television, and reading, all tend to crowd out the source of true mental health which is a prayerful, Spirit-filled study of God's Word.

---

1. See Romans 7:14–24.

One of the greatest problems has been the fact that even psychologists, psychiatrists, and counselors professing to be Christians, have frequently followed precisely the same kind of program that has been used by non-Christian professionals. Now it seems reasonable to believe that the very best programs established by men will always fall short of that which God can provide for His children.

One of the most commonly used programs in community mental health involves the whole family in therapy. This procedure is commendable in itself, but it is the way in which the family is often involved that causes problems. For example, if a husband is exhibiting strong mental disturbance, it is usual to invite the wife and maybe other members of his family, particularly older children, in an attempt to do something to help the disturbed patient. Often this therapy is built around the principles of L.A.W. (Love, Assurance, and Worthwhileness). It is suggested that because the person has probably had inadequate demonstrations of love in his home, he has grown up without love, true acceptance, and feelings of self-worth. The program is designed to reestablish love to increase his awareness of acceptance and self-worth.[2]

Now, these three attributes are important to each of us. Love has a vital role to play in human behavior. Acceptance and worthwhileness both are critical to adequate human performance. However, it is usual in these programs to invite the family, and perhaps close friends, to discover ways in which they can aid the disturbed person in knowing that he is loved and is being accepted and that his efforts are counted as worthwhile. Therefore, the patient becomes the center of attention and focus in this treatment. It soon becomes obvious, however, that relatives are the very last to admit that another member of their family has a mental illness. Thus long before the patient has been brought for counseling, the family usually has gone to inordinate lengths to placate the maladaptive behavior of the disturbed member. Therefore prior to the patient's being brought, encouraged, persuaded, or coerced to come to see the counselor, there has been a whole history of attempts to cover his unbalanced practices. When a family tries to build up the self-worth of the person, he becomes the center of everything happening in the home. And rather than helping him to change his abnormal behavior, this attention tends to reinforce it. These

---

2. See chapter 6 entitled "Law and Love."

persons almost without exception have long before developed an insecurity built around low self-evaluation.

It is true that the poor home environment has probably contributed to the inadequacies of adulthood. However, the problem is not so much the lack of love, though this has been the initial problem. The central problem is that because people are basically mimics, and the home did not provide adequate demonstrations of love, that *he* did not learn how to love. Therefore, instead of reaching out to others, he has developed an insatiable desire to be loved. All the efforts of men and women, of friends and family, will not help him to obtain security.

What he really needs above everything else is to learn how to extend himself to others; how to build up acceptance and self-worth through centering his attention upon others rather than upon self. Thus the involvement of the family is critical, not in making the patient the center of attention, but in helping him to reverse his egocentric concerns and behavior in outreach to family and to friends.

There is nothing more effective in destroying self-love, and therefore the danger of a fragile self-image, than love for others. However, the role of home environment is critical in giving children the maximum opportunity to develop selfless outreach to others. The time parents spend with their children, demonstrating loving care and teaching them how to share and to be concerned with others is perhaps the most valuable time spent with them. This example of loving concern militates against the self-seeking which is inherent within the life of each human being. There is an imperative need to educate children to look beyond themselves to find true happiness and true contentment. But it is also important for parents to respect their children, thus aiding them to develop self-respect. Children should also be taught respect for others, as all Christian love is based upon such respect. As the child develops he must be led to understand that industry and self-support also are keys to self-respect.

Because self is the root of all sin, and as sin inevitably leads to feelings of guilt, it is only to be expected that the insecure person with a low self-image will suffer severely from feelings of self-incrimination. Because of his own insecurity he finds it very difficult to forgive and forget the excesses of others against him, and thus he tends to harbor feelings which in turn, in a circular way, militate against his self-image. Therefore because of the difficulty he has in forgiving others, he finds it difficult to believe that God will and can forgive him. Thus very frequently he suffers from fear that he has committed the unpardonable sin. Unfortunately, many of us have accepted a wrong understanding of guilt. Too often guilt has been limited in our thinking to that disabling of men and women that results in shattered emotional lives. Guilt does have a proper and critical place in the life of every human being. It must not be ignored. Too often we have tried to camouflage guilt by discussing noninhibitory approaches. This strategy in fact has suppressed our guilt feelings, which in turn leads to greater psychological problems.[3]

The Christian whose life is established upon the selfless principles of Jesus Christ; who in full repentance places his burdens upon the burden Bearer, may have peace and contentment and a security against emotional breakdown. Thus the Christian counselor freely acknowledges that neither he nor his counselee has the answer to emotional illness, but he looks to the One who has that understanding and he points the counselee to Christ and His principles of human security.

---

3. See chapter 7 entitled "The Problem of Guilt."

14

Success and Failure

MASSIVE social pressures to be successful and to avoid failure devolve upon most human beings from an early age. Success is usually thought to be achieved through the struggle for victory, notoriety, fame, and acceptance. Failure results when we are defeated, when we fail to meet arbitrarily set goals, when we are rejected, when we remain unknown. A highly competitive society sets the stage for a massive social failure syndrome.

Most concepts of success revolve around power, position, pride, praise, popularity, prestige, property and possessions. And frequently, parents wittingly or unwittingly fire their children with unholy ambitions which stimulate and reinforce egocentric motives and minimize those goals which allow the child to more effectively see success in the light of selfless extension. Failure thus is thought to occur when either those goals we have set for ourselves, or which others have set for us, are not achieved, resulting in frustration, shattered self-worth, guilt and even aggression.

Too frequently the success-failure evaluation is determined by immediate results. Delayed evaluation is often far wiser and is much like the miner who has dug for gold unsuccessfully for weeks, but with continued digging finds the rich vein. Was he a failure in those previous weeks, or was indeed the effort expended worthwhile for the achievement of the ultimate goal? It is obvious that the greatest apparent failure of earth's history, the crucifixion of Christ, was also the basis for the greatest success of human history. Yet at the moment of trial, crucifixion and death, Christ's disciples were thrown into great sorrow, despondency and a sense of failure.

Because success and failure are antonyms, it may be helpful to explore them in terms of the opposites which lead either to success or failure.

1. Selflessness versus self-centeredness

Much is said in this volume concerning the centrality of selflessness and self-centeredness, and certainly these traits have a primary role to play in failure and success. Paul explains the potency of love:

> Charity never faileth: but whether there be prophecies, they shall fail; whether there be tongues, they shall cease; whether there be knowledge, it shall vanish away.   1 Corinthians 13:8

But when self-sufficiency rather than love is the basis of motivation, a sense of failure is inevitable, irrespective of some immediate evidence of success. Selfishness mars the work of all those who are unconsecrated to Christ, and many fail because they trust in themselves. There is a failure to recognize—

> that all things work together for good to them that love God, to them who are the called according to his purpose.   Romans 8:28

This dichotomy between selflessness and self-centeredness is well described in the experiences of King Nebuchadnezzar of Babylon. After he had been warned of serious consequences should he continue in his self-centeredness, pride was still his primary motivation. This pride was evidenced in his evaluation of the basis of his successful kingdom:

> The king spake, and said, Is not this great Babylon, that I have built for the house of the kingdom by the might of my power, and for the honour of my majesty?   Daniel 4:30

This proud man, king of the greatest nation on earth at the time, subsequently spent many years in a state of insanity. True lasting success can be achieved only in the climate of selflessness.

2. Commitment to Christ's leading versus following one's own impulses

Human impulse is inevitably selfish. Man suffers from an overanxiety to seek his own success and to plot his own future. The experience of Peter's walk upon the water[1] is indicative of what happens when man turns away

---

1. See Matthew 14:26–31.

from trust in Christ to trust in self. As soon as Peter turned from Christ he began to sink. Commitment to Christ's leading involved the following of God's commandments and instruction. The Lord emphasized this truth to Joshua:

> This book of the law shall not depart out of thy mouth; but thou shalt meditate therein day and night, that thou mayest observe to do according to all that is written therein: for then thou shalt make thy way prosperous, and then thou shalt have good success.   Joshua 1:8

Frequently men wait for God's leading as if there will be some miraculous revelation to them, but within His Word are to be found the bases of moving forward and of following His leading. All who construct their lives consistent with these principles are in fact following the leading of Christ. They will not fall into the trap of being directed by their own selfish impulses.

3. Christ-control versus lack of control

Whenever man loses sight of the fact that Christ is the ultimate basis of success, he loses the real focal point of his life. By allowing Christ to do His work in us, and by following His pathway, we experience the all-sufficiency of Christ. If our confidence is completely in Him there can be no failure, for with Christ there is no defeat. The battle no longer is ours, but it is Christ's. Often we take the burden and responsibility upon ourselves. The Lord taught this lesson to the prophet Samuel. Samuel was grieved and felt rejected when the people of Israel asked for a king, but God pointed out it was not he they were rejecting, but God.

> And the LORD said unto Samuel, Hearken unto the voice of the people in all that they say unto thee: for they have not rejected thee, but they have rejected me, that I should not reign over them.   1 Samuel 8:7

Paul puts it beautifully:

> Christ liveth in me: and the life which I now live in the flesh I live by the faith of the Son of God, who loved me, and gave himself for me.
> Galatians 2:20

It is put even more explicitly in the epistle to the Colossians.

> Christ in you, the hope of glory.   Colossians 1:27

When our lives are under the control of Christ, success is assured.

4. Submission to God's will versus fear of failure

It may seem strange to place fear of failure as a contributor to failure, but many become inefficient and unsuccessful because they avoid responsibility, fearing that they might fail. Strangely, there are those who, rather than putting all they have into a challenge, will do absolutely nothing to meet it, thus assuring failure. They feel less threatened by the fact that they have failed because they haven't tried, than they would if "failure" occurred after a total effort. This dilemma is not uncommon among students at school or college. We live in a society where many feel that they would rather be judged as lazy than as low in ability or aptitude. Many achievable aspects of their lives are never attained because of fear of failure. Failure inevitably looks to human limitations, and judges them according to human standards.

Two of the strangest experiences of expressed failure occurred in the lives of the prophets, Elijah and Jonah. Elijah had just shown his courage in standing for God on Mount Carmel against the masses of the prophets of Baal. Yet subsequently this man who had demonstrated such trust in God became afraid of the threats of Queen Jezebel and ran into hiding, where he pled with the Lord to take his life.[2] Yet Elijah was on the verge of the greatest honor that God could bestow upon any man—that of life in heaven.

Jonah had attempted to run from responsibility, but God brought him back by a miracle to warn the city of Nineveh of God's impending judgment. So successful was the warning of Jonah that under the direction of its leadership the city repented, and God withheld His judgments. Yet Jonah was filled with consternation when the predictions he had made were not fulfilled. He felt humiliated and he blamed God, justifying his previous flight from duty explaining that he knew that God was gracious and merciful and slow to anger and of great kindness. Therefore he did not believe that God would fulfill His judgment upon Nineveh.[3] Somehow, Jonah failed to realize that through his preaching the Holy Spirit had been able to lead a whole city back to God and what Jonah saw as abject failure was indeed the pinnacle of success. Perhaps there is no greater evidence of the submission to God's will than that expressed by Job:

---

2. See 1 Kings 19:1–4.
3. See Jonah 4:1–3.

Though he slay me, yet will I trust in him.   Job 13:15

Such submission to God's will is the most perfect basis for success.

5. Regard for God's approval versus concern for human approval

It is easy to place our approval status in the hands of man—to be concerned about his evaluation and his judgment. Yet the ultimate responsibility for every human being is a regard for God's approval. While sometimes these will correspond, frequently they will be in conflict, just as Christ, in seeking to do the will of His Father, often evoked the disapproval of the leadership of the Jews. Too often we respond on the basis of what others will think of what we do. Parents can put tremendous pressure on their children, motivating them by indicating how humiliated they are by the failure of their children. Such motivation is born of deep-seated low self-image. Many parents seek to achieve vicarious success through the success of their children, and when their children fail to measure up, they feel thwarted and frustrated. But God's approval is surely the supreme criterion. This truth is fully indicated in Paul's counsel to Timothy:

> Study to shew thyself approved unto God, a workman that needeth
> not to be ashamed, rightly dividing the word of truth.
>
> 2 Timothy 2:15

God's approval is based upon man's wholehearted response to duty, not upon absolute achievements.

6. Acceptance of responsibility versus evasion of responsibility

Failure results from any attempt to evade responsibility, for such evasion is born of looking at personal limitations, rather than placing complete trust in God. Some of the greatest success stories of the Scriptures have come when men have responded to the call of God to bear heavy and difficult responsibilities. As a lad, under the direction of the high priest, Eli, Samuel responded to the call of the Lord, saying,

> Speak, for thy servant heareth.   1 Samuel 3:10

The young Isaiah made a similar response to the call of God.

> Whom shall I send, and who will go for us? Then said I, Here am I;
> send me.   Isaiah 6:8

Paul, after his conversion, prayed to the Lord,

> Lord, what wilt thou have me to do?   Acts 9:6

God never calls a man or woman to accept responsibility unless He also provides the enabling. A call for responsibility is an assurance and promise of His complete power to achieve all that will be required. As men and women accept responsibility, they can confidently pray for and acknowledge the strength and power that God gives them for the task.

7. Desire for greater good, versus a fascination with evil

Far too often we fail because of a fascination with sin. Because true success can come only as a gift from God, it must flow from a pure heart. God deals through pure channels only, and what is not pure He Himself purifies. While the choice of goodness may often involve a pathway of greater difficulty, it will inevitably result in ultimate success. This choice Moses made when he was educated in the court of the Pharaohs.

> By faith Moses, when he was come to years, refused to be called the son of Pharaoh's daughter; choosing rather to suffer affliction with the people of God, than to enjoy the pleasures of sin for a season; esteeming the reproach of Christ greater riches than the treasures in Egypt: for he had respect unto the recompence of the reward.
>
> Hebrews 11:24–26

If Moses had chosen a life of sin and ease, he probably would have remained unknown. But today he is an object of great honor to three great world religions: Christianity, Judaism and Islam. On the other hand, there are those who have chosen what seemed the easy way—the way of worldliness. Thus Paul sadly informed Timothy,

> Demas hath forsaken me, having loved this present world.
>
> 2 Timothy 4:10

However, while the life of sin may seem easy and more attractive, the reality is exactly the opposite, as Solomon warns:

> The way of transgressors is hard. Proverbs 13:15

8. Indomitable will, versus a weak and vacillating will

The weak and vacillating person cannot be successful. A will strengthened by faith and trust in Christ is a will that will achieve success and victory in life. It must be emphasized, however, that the strength of the will is not dependent upon human heredity or background, but upon submission of the will to Christ. A weak and vacillating will is a will that has never been directed by the power of Christ. An indomitable will is developed when the mind of man is transformed and renewed by Christ:

> And be not conformed to this world: but be ye transformed by the renewing of your mind, that ye may prove what is that good, and acceptable, and perfect, will of God.   Romans 12:2

Weakness and vacillation can be seen in response to the challenge of Elijah on Mount Carmel. When challenged by Elijah to choose between God and Baal, the people refused to make a decision.

> And Elijah came unto all the people, and said, How long halt ye between two opinions? if the LORD be God, follow him: but if Baal, then follow him. And the people answered him not a word.
>   1 Kings 18:21

It was only after the great manifestation of the power of God in the acceptance of Elijah's sacrifice and the rejection of the sacrifice of the prophets of Baal that the people had the "courage" to say,

> The LORD, he is the God; the LORD, he is the God.   1 Kings 18:39

God always allows a choice. At the end of his life, Joshua challenged the Israelites to make that choice for or against God, but then showed his own unwavering stand with the words,

> but as for me and my house, we will serve the LORD.   Joshua 24:15

Such a determination results when the fragile will of man is linked with the invincible will of God.

9. Strenuous application versus laziness

The parable of the talents[4] stresses the importance of application. One servant was lazy and sought to make excuses for the lack of development of the talent he was given. The other two, by careful and energetic application, were able to multiply the talents entrusted to them. Hard work, perseverance and determination are all essential components of success. Indolence is a sin. Some simply rest, thinking that they need only put their trust in God for the best good to be achieved, but man cannot expect God to do for him that which he is capable of doing for himself. It is when man has reached the extremity of his resources that God intervenes. Man must move as far as he can, relying upon God to make the difference between his limitation and what he needs for success.

---

4.   See Matthew 25:14–30.

10. Perseverance, versus discouragement

Those who give up easily and who are easily discouraged will also find failure the usual lot of their lives. To continue in the morass of despondency is to establish a climate whereby success cannot survive. Christ made this point when He said,

> And ye shall be hated of all men for my name's sake: but he that endureth to the end shall be saved. Matthew 10:22

Paul's perseverance and continued thrust can be seen in his declaration to Timothy,

> I have fought a good fight, I have finished my course, I have kept the faith. 2 Timothy 4:7

Success cannot be built on timidity or tentativeness, but upon a perseverance which admits no barriers, no obstacles, no obstructions as man maintains his partnership with Christ.

11. Facing trials courageously, versus avoiding difficult roles

It is easy to allow others to shoulder the heavy burdens and the difficult responsibilities. It is easy to excuse ourselves on the basis of lack of background, experience, education or preparation. But honesty frequently reveals that difficulties are avoided because we do not want to face the challenges and trials that we know are frequently part of God's calling. Yet we can rest in the assurance that we face nothing alone. All our talents, abilities, intelligence and physical energy are supported by the great God of the universe, and we need to be reminded of this fact, as Moses was when he wanted to avoid the heavy responsibility that God placed upon him to lead His people out of Egypt.[5] God is the author of our being, responsible for the success of our calling. The ultimate realization of success is in union with Christ, as may be seen in the light of the great crescendo of the last five verses of Romans 8. The question is asked,

> Who shall separate us from the love of Christ? shall tribulation, or distress, or persecution, or famine, or nakedness, or peril, or sword? Romans 8:35

Then comes the assurance,

> Nay, in all these things we are more than conquerors through him that loved us. For I am persuaded, that neither death, nor life, nor angels,

---

5. See Exodus 3:10–17.

nor principalities, nor powers, nor things present, nor things to come, nor height, nor depth, nor any other creature, shall be able to separate us from the love of God, which is in Christ Jesus our Lord.

Romans 8:37–39

Christ not only invites us to accept His salvation, but He also provides the strength to face all difficulties, for the success is *His*.

12. Faith versus presumption

Faith involves a trust relationship with God—a total commitment to Him and His leadings. Presumption on the other hand seeks to achieve the same ends, but in human strength. No better example of the difference between faith and presumption can be seen than in the experience of Abram. Abram exhibited great faith when he followed God's instruction to leave Ur of the Chaldees for a land unspecified.[6] Yet the same Abraham responded presumptively when he accepted Hagar as a second wife in an attempt to obtain the son that God had promised to him. Ishmael, the son of that union, was not the son of promise, but the son of presumption. God responded to faith long after Sarah's normal childbearing age. In the birth of Isaac was truly given the son of promise.

Another example of presumption is given in the experience of Samson. Samson had covenanted with God not to reveal that the secret of his great strength lay in his unshaven hair. But Samson betrayed that covenant by revealing it to his wife, Delilah. Though from previous experience Samson had every reason to believe that Delilah was seeking to deprive him of his strength, he now felt such self-sufficiency that when his head was shaven he still felt that he could achieve the great feats of strength of previous experiences.

I will go out as at other times before, and shake myself. Judges 16:20

And then come the sad words,

And he wist not that the LORD was departed from him.   Judges 16:20

From this traumatic experience Samson learned to trust God. This fact is revealed just prior to his death.

O Lord GOD, remember me, I pray thee, and strengthen me, I pray thee, only this once, O God, that I may be at once avenged of the Philistines for my two eyes.   Judges 16:28

Presumption leads to failure. Faith leads to success.

---

6. See Genesis 12:1–4; Hebrews 11:8–10.

13. Shaping circumstances versus being shaped by circumstances

The truly committed Christian does not allow circumstances to shape his life or to direct him. He exerts positive virtues such as diligence, honesty, integrity and purity, seeking to use circumstances to achieve the great goals that God has set for him. Yet even among professing Christians there are those who are susceptible to every circumstance. Paul pointed out that those who come—

> unto the measure of the stature of the fullness of Christ. . . . [would] henceforth be no more children, tossed to and fro, and carried about with every wind of doctrine, by the sleight of men, and cunning craftiness, whereby they lie in wait to deceive.   Ephesians 4:13–14

Circumstances must be shaped by the Christian, knowing that as God leads He will allow nothing to limit the fulfillment of His purpose. Joshua realized this truth as he faced the river Jordan. The priests were commanded to move forward and the river opened up so that Israel might proceed to the Promised Land.[7]

14. Looking forward versus looking backward

Often failure is built upon a backward look. The failures of our past life should be forgotten. There is no purpose served by reiterating the failures of the past or the circumstances which have produced negative consequences. God calls men and women to believe that the failures of the past have been forgiven, and to look to the future and the glorious hope that He has set before all mankind. Thus Paul was able to say,

> I press toward the mark for the prize of the high calling of God in Christ Jesus.   Philippians 3:14

The destruction of Lot's wife when she looked back upon Sodom,[8] is symbolic of the failure that attends the continued backward look of those who profess Christianity. Success is the inevitable result of a total commitment to Christ. Just prior to his death, David repeated to Solomon God's promise that He would never fail him during the building of the temple.

> He shall build an house for my name; and he shall be my son, and I

---

7. See Joshua 4:5–8.
8. See Genesis 19:26.

will be his father; and I will establish the throne of his kingdom over Israel for ever.   1 Chronicles 22:10

At the dedication of the temple Solomon's prayer acknowledged that his father's trust in God had been honored.

> Blessed be the LORD, that hath given rest unto his people Israel, according to all that he promised: there hath not failed one word of all his good promise, which he promised by the hand of Moses his servant.   1 Kings 8:56

Success is not dependent upon intellectual greatness or personal power, but upon submission to God's leading. God, not man, is responsible for success. How would man value the success of William Carey, the great pioneer missionary to India? As Carey labored for many years without a convert, would these years be considered a failure? Not as we view his work from the vantage point of time.

Success is built upon spending time in prayer and earnest Bible study so that one may become an effective co-worker with Christ. We should not seek to avoid difficulties or struggles, for these are frequently the building blocks of success as we learn wisdom from human failure and as we learn greater trust and faith in God. It is easy to feel humiliated when things do not go according to human plans, but if our security is in Christ, our success will not be evaluated in finite terms. Only those who have faced, and, in the power of Christ, surmounted great difficulties can know the true bases of success.

In eternal reflection we will know the limited view we now have of success. Human plans will then be seen to have been foolish, inadequate and unfulfilling.

15

Motivation

IT is generally held that no behavior results unless there is motivation, for motives incite to action. Motivation can be broadly equated with drives, incentives, appetites, aversions and needs. It is the motive which determines the real nature of man's acts. Christ emphasized this fact in commending the widow who gave all that she had—two mites—for the treasury of the temple. She had in fact given much more than the wealthy who had given large donations from their abundance.[1] God regards most highly every act initiated by selfless concern for others, whereas the most lavish gifts initiated by self-centered motives, are unacceptable to Him and fail to bless the giver. Thus the act of giving must be initiated by generous motivation.

> Every man according as he purposeth in his heart, so let him give; not grudgingly, or of necessity: for God loveth a cheerful giver.
>
> 2 Corinthians 9:7

While it is frequently easy to determine the basis for particular behaviors, that is not always the case. For example, it is usually reasonable to assume that someone eating is satiating the hunger drive. Yet, with present-day knowledge, it is obvious that this assumption is not necessarily so, and the motivation may be related to a wide range of social motives, anxieties or even group pressures; so that just by the behavior *per se* we can never be sure of the precise motivation which has incited that behavior.

It is, however, possible to assume that most bad behavior is incited by wrong motives. For example, stealing will almost inevitably have been incited by some form of self-indulgence; adulterous behavior by lustful

---

1. See Luke 21:1–4.

motives. On the other hand, it is much more difficult to assume that "good" behavior" has automatically resulted from good motives. Frequently, very "good" acts have resulted from impure and self-centered motivation—motivations that are related to one's drive for self-approval, self-acclaim, and social acceptability and prestige. Yet the Christian cannot overlook the fact that motives are the basis upon which his relationship with God is secured. God has declared,

For as he thinketh in his heart, so is he.   Proverbs 23:7

The real determinant of the character of man is not in actions per se, but in the relationship of the heart to Christ. Thus while it is true that compassionate and selfless action will be the fruit of the one whose life Christ has transformed, similar actions may, in many instances, be performed by those whose hearts are totally uncommitted to Christ.

Generally, drives are divided into two groups—those which are of a biological origin, usually referred to as universal drives, and those which are acquired during the lifetime, which are often referred to as social drives. It is conventional to designate the biological drives as primary and the social drives as secondary. However, this designation should not be taken to indicate that the biological drives are necessarily stronger than the social motives. It is true that at birth the dominant drives are biological, such as air, hunger, thirst, avoidance of pain, rest, and excretion. However, during the process of acculturation, frequently the social drives will develop to a marked extent, and in many instances will even dominate the biological drives. For example, the miser who hoards his money may suffer or indeed even die from malnutrition. A student highly motivated for academic success may deprive himself of much rest; and the sex drive may become largely or totally subservient to a wide range of social goals or motives. Thus the primary drives are only primary in the sense that they are innate, and the secondary drives only so classified because they are developed subsequent to the primary drives.

Much discussion has been undertaken to determine the nature of emotive drives such as love, joy, sympathy, and security, together with the aversive emotions of guilt, grief, anxiety, fear, depression, pain, anger, jealousy and hatred. It is felt by most psychologists that the majority of emotions are learned, and certainly the specific expressions of emotions are learned. However, many psychologists agree that probably the emotion of fear and the need of security are inherent, the latter probably forming the basis for the development of love. In adult life emotions form some of the strongest incitements to action. While it may seem that some emotions are positive and others negative, a careful analysis by the Christian will indicate that every emotion can be expressed in a positive, God-centered way or in a negative, self-centered way. The way in which some of the biological motives such as air, thirst and hunger have been diverted and the sex drive has been perverted are dealt with elsewhere.[2] On the other hand, the emotions themselves also offer positive and negative expression. Even the best of motives, such as love, offers negative connotations and the worst, such as hate, positive connotations.[3]

By the time that the claims of Christ are being experienced in the lives of human beings, many of the motives, both biological and acquired, have strong directions toward evil. In many instances it may seem almost impossible for these negatively developed motives to be changed, but God does have the complete power, through the victory of His Son, for all who will to gain victory over every biological and acquired direction toward evil.

Frequently our minds have become polluted because of the mass of unprofitable stimulation that has impinged upon the senses from the earliest age. But there is an answer to this mind pollution. Slowly but surely this accumulation of mental corruption can be removed from the mind by studying and meditating upon the Word of God. David's analysis is pertinent here:

Thy word have I hid in mine heart, that I might not sin against thee.

Psalm 119:11

The purity of truth eliminates the corruption of past experience. But it is in the total commitment of the life to Christ, foreshadowing the new-birth experience, that men and women develop a totally new pattern of motivation.[4] Paul assures us that when man is born again he is a new creation.

Old things are passed away; behold, all things are become new.

2 Corinthians 5:17

---

2. See chapters 20, 25, 26 entitled "Physical Factors in Mental Health," "Morality and Sex" and "Homosexuality."
3. See chapter 8 entitled "Negative Emotions."
4. See John 3:3–6.

It is this new-birth experience which alone can empower a total transformation in the motives of man.

In many passages of Scripture the natural state of man is clearly defined. Paul declares that the possession of a carnal mind (that is, the natural intents and motivations of man) is inimical to the possession of righteous motivation.

> Because the carnal mind is enmity against God: for it is not subject to the law of God, neither indeed can be. So then they that are in the flesh cannot please God. Romans 8:7–8

Jeremiah stated it graphically:

> The heart is deceitful above all things, and desperately wicked: who can know it? Jeremiah 17:9

Solomon declares,

> The thoughts of the wicked are an abomination to the LORD: but the words of the pure are pleasant words. Proverbs 15:26

Jesus stated,

> For out of the heart proceed evil thoughts, murders, adulteries, fornications, thefts, false witness, blasphemies. Matthew 15:19

While man may be able to change some of the behavior patterns normally arising out of such thought processes, he is totally incapable, of himself, to change the state of his heart.

It is only when man admits his total inability to change his thoughts and motives, that he will turn to Christ for the answer. This struggle is vividly depicted by Paul in Romans 7, where he portrays a man who is carnal, a slave to sin, who in his own strength attempts to find that right relationship with God through his own human effort. He discovers that everything that he wants to do he fails to do, and those patterns of life he sincerely wants to avoid are the very patterns he is following, until in desperation he cries out,

> O wretched man that I am! who shall deliver me from the body of this death? Romans 7:24

Immediately the answer comes back,

> I thank God through Jesus Christ our Lord. Romans 7:25

Here Paul shows the simple but perfect answer to man's motivational dilemma. Without the indwelling power of Christ, at the very best we have tainted motives. It is in acknowledgment of this truth that Paul in Romans 8 continues,

> But if the Spirit of him that raised up Jesus from the dead dwell in you, he that raised up Christ from the dead shall also quicken your mortal bodies by his Spirit that dwelleth in you.   Romans 8:11

It is through the indwelling power of the Holy Spirit that man's heart is transformed from selfish motives to motives of love. It is with this understanding that we recognize the significance of Paul's counsel:

> Let this mind be in you, which was also in Christ Jesus.
>
> Philippians 2:5

It is only as Christ's motives activate man's behavior that his actions can flow from a heart of love. It now can be perceived what Solomon meant when he said,

> The thoughts of the righteous are right.   Proverbs 12:5

These thoughts can be right only as the mind of Christ is the controlling power of the life. Therefore the significance in the surrender of the total heart to God cannot be overemphasized. The Lord calls man to turn to Him with all his heart.

> Therefore also now, saith the LORD, turn ye even to me with all your heart, and with fasting, and with weeping, and with mourning.
>
> Joel 2:12

Paul urges us to bring into captivity—

> every thought to the obedience of Christ.   2 Corinthians 10:5

David further prayed to the Lord that—

> the words of my mouth, and the meditation of my heart, be acceptable in thy sight, O LORD, my strength, and my redeemer.
>
> Psalm 19:14

Yet it is impossible for man to change his heart or of himself to receive the mind of Christ. Even the changing of the mind must be an act of God. All may pray the prayer of David:

> Create in me a clean heart, O God; and renew a right spirit within me.
>
> Psalm 51:10

The very motives of man may be changed only as Christ is allowed to remove the carnal mind and replace it with His own mind. Perhaps nothing is a better barometer of spiritual growth than our relation to possessions and wealth. God has designated one-tenth of man's increase, the tithe, as His and allows man to be blessed by giving of offerings and caring for the needy as he is capable.

We cannot give our minds to Christ; we cannot control our thoughts, but we can daily request Christ to take them so that the very motives that initiate our words and actions may be sanctified by the divine life. The promise of the renewed mind is clear. The Lord declared,

> And I will give them an heart to know me. Jeremiah 24:7

And in even more specific language He promises,

> A new heart also will I give you, and a new spirit will I put within you: and I will take away the stony heart out of your flesh, and I will give you an heart of flesh. Ezekiel 36:26

It is in this context that the mind of the Christian is remade. No human effort, no struggle or deprivation can produce it, but the simple submission to Christ of the totality of life will achieve it. It is only thus that man can keep the law of God. In his own strength obedience is impossible, for his very thoughts are perverse and polluted. Jesus declared that adulterous thoughts are a violation of the seventh commandment:

> But I say unto you, That whosoever looketh on a woman to lust after her hath committed adultery with her already in his heart. Matthew 5:28

John declared that hatred is equivalent to murder:

> Whosoever hateth his brother is a murderer: and ye know that no murderer hath eternal life abiding in him. 1 John 3:15

The law of God is kept when the mind is controlled by Christ,[5] and it is in this sense that God has promised the fulfillment of his covenant:

> I will put my law in their inward parts, and write it in their hearts; and will be their God, and they shall be my people. Jeremiah 31:33

When the actions are inconsistent with the motives, man's service is unacceptable to God.

---

5. The reader must not confuse thoughts of temptation with sin. The devil will put evil temptations in our minds as he did in Christ's. These become sin only when we cherish the temptation. Indeed, great blessings are promised to those who do not yield to temptation.

> Ye hypocrites, well did Esaias prophesy of you, saying, This people draweth nigh unto me with their mouth, and honoureth me with their lips; but their heart is far from me.   Matthew 15:7–8

When the words and actions are inconsistent with the motives, confusion and inevitable conflict result. Therefore the purifying of the mind is perhaps the most critical issue in determining the mental health of men and women.

In His sermon on the mount, Jesus said,

> Blessed are the pure in heart: for they shall see God.   Matthew 5:8

Mental health is further assured by Isaiah:

> Thou wilt keep him in perfect peace, whose mind is stayed on thee: because he trusteth in thee.   Isaiah 26:3

Nothing could summarize the motivation of a Christian better than Paul's conclusions to Timothy:

> Now the end of the commandment is charity out of a pure heart, and of a good conscience, and of faith unfeigned.   1 Timothy 1:5

16

Habituation

WHILE Christians reject the behavioristic position that man is
the sum total of all his environmental influences,[1] it is nevertheless certain that present behavior, as well as attitudes and
beliefs have been developed and strengthened by the process of habituation. The Christian understanding of habituation, however, is not independent of choice and decision making. The establishment of habit patterns and characteristic ways of behaving are subject to the modifying
and controlling influence of higher brain processes which, if well developed and rightfully employed, will be increasingly reflected in thoughts,
words and action.

During prenatal development, infancy and childhood, habit patterns
are primarily developed in accordance with the influence of hereditary,
maturational patterns and parental influences. The interaction of these
factors lays a very strong foundation upon which future habits and behavior will be established. As the child arrives into the years of increasing
independence, much will depend upon the resources of these earlier experiences, which will determine the extent to which he is able to behave
according to principles and purposes established by the higher powers of
reason. However, while early experience is held to have a profound effect
upon later choices, it cannot be accepted that this one factor is the only
basis of behavior. It is agreed, however, that the repetition of actions
strengthens behavioral habits, but humans do have the power to modify,
substitute or delete even long-established habit patterns. The conversion
of any human being to Christ involves not only a choice of leadership in

---

1. See appendix A entitled "The Nature of Man."

the life, but also a change of life-style which in many instances is quite radical. If man did not have the power of choice, he would have no way to accept Christ's power in his life. Then there would be no hope that those traits of character defining the unconverted life would be put aside for a life patterned upon the life of Jesus Christ. If a simple stimulus-response view of life were accepted, it would offer at the best a slow and unsure hope of life change and would especially offer little, if any, hope for the middle-aged and elderly to accept the claims of Christ upon their lives. Yet the Bible is replete with examples of the sudden changes wrought by conversions. Zacchaeus,[2] the thief on the cross,[3] and Paul[4] are examples.

The laws of primacy and recency—especially the former—play a role in habit formation. The law of primacy says that early experiences are stronger than later experiences in habit formation. Thus those habits begun in the prenatal and early postnatal life of the child are much more likely to dominate than habits established later. Therefore much care by parents is required during these formative months.[5] Poor habits early established, militate against the work of the Holy Spirit in later life. On the other hand, wise parental efforts will help the infant to develop life patterns which will facilitate his later responses to the Holy Spirit.

The law of recency says that most recent habits tend to be strong. This law is also significant to Christians, for if the last response is consistent with Christian commitment, there is greater likelihood that the response will be repeated subsequently in similar circumstances. But a yielding to temptation increases the likelihood of yielding again.

A most important law is the law of exercise. The frequency with which behavior is repeated determines to a large measure the strength of a habit. Those habits which are motivated by self-centered purposes are more easily strengthened by exercise than those which are selflessly motivated. Thus greater efforts and more specific decisions are needed to establish good habits. On the part of parents, patient, consistent effort is required, and later it is also required of the person himself when he is developing his own independent life responses. The greatest basis for the formation of good habits is self-control, and this quality is strengthened by exercise.

---

2. See Luke 19:1–10.
3. See Luke 23:39–43.
4. See Acts 9:1–6.
5. See chapter 18 entitled "Diet."

The involvement of the will is essential to the breaking of bad habits and their eradication, as well as to the establishment of worthwhile habits. While man is incapable of breaking the evil habits without the power of Christ, neither can they be broken without an acknowledgment that they are wrong, a desire to break from the bondage of sin, and a wholehearted effort to eliminate the evil. Victorious living results only when inadequate human effort is surrendered in faith to the power of Christ who alone effects the transformation that changes self-willed habits into Christlike behavior patterns. This change is what Christ meant in His dialogue with the Pharisee, Nicodemus.

Except a man be born again, he cannot see the kingdom of God.

John 3:3

There must be divine intervention in the life before human effort can effect a transformation from self-centered to God-centered life patterns. Paul fully endorses this truth when he declares,

Therefore if any man be in Christ, he is a new creature: old things are passed away; behold, all things are become new.

2 Corinthians 5:17

The importance of habituation is seen in the response to temptation. If we yield to temptation, the power of resistance is weakened and the conscience is stifled. Every continued repetition furthers the weakening, and if indulged long enough, the reversal of the habit might be almost impossible. However, if temptation is resisted, and in the power of Christ the temptation is overcome, the moral fiber of man is strengthened rather than being weakened.

The Bible stresses the relationship between causal events and their consequences. Paul says,

Be not deceived; God is not mocked: for whatsoever a man soweth, that shall he also reap. For he that soweth to his flesh shall of the flesh reap corruption; but he that soweth to the Spirit shall of the Spirit reap life everlasting. And let us not be weary in well doing: for in due season we shall reap, if we faint not.   Galatians 6:7–9

Choices made, often lead to consequences far beyond the initial issues, and wisdom dictates that even the little choices of life must be made with care. Solomon in metaphoric language indicates this truth when he states,

[It is] the little foxes, that spoil the vines.   Song of Solomon 2:15

That is, it is the little sins that spoil the life.

The acceptance of Christ may be instantaneous, and the life transformation of allegiance from Satan to Christ is instantaneous. This commitment inevitably leads to immediate behavior change, often of a dramatic nature. Nevertheless, while the change in the direction of the life is instantaneous, growth and development of the true Christian are continuous and lifelong. Thus the Christian life is frequently referred to as a growth (1 Peter 2:2),[6] and as a learning experience (Deuteronomy 4:10).[7] Therefore, while the transfer of allegiance is instantaneous, there is the need for daily growth which results from the study of God's Word, from the promptings of the Holy Spirit and from a rich prayer life, thus enabling new dimensions of Christian living to be understood and practiced. Further, while conversion leads to many immediate changes of overt behavior, old habits may reappear when sudden, unexpected adverse circumstances arise. For example, one who at conversion has eliminated blasphemy and cursing from his vocabulary, may nevertheless, to his great consternation, revert to it if suddenly he stubs his toe. However, as he confesses the sin and as he grows and habituates the purity of Christ in his life, less and less in such aversive situations will un-Christlike speech be used even in reflex action. The practicing of Christianity leads to complete victory, and the time eventually comes when never under any circumstances is un-Christlike language used.

It is not possible to ignore the influence of hereditary and maturational factors in determining the possible direction of habit patterns, but it must not be accepted that these are either unchangeable or best for one. It must be acknowledged that Christianity calls for a change from inherent tendencies, and that the power of Christ is able to change men from those patterns inherited or learned, which are self-destructive and lead to eternal separation from God. It is not acceptable to assume that because a man has a characteristic pattern in life that is "just him," and he cannot or need not be changed. Anything that is not Christlike, Jesus has assured us in His strength we can overcome. Every sinful way indulged, strengthens habits of wrong and weakens control. Not only is goodness destroyed by self-indulgence, but contentment and peace of mind are also destroyed.

---

6.   See also 2 Peter 3:18; Ephesians 4:15.
7.   See also Deuteronomy 14:23; Deuteronomy 31:12.

Because it is much easier to be educated for evil, it is more difficult to change strong negative habits. There is much warning against the wilfull indulgence of sin. Solomon expresses the danger forthrightly:

> The way of the wicked is as darkness: they know not at what they stumble.   Proverbs 4:19

Peter also sees a similar relationship for the wicked.

> But chiefly them that walk after the flesh in the lust of uncleanness, and despise government. Presumptuous are they, self-willed, they are not afraid to speak evil of dignities. Whereas angels, which are greater in power and might, bring not railing accusation against them before the Lord. But these, as natural brute beasts, made to be taken and destroyed, speak evil of the things that they understand not; and shall utterly perish in their own corruption; and shall receive the reward of unrighteousness, as they that count it pleasure to riot in the day time. Spots they are and blemishes, sporting themselves with their own deceivings while they feast with you; having eyes full of adultery, and that cannot cease from sin; beguiling unstable souls: an heart they have exercised with covetous practices; cursed children, which have forsaken the right way, and are gone astray, following the way of Balaam the son of Bosor, who loved the wages of unrighteousness.
>   2 Peter 2:10–15

David's prayer was that the Lord would keep his heart from any evil thing.

> Incline not my heart to any evil thing, to practise wicked works with men that work iniquity: and let me not eat of their dainties.
>   Psalm 141:4

All the urging and encouragement of Christian friends and families to reverse or avoid sinful habits will be useless unless the carnal mind is subdued and the Holy Spirit is permitted to control the mind.[8] It is the secret to the eradication of wrong habits and the establishment of good habits.

Pure and holy thoughts do not arise naturally in the mind of the unconverted man or woman. The carnal (natural) mind is not able to obey the law of God.

> Because the carnal mind is enmity against God: for it is not subject to the law of God, neither indeed can be.   Romans 8:7

---

8. See Romans 8:6–14.

Therefore the carnal mind follows pathways of sin. Yet the Christian is not an automaton. The choice is his, whether to allow the Holy Spirit to transform his life, and he also must exert his effort and influence on the side of right to the fullest extent.

The development of useful habits is critical not only to self-worth but also to contentment and purity of life. The availability of unstructured leisure time can be most harmful. Idleness and laziness provide the platform for a wide range of unproductive and unprofitable behavior. Thus from their earliest years children should be taught habits of industry. This training offers a great barrier against discouragement and despondency. Also the development of habits of regularity and order lays a foundation for profitable activities in other spheres of life. The way in which the young are educated is vital to later habit patterns. Thus Paul advocates that fathers bring up their children in the nurture and admonition of the Lord.

> And, ye fathers, provoke not your children to wrath: but bring them up in the nurture and admonition of the Lord.   Ephesians 6:4

Solomon gives the assurance that right education of the children will be rewarded by right conduct in manhood.

> Train up a child in the way he should go: and when he is old, he will not depart from it.   Proverbs 22:6

However, we must recognize that the final choice is that of each individual, and personal effort allied with the power of the Holy Spirit is needed to obtain victory over sinful habits.

> Submit yourselves therefore to God. Resist the devil, and he will flee from you.   James 4:7

While it is usual to associate habits with overt behavior, it is necessary to recognize that habits have their source in the mind. Thus Solomon says,

> For as he thinketh in his heart, so is he.   Proverbs 23:7

Further, Solomon admonishes,

> Keep thy heart with all diligence; for out of it are the issues of life.
>   Proverbs 4:23

And Jesus said,

> Out of the abundance of the heart the mouth speaketh.
>   Matthew 12:34

It is undoubtedly in the light of this relationship between thoughts, words and actions that the Psalmist wrote,

> Let the words of my mouth, and the meditation of my heart, be acceptable in thy sight, O Lord, my strength, and my redeemer.
>
> Psalm 19:14

The monitoring of thought patterns is essential to the formation of profitable behavioral habits which are the foundation of character and are fundamental to Christian growth. The overcoming of evil habits requires the choice to serve God, for it is through the will that sin gains its victory over man until the will is almost paralyzed, to the extent that it is hardly possible to make right decisions. It will take effort and control by the will, for one to turn away from wrong to profitable habits, but the results will be greatly rewarding. The Scripture frequently admonishes us to practice doing good, while departing from evil.

> Depart from evil, and do good; seek peace, and pursue it.
>
> Psalm 34:14

> Let him eschew evil, and do good; let him seek peace, and ensue it.
>
> 1 Peter 3:11

Further, the practicing of good is depicted in the Scripture as a learning process:

> Learn to do well; seek judgment, relieve the oppressed, judge the fatherless, plead for the widow.　　　Isaiah 1:17

> With my soul have I desired thee in the night; yea, with my spirit within me will I seek thee early: for when thy judgments are in the earth, the inhabitants of the world will learn righteousness.
>
> Isaiah 26:9

> And it shall come to pass, if they will diligently learn the ways of my people, to swear by my name, The Lord liveth; as they taught my people to swear by Baal; then shall they be built in the midst of my people.　　　Jeremiah 12:16

But it is more than a learning experience. The will can be exercised consistently for good only when it is linked with an unwavering trust in God.

> Trust in the Lord, and do good; so shalt thou dwell in the land, and verily thou shalt be fed.　　　Psalm 37:3

It is this trust that enables one determined to depart from evil and do good, to be successful.

Depart from evil, and do good; and dwell for evermore.

Psalm 37:27

Trust in God provides power to overcome both learned and inherent patterns of behavior which are inconsistent with the fullness of life. The prophet Jeremiah makes it plain that man on his own is unable to change his evil habits.

Can the Ethiopian change his skin, or the leopard his spots? then may ye also do good, that are accustomed to do evil. Jeremiah 13:23

Thus we must squarely face every sinful habit, and by irrevocable trust in Christ change our old ways. This trust can be exercised only when self is fully renounced, for only then can man's will be safely reunited with the will of God. When God controls our will, then our thoughts, words, emotions and deeds are controlled. It is only then that we can fulfill the rewarding command,

But love ye your enemies, and do good, and lend, hoping for nothing again; and your reward shall be great, and ye shall be the children of the Highest: for he is kind unto the unthankful and to the evil. Be ye therefore merciful, as your Father also is merciful. Judge not, and ye shall not be judged: condemn not, and ye shall not be condemned: forgive, and ye shall be forgiven: give, and it shall be given unto you; good measure, pressed down, and shaken together, and running over, shall men give into your bosom. For with the same measure that ye mete withal it shall be measured to you again. Luke 6:35–38

While reward seeking will never be the motive for good acts, there is inevitably a rich reward that finds its expression in physical, emotional and spiritual healing and strengthening. It is the Spirit of God which educates the mind to seek spiritual values, and motivates to actions of purity and holiness.

Habits are the foundation of character.[9] Even the minutest act constitutes character. Therefore persistent and consistent right doing is the basis of perfecting a Christian character. There must also be a constant reminder of God's will and His way so that a well-established, understanding basis for right doing is developed. For example, God instructed Israel to teach His law constantly to their children while implanting its precepts in their

---

9. See chapter 3 entitled "Mental Health and Character."

own hearts.[10] Yet each test, trial and temptation must be surmounted one at a time. There are those who have been ensnared in sin for many years. It is the Christian's responsibility to demonstrate to these tempted ones that God offers an entirely superior way of life while also providing the power to live that life.

But the laws of habituation are such that while Christ forgives and restores, the life is marred proportionately to the temptations to which one has yielded. Further, our God-given talents are limited to that extent. It is a serious decision to continue in sin once the knowledge of truth is obtained, for each wrong habit weakens the physical, emotional and spiritual development. Those who feel they are at liberty to persist in worldly pursuits for a while, expecting to turn to God later in life, make a fearfully dangerous decision. Not only are they seriously limiting both the time and effectiveness of their usefulness to God, but they also face the consequences of persisting in wrong habits which will constantly weaken their resolve until they may no longer even desire to walk in the paths of righteousness.

Test and temptations are permitted that many may choose: by yielding, to strengthen the habits of wrongdoing; or by resisting, to strengthen the habits of right doing. Each defect weakens, and each victory strengthens the ways of righteousness. The power of Christ is readily available to all who earnestly seek to break the bonds of wrong habits established upon inborn tendencies to evil. Human desire and effort are a necessary, but not a sufficient, basis for the formation of habits of goodness and purity. Continuous victory results only when our desires and efforts allow Christ to remove all self-idolatrous motives, that the power of His Spirit may work the works of sanctification in our lives.

---

10. See Deuteronomy 4:4–9.

17

The Senses

MAN monitors his external environment by way of his twelve to fifteen sense modalities,[1] and it is through these modalities that the brain and the central nervous system receive input. To a large measure the sensory input controls the output of the mind. Evils in the environment evoke evil within the mind.

Emotional and mental health have much to do with the sensory input we receive, as well as with the individualized responses to this input. These responses are in turn integrally bound up with one's spiritual health. It is obvious that we do not have total control over the stimuli monitored by sense organs. It is also true however that we do have considerable control. It stands to reason that if our input is consistently of a negative nature we cannot fulfill the dynamic potential that God has for us. The Scripture says,

> For they that are after the flesh do mind the things of the flesh; but they that are after the Spirit the things of the Spirit. For to be carnally minded is death; but to be spiritually minded is life and peace.
>
> Romans 8:5–6

Thus the spiritual life established upon the imputed and imparted righteousness of Jesus Christ not only is a preparation for eternal life, but also offers a guarantee of peace. An emotionally disturbed person lacks internal peace, but the Christian has the foundation of ultimate peace. Much depends upon what our sense modalities translate to our brains. Paul emphasizes the need for careful input to our mind:

---

1. These include cold, hearing, heat, kinesthesia (position sense), pain, light, pressure, deep pressure, smell, stereognosis (sense of shape), taste, touch, two-point discrimination, vibration, and vision.

Finally, brethren, whatsoever things are true, whatsoever things are
honest, whatsoever things are just, whatsoever things are pure, whatsoever things are lovely, whatsoever things are of good report; if there
be any virtue, and if there be any praise, think on these things.

Philippians 4:8

It is impossible for humans to think about things that have absolutely no
relevance to their experiences. For example, it would be impossible for
an infant to think about nuclear physics. It is completely outside the range
of his experience, and indeed is outside the experience of many adults.
But we do think upon and contemplate those things which come within
the purview of our perceptual experiences. Every sense modality is constantly receiving information concerning the environment. This reception begins long before we are born, while we are in the prenatal state,
and of course is vastly expanded shortly after birth. In the varied world in
which we live, the perceptual possibilities are almost unlimited. All sorts
of stimuli are, as it were, fighting for our attention.

Mankind has become more and more aware of all the various aspects
of human attention, the various efforts of the advertiser, the person who is
trying to get his point across through the mass media, those who are trying to sell their wares. Those seeking to gain our attention direct their
efforts toward the widest range of human audience. Some of these things
are good, some of them are profitable; but a vast number are directed
toward soul destruction. It is not wise for us to desire to experience all the
possible experiences that are available, and many times we are very greatly
advantaged by avoiding those experiences which would be likely to militate against sound mental health and spiritual growth.

Not all knowledge is power. This lesson was sadly learned by Adam
and Eve in the Garden of Eden.[2] Human perception is beclouded by pride,
selfishness, and negative emotions. Persistent sin diminishes perceptual
keenness. It is by beholding that man is changed either for good or for
evil. Paul points out that by beholding the glory of the Lord we—

are changed into the same image from glory to glory, even as by the
Spirit of the Lord.   2 Corinthians 3:18

Some young people see a tantalizing mysticism in that which is dissimilar
to the life-styles to which they have been accustomed. But Christian-ori-

---

2. See Genesis 3:1–19.

ented young people need to realize with great thankfulness, that from which they have been preserved, rather than to allow their curiosity to draw them into a way of life which is self-destructive. While the Christian does not subscribe to the rigid deterministic view that we are simply the total of our perceptual experiences, we cannot deny that the Word of God points out that what we see and what we hear, and what we taste, and what we smell and feel have profound influence on the way in which our minds function.

While it is almost impossible for us to escape at least some of the corrupt influences in our environment if we are going to live anything like a normal life, yet we need not enter completely into a full feasting of our senses upon the kinds of things that are morally destructive. Thus David entreated the Lord to keep his eyes from beholding the false and the vain.

> Turn away mine eyes from beholding vanity; and quicken thou me in thy way.
>
> Psalm 119:37

It is especially critical that infants and children be provided with a wholesome and morally sound environment. Their appreciation of the simple values of life is destroyed by focusing the mind upon the imaginary. In their formative years, the attitudes, beliefs and value systems are being formed. Also, at this time of life it is difficult to discriminate between the real and the unreal. Most children go through a stage of fantasy when they are convinced that the make-believe is in fact reality. This fantasy is often associated with apparent playing with animals which do not exist. Many parents are deeply concerned by this behavior and consider it to be lying on the part of the child. But it is not lying in the normal sense of deliberate fabrication. We cannot help the child either by punishing him for the act, which often leads to repression on the part of the child, or by going along with the fantasy. But it is important to help the child realize that we discriminate between the real and the unreal by saying something like, "Yes, but it isn't a real monkey, is it?"

An environment in which the child is able to relate in a constructive way to the real world is especially important at this stage. The child is further helped by the parent in reinforcing a real object or activity that has taken place, by an appropriate comment. Too often at this age children are fed with the make-believe built around fantasy stories. These in themselves are not helpful to the child's development and are even more devastating when they become part of the regular fodder of the television diet of the child. Parents need to make every effort to help the child to discriminate between the real and the unreal.

Television is especially devastating to the young child, for young children do not have the background or the experience to be able to handle effectively these fantasy experiences. Thus they tend to integrate them within their real life. Therefore that which may be of minor influence upon an adult (and even this assessment is questionable) can be a major influence upon the child. The television has been largely responsible for the entertainment syndrome that makes it increasingly difficult for young people to relate to, or to enjoy the solid and practical pursuits of life. Studies have shown that extended television viewing produces the slow alpha wave brain patterns of the sleep and resting state rather than the faster beta wave brain patterns of normal intellectual activity. This passive reception of what is viewed underscores the dangers of television viewing.

It must be realized that the mind is a dynamic entity which does not turn off when the television is turned off. Young people receive much of their experience vicariously, often four or five hours a day minimum, through the avenue of the television set, and are getting less and less experience in the real world. This orientation has devastating implications, and some psychologists have attributed the increase in child and adolescent schizophrenia and autism to this specific source.[3]

Furthermore, unlike a book, the television or radio does not allow for careful evaluation of what is heard or what is presented, for immediately it has passed on to another topic. The reader of a book has the opportunity to reread, to contemplate and to evaluate very much more effectively. But even here the wrong kind of reading can have effects similar to those of the television, where the world of fiction is interwoven into the fantasies of the mind. Nor can one overlook the impact of music. Not only does hard rock music have devastating physiological implications, and certainly militates against the tranquility of mind that God provides for man; but much other music has similar consequences.

In a pleasure-loving age, it is easy for the minds of both children and adults to be engrossed in amusements which cannot profit and are unre-

---

3. See chapter 22 entitled "Childhood."

warding. Amusements pursued simply for the sake of excitement and plea-sure are always ultimately unsatisfying because they are self-gratifying, and are neither useful nor a blessing to others. The worthwhile pursuits of the Christian draw him closer to God and make him a greater blessing to others. Any amusement excites the imagination, whether it be the theater, sporting events, or novel reading. Thus amusements are destructive of a tranquil life and spiritual growth. Though exciting at the time, they tend to be followed by depression demanding even greater excitement and thus they do not contribute to lasting happiness. The wise Christian so controls his environment that he avoids as far as possible, reading, seeing or listening to that which is harmful to spiritual growth. Neither should he overlook the influence of the senses of feeling, of taste, and of smell.

Children usually learn to enjoy the type of food they are given to eat as little children. Thus the parents have an obligation to direct their tastes in such a way that they will enjoy wholesome food. If they are given spicy foods when young they will desire those foods later in life. Simi-larly those who are given foods designed for health of mind and body will value such a diet in adulthood.

It is worthwhile on the other hand to look at those influences which do provide a positive atmosphere for monitoring the perceived world of the infant, the child and the adolescent. Obviously a beautiful relaxed, rural environment is superior to the contrived, bustling environment of the ur-ban areas. The results of good reading, of good companionship, of music that is relaxing and spiritually uplifting, of Bible study—all have a posi-tive, strengthening effect upon the development of mental health. Spiri-tual things are discerned through the promptings of the Holy Spirit.

> But the natural man receiveth not the things of the Spirit of God: for
> they are foolishness unto him: neither can he know them, because
> they are spiritually discerned.   1 Corinthians 2:14

This discernment is accomplished more effectively as the earnest study of God's Word fortifies the mind against evil and the deception of Satan. Spiritual growth is dependent upon clear perception which emanates from God through the Holy Spirit, and is more readily achieved when the life is, as far as possible, surrounded by that which is pure and holy and when the mind is fed with wholesome intellectual and spiritual food. With great care should parents choose the books and magazines provided for their children. Those materials encouraging thoughts of dedication and of service should ever be available, to the exclusion of the imaginary, the sensational and the fictitious. Parents also have a responsibility to provide recreational activities which, in a noncompetitive way, draw their children toward the great natural handiwork of God, and which provide opportunity for spiritual growth and service to others.

18

Diet

PREVIOUSLY we have explored the influence of the perceptual processes of our sense modalities upon mental health.[1] There are, however, other ways of influencing brain functioning. The brain is the anatomical structure mediating mind processes, and is the basis of the neurological processes that stimulate the thought mechanisms of every human being.

While the sense modalities and the peripheral nervous system play a major role with their input to the brain, it cannot be overlooked that the functioning of the brain is also greatly affected by the blood circulatory system. It is therefore to be expected that our mental health is related to the eating and drinking patterns that we follow, as the quality of the nutrients in the blood is greatly affected by dietary habits. Paul certainly saw this clear relationship of diet to our spiritual life when he said,

> Whether therefore ye eat, or drink, or whatsoever ye do, do all to the glory of God.   1 Corinthians 10:31

The apostle Peter, referring not only to diet, but also to the link between diet and spiritual life, says:

> Dearly beloved, I beseech you as strangers and pilgrims, abstain from fleshly lusts, which war against the soul.   1 Peter 2:11

There is no doubt that Satan is frequently successful in controlling lives through appetite.

In the sophisticated age in which we live, human dietary input has been revolutionized. Much of our diet is based upon refined foods, and

---

1. See chapter 17 entitled "The Senses."

the liquid consumed tends to be other than the pure water primarily given by God for the satiation of man's thirst. Governments today are pouring millions of dollars, through various agencies, into research which has uncovered the fact that many processed foods commonly ingested by humans have great health risks attached to them. Because of the interrelationship between the physical, emotional and spiritual life of man, it is understandable that these foods also affect his emotional stability. The safest and best approach to living revolves around simple foods that are not highly seasoned nor highly refined, for there is a close relationship between simplicity of diet and human growth and development.

Diets free from refined sugars, fats and oils and spices do much to reverse degenerative diseases such as cardiovascular disease, cerebrovascular disease, diabetes, arthritis and obesity. Much evidence indicates that a diet high in complex carbohydrate, high in fiber, and relatively low in fats and protein is the most suitable for human needs. Such a diet would have not more than about twenty percent unrefined fat and twenty percent unrefined protein and not less than sixty percent complex carbohydrate. This diet, simply but tastefully prepared, is not only conducive to good health, but is also comparatively inexpensive.

The use of refined fats, both saturated and unsaturated, is advocated less and less. The fats occurring naturally in nuts and grains are superior to the concentrates. This principle is true also for refined carbohydrates and protein concentrates. Up until a century or so ago, the majority of people found little difficulty in living a life that included a simple and often relatively healthful diet. But today, for the city dweller especially, such a diet has to be carefully planned and thoroughly understood. It is significant to note that God chose a simple environment—a beautiful garden, in which man was to make his first home.

> And the LORD God formed man of the dust of the ground, and breathed into his nostrils the breath of life; and man became a living soul. And the LORD God planted a garden eastward in Eden; and there he put the man whom he had formed. . . . And the LORD God took the man, and put him into the garden of Eden to dress it and to keep it.
>
> Genesis 2:7–8, 15

It may be further noted that the cities had their origin with the first murderer, Cain.

And Cain knew his wife; and she conceived, and bare Enoch: and he builded a city, and called the name of the city, after the name of his son, Enoch.

Genesis 4:17

The simple diet is still best for man's health. Especially today when cancer, tuberculosis, and other diseases are much in evidence in animal flesh,[2] there can again be great benefit derived from a vegetarian diet. Further, the constant frequenting of restaurants and cafeterias makes it more difficult to select the kind of diet more likely to preserve the mental, emotional and physical health. It is in the home that the diet can be most successfully monitored.

Much of wrong diet can be traced to self-centeredness. Overeating, and eating the wrong kinds of food, have foundation in an uncontrolled self-seeking which militates against spiritual and emotional health. It will be noted that the infant has great preoccupation with oral satisfaction. Much of his early life is bound up with the gratification of his hunger needs, and one of his basic compulsions is to place almost everything he can manipulate into his mouth. Much education is required to transform the indiscriminacy of infancy into the balanced and selective patterns of sound dietary principles. There is no question that a poor diet, built around improper health habits, can be a strong factor in the demonstration of poor temperamental characteristics. Overeating tends to draw the blood from the brain, and frequent eating between meals has a negative effect upon the emotional being. Eating should not be continued until one feels uncomfortable; neither should the appetite be indulged between meals.

There are very good reasons why the glutton is grouped with the drunkard in Scripture.

For the drunkard and the glutton shall come to poverty: and drowsiness shall clothe a man with rags.

Proverbs 23:21

And they shall say unto the elders of his city, This our son is stubborn and rebellious, he will not obey our voice; he is a glutton, and a drunkard.

Deuteronomy 21:20

---

2. When the King James Bible was translated, the English word *meat* meant food derived from grain, not from flesh: "And when any will offer a meat offering unto the LORD, his offering shall be of fine flour; and he shall pour oil upon it, and put frankincense thereon. (Leviticus 2:1)

Both produce a certain "intoxication" of the mind which reduces the effectiveness of moral judgment, and limits one's spiritual growth, leading to reduced emotional growth. In fact, there has been considerable research involving the relationship between diet and mental illness, and some investigators claim to have been able to establish a very strong correlation between diet patterns and the tendency to neurotic and psychotic behavior.

Christians have a great responsibility to carefully monitor their eating and drinking habits, regularizing them and taking care as to the quality and the amount of food eaten. The regularity of eating is important. It is almost always best if not more than three meals be eaten each day, and some who are not engaged in heavy physical labor may be better with two meals per day. These meals should be spaced at least five hours apart, with nothing other than water taken between them. The last meal is best eaten at least four hours before bedtime. It is also beneficial to digestion if no liquid is drunk with the meal so that digestion is not inhibited. However, good quantities of water should be drunk between meals. Health is further stimulated when meals are eaten slowly in a happy, social atmosphere with deep gratitude to the great Provider of all our sustenance. Digestion is also assisted by light exercise after eating, as in brisk walking or light gardening. Is it not a moral wrong to eat or drink in a manner which saps our physical strength and leaves our minds less capable of discernment between good and evil?

Further, intemperance in eating affects our emotions, for those desirable emotions of love, tenderness, kindness, and sympathy are dependent upon clear minds and unselfish behavior patterns. On the other hand, the undesirable emotions such as hatred, envy, jealousy and covetousness are no doubt strengthened by habits which are based upon self-seeking and self-serving.[3] Often we try to disassociate the intellectual aspects of life from the emotional aspects, but it is well nigh impossible to do so. Some have looked upon religion in this way, suggesting that emotions should play no part in religious acceptance or in religious practice. However, the totality of the human experience is related to our religious life, and our emotions are critically bound up with religious decisions. This is not to suggest that overly emotional responses cannot be counterproductive, and

---

3. See chapter 8 entitled "Negative Emotions."

a religion leading to the building up of a frenzied reaction could hardly be considered to have produced a holy emotion; but love and kindness, tenderness, and sympathy are emotions which themselves have been expressed by God to His people through the sacrifice of Jesus Christ, and Christianity is part of these positive emotions. Such emotions are also intimately connected with sound mental health.

On the other hand, Christians must seek to avoid undernourishment. Some go to extremes, making various aspects of diet virtually the prime characteristics of their faith. We cannot imagine Adam and Eve as thin and emaciated, any more than we envision them as obese. "Much evidence now exists as to the dangers to longevity of being underweight" (*The British Medical Journal*, 4th October 19380, vol. 281 p. 894). Of course it is recognized that some people have, genetically, a predisposition to slender figures, just as others have genetic tendencies to obesity. However, Scripture does counsel against extremes in diet. While under- and overnutrition are not always reflected in one's physique, the principles of dietary control apply to all.

Today the problem of narcotic drugs has escalated to mammoth proportions. Research is replete with evidence of the negative effects of tobacco, alcohol and other drugs upon the emotional and physical development and stability of the person. A dependency develops which may indeed facilitate neurotic disabilities rather than solving the cause of the nervousness and tension. In fact, in using any stimulant one fails to get at the very cause of physical problems, and a dependency situation is developed, leading to continuous deterioration and increased dependency upon the stimulants and drugs. Further, the use of any narcotic strengthens selfish indulgence and consequently weakens the will. Even the consistent use of headache preparations can produce serious physical and emotional dependencies, which in themselves militate against the power of the Holy Spirit and the calm and tranquil pursuit of life. Yet, sadly, there are many who would prefer the inevitable results of poor diet rather than submit to self-discipline.[4]

The Christian church as well as society at large now faces a serious problem in the use of hard drugs of various kinds. The minds and bodies of children and teenagers are being destroyed, frequently because of the

---

4. See chapter 19 entitled "Mental Health and Legal Drugs."

appeal of the unknown and the appeal of the mysterious and the forbidden. This appeal is accentuated by the inordinate peer-group pressure which is often facilitated by free samples of drugs from designing pushers. There is no complete assurance that any child will not experiment with drugs and thus be lured into the tragedy of addiction. Parents must not turn a blind eye to the possibilities even with their own children. However, if open communication has been established, and if the child has learned to love and relish a simple life-style, there is less likelihood that he will show an interest in the drug scene. But perhaps the greatest safeguard against yielding to this temptation is the previous development of a firm basis upon which to make those decisions which will permit a child to remain firm even in the face of rejection or scorn. Often lectures on the danger of drugs do little to turn youth away from them, and may even increase drug usage.

There can be no doubt that in the complex and confusing age in which we live, there is a need for an active choosing of life-styles and practices which have as their base simplicity and naturalness, facilitating the development of strong physical, emotional and spiritual lives. This ideal does not develop by chance, but results from careful and deliberate efforts to structure one's life-style consistent with the best practices of physical health. Wrong habits of eating and drinking lay a foundation for faulty patterns of thinking and acting. Perhaps no factor is of greater physical, emotional, intellectual and spiritual importance to our health than the habits of eating and drinking.

19

Mental Health and
Legal Drugs

ALCOHOL causes more murders, more crimes of violence, more marital disharmony, more mental breakdown and more motor vehicle accidents than heroin, morphine, cocaine, amphetamines, marijuana and all other drugs combined. Yet alcohol is a legal drug. On the other hand, men and women commonly receive the severest of penalties for selling the other drugs cited. Some countries execute heroin pushers while marketing alcohol to their citizens.

Let us imagine, hypothetically, what would happen if alcohol had been discovered for the first time in the 1980s. It would naturally be tested first in animal studies. The investigators would find that the learning processes are slowed, coordination impaired, the liver, heart, brain, nervous system and gastrointestinal tract severely damaged and that emotional changes have occurred. The result of such findings could lead to only one result— alcohol would be banned in every civilized nation upon this earth. One does not have to be particularly insightful to know how the stringent American Food and Drug Administration would treat such a drug.

The same is true of other legalized drugs, such as nicotine and caffeine. These drugs, however, became established in the life patterns of the populace before their dangers were fully appreciated, and today the economic and political power exerted by the manufacturers and the users of these drugs is so great that few governments dare to energetically tackle the problem.

The sad truth is, that ignoring the divine warnings concerning the dangers of these drugs, warnings given well in advance of the findings of medical science, many Christians are consuming them. The situation has grown so imposing that at least one denominational publication has felt constrained to confront the problem of Christian alcoholics. Many believe that the consumption of alcohol in moderation is consistent with their Christian commitment. But experience shows that those adopting this view are spiritually weak and commonly lose their way. Further, peace of mind is lost.

Almost forty-five years ago one of the authors and his wife were invited to a social evening at the home of another church member. To our dismay we found fellow church members, one church elder and two trainee nurses from our own hospital consuming alcohol. Indeed, we were the only ones who refrained. Altogether about twenty church members were involved. Today not a single one of those present remains faithful to the Lord. In most cases their lives have been utter failures, with career disappointments and marital infidelity. No one became drunk on that occasion. All felt safe in their "moderation."

The dangers of the use of alcohol "in moderation" are enormous. As a tissue poison, even small amounts work their havoc. But it is upon our spiritual lives that alcohol does most damage. Alcohol is a sedative which initially depresses the high cerebral centers, releasing us from the control of those brain areas which mediate our response to the Holy Spirit. To be a loyal follower of the Lord Jesus Christ takes moral vigilance, and even small amounts of alcohol decrease this safeguard. We read of only a single instance of Christ being offered alcohol. This was at the time of His extremity, yet He dared not take the drug, for Christ required total clarity of spiritual perception in order to save us from our sins.

> And they gave him to drink wine mingled with myrrh: but he received it not.   Mark 15:23

No true Christian could weaken his resolve to follow his Savior by partaking of that which subdues conscience.

Another danger of "moderate" alcohol intake is that some people are prone to alcoholism. There is no way to determine who is thus predisposed. Invariably the alcoholic commences as a "moderate" drinker. Only those who abstain from alcohol are assured of the avoidance of such a tragedy. And even if we ourselves do not become alcoholic, it would be a matter of great heartache if we, by our acquiescence to the intake of alcohol, gave an example to our children which led them to such a dire condition.

Many Christians argue endlessly about whether Scripture condones the drinking of alcohol in moderation. What is true is that the Bible frequently warns of the dangers of strong drink and also admonishes God's chosen people to avoid it. A few representative examples are set out below:

> Wine is a mocker, strong drink is raging: and whosoever is deceived thereby is not wise. Proverbs 20:1

> It is not for kings, O Lemuel, it is not for kings to drink wine, nor for princes strong drink: lest they drink, and forget the law, and pervert the judgment of any of the afflicted. Proverbs 31:4–5

> Now therefore beware, I pray thee, and drink not wine nor strong drink, and eat not any unclean thing. . . . Behold, thou shalt conceive, and bear a son; and now drink no wine nor strong drink, neither eat any unclean thing: for the child shall be a Nazarite unto God from the womb to the day of his death. Judges 13:4, 7

> For a bishop must be blameless, as the steward of God; not self-willed, not soon angry, not given to wine, no striker, not given to filthy lucre. Titus 1:7

> For he shall be great in the sight of the Lord, and shall drink neither wine nor strong drink; and he shall be filled with the Holy Ghost, even from his mother's womb. Luke 1:15

> But ye gave the Nazarites wine to drink; and commanded the prophets, saying, Prophesy not. Amos 2:12

Hosea accurately set forth the crux of the problem with alcohol when he asserted:

> Whoredom and wine and new wine take away the heart. Hosea 4:11

This perception was expanded by King Solomon and the prophet Isaiah:

> Who hath woe? who hath sorrow? who hath contentions? who hath babbling? who hath wounds without cause? who hath redness of eyes? They that tarry long at the wine; they that go to seek mixed wine. Look not thou upon the wine when it is red, when it giveth his colour in the cup, when it moveth itself aright. At the last it biteth like a serpent, and stingeth like an adder. Proverbs 23:29–32

But they also have erred through wine, and through strong drink are out of the way; the priest and the prophet have erred through strong drink, they are swallowed up of wine, they are out of the way through strong drink; they err in vision, they stumble in judgment.

Isaiah 28:7

Isaiah's counsel is most pertinent. As Christians each one of us is a priest. Protestants quite rightly are confirmed in the concept of the priesthood of all believers, yet many shun this wise reflection upon the effects of alcohol upon priests. Our calling as God's children is far too high to reject the obvious implications of this passage of inspiration.

Some Christians argue that the Bible nowhere specifically condemns the moderate intake of alcohol, and use this argument as grounds for their drinking. One could use a similar argument for the taking of heroin, the practice of gambling and the indulgence in polygamy. The list of sins which could be practiced if such biblical reasoning is used is a very long one indeed.

A visit to a busy emergency room on a Friday or Saturday evening would convince any reader of the disproportionate effect of alcohol upon road fatalities. As case after case is brought in by ambulance, very soon the odor of stale alcohol hangs like a heavy cloud over the whole department. In Melbourne's Austin Hospital it was found that approximately twenty percent of the inpatients were there as a direct result of alcohol. We can scarcely imagine the cost of this drug to the community in terms of money and lost production. In addition, the greater problem is the human heartache.

Further, many parents are amazed and distracted when their children become addicted to "hard" drugs. They have set the example to those children which has led them to use narcotics. The parents of one young man came to see one of the authors. As Christians, they were emotionally devastated by the arrest and imprisonment of their son for the robbery of a pharmacy in an attempt to obtain narcotics to satisfy his addiction. It was indeed a very tragic situation, since the family members had lived lives of apparent rectitude. However, upon questioning it became evident that the parents had set an example of caffeine ingestion and later of wine consumption with the evening meal and at occasional socials. Such an example had clearly had repercussions in the life of the son.

Of the legal drugs, nicotine is possibly the least used in certain denominations. Nevertheless some have succumbed to it. Of the three drugs here discussed, none is more difficult to break from than nicotine. Excluding those drinkers who have become alcoholics, the vast majority of alcohol drinkers find it much less difficult to discontinue alcohol than to cease smoking. Being an irritant, nicotine has effects upon emotional stability in addition to its well-documented physical consequences. Once addiction is established, the lack of a cigarette causes irritability which can be relieved only by further consumption of the drug. Many believe that cigarettes calm their nerves, overlooking the fact that in reality the cigarette is simply subduing the nervous instability which its lack is causing.

No Christian dare defile his body by some chemical which destroys in him the Spirit of Christ. How well the archenemy of souls used these drugs to entrap us, to destroy our equanimity, and to lead us from the Lord.

Probably the most-used drug in Christian homes is caffeine. Once again, it is a poison with amply documented effects. It is in the area of mental health, however, that it has some of its most devastating consequences. In the standard pharmacological text book originally edited by Goodman and Gilman, over eleven finely printed, double-columned pages are devoted to the serious pharmacological effects of this drug. Many of these effects are upon the brain and the nervous system. Yet a cup of tea or coffee of average strength contains a full pharmacological dose of caffeine.

One of the authors was confronted in his office by a distraught housewife, 28 years of age. She was in a particularly agitated state and demanded to be sedated. She could not stop shouting at and quarreling with her husband, and was continuously irritated by the children. She confessed that she truly loved her husband and children, but she knew she was headed for a marriage breakup unless her entire personality changed. She herself was powerless to do anything to control her rantings and ravings. She virtually demanded help immediately. Because of her present state of neurotic behavior, the task seemed hopeless. It appeared that only a general anesthetic could have prevented her highly emotional conduct. Naturally it was vital to find the cause of her problem. Despite much questioning, to the discomfort of many patients waiting to be seen in the clinic, no real environmental source of her problem was elucidated. It was only when she was specifically questioned that it was ascertained that she drank about ten cups of coffee per day. Suspecting that it was possible that the patient was suffering from severe caffeine intoxication, the doctor advised her to cease her caffeine intake. She felt that such a request was impossible to follow because of the severe withdrawal effects she anticipated. It was pointed out that this was a test of just how much she did love her family.

The patient left the clinic rather dejected by the advice given, and obviously with little confidence in its efficacy. She was not seen for two months. When she did return, her countenance was so changed that it was not possible to recognize her. From a tormented person she had been transformed to a radiant young mother and wife. This transformation of personality had not been mediated by any medication; it had not been the result of psychotherapy; it had simply resulted from the discontinuance of the potent drug, caffeine.

The growing habit of Christian parents in giving cola drinks to their children further prepares them for emotional difficulties since the cola bean, like the coffee bean and the tea leaf, contains caffeine and is a dangerous commodity. Others, while vocally condemning the drinking of tea, coffee and cola beverages, take excessive amounts of headache preparations containing caffeine. The source of the drug is irrelevant. It is equally debilitating from all preparations.

As Christians, it is impelling that we avoid the intake of these drugs, for they militate against the expression of the Christian virtues and lead us from God, and in so doing destroy our personal happiness.

20

Physical Factors in Mental Health

GOD has provided in nature that which is designed for man's physical health and regeneration. To His chosen people, Israel, He promised the speedy restoration of health if they would minister the love of God to the needy and the oppressed.

> Is not this the fast that I have chosen? To loose the bands of wickedness, to undo the heavy burdens, and to let the oppressed go free, and that ye break every yoke? is it not to deal thy bread to the hungry, and that thou bring the poor that are cast out to thy house? when thou seest the naked, that thou cover him; and that thou hide not thyself from thine own flesh? Then shall thy light break forth as the morning, and thine health shall spring forth speedily; and thy righteousness shall go before thee; the glory of the LORD shall be thy rereward.
>
> Isaiah 58:6–8

The relationship of selfless concern for our fellow man to strength and mental health has been explored elsewhere,[1] but Isaiah also assures us that physical health is greatly enhanced when in the strength of Christ, selfishness is removed, so that the joy of service may be achieved. Self-centeredness has a significant effect upon man's physical resources. The emotional stress of constantly defending self, together with the anxiety of personal hurt, almost certainly increases the predisposition to severe cardiovascular and other degenerative diseases. Thus what affects emotional health affects physical health, as both are greatly influenced by the action of the sympathetic nervous system.

Because of this close interrelationship between physical and emotional health, an essential understanding of the principles of physical health is

---

1. See chapter 5 entitled "Love and Mental Health."

vital to those seeking the restoration or maintenance of mental health. Provided within earth's environment is all that is required for the development and continuation of maximal physical health. While, in a world largely distorted by sin, physical health may be impaired by accidents, physical causes and genetic limitations, yet to a marked extent our physical health is within our own control. It is a responsibility that pays enormous personal dividends. When Paul appeals to Christians to offer their bodies a living sacrifice, completely acceptable to God, this admonition, like all God's commands, is for man's great benefit.

> I beseech you therefore, brethren, by the mercies of God, that ye present your bodies a living sacrifice, holy, acceptable unto God, which is your reasonable service.   Romans 12:1

David declares that God is the source of health.

> Who forgiveth all thine iniquities; who healeth all thy diseases.
>   Psalm 103:3

Certainly God's health principles are designed to provide the fullest physical benefits for all who follow His simple health rules. These rules can be summarized in eight principles:

1. A simple, well-balanced diet

2. A following of the laws of temperance

3. The use of pure water

4. Fresh air

5. Regular exposure to sunlight in moderation

6. Daily exercise

7. Adequate and regular rest patterns

8. A daily trusting relationship with God

In chapters 18 and 19, principles of diet, temperance and use of water were explored. But it might be further emphasized that true temperance calls for the elimination of all narcotic drugs, of irregular and poor eating habits, of the use of condiments and all that is harmful by use or by overuse. In developed societies it has become increasingly difficult to find water that is unpolluted. The situation has been further complicated by the necessity to add chemicals to almost all urban water supplies. Whenever possible, distilled, rain or spring water should be used. Obviously, a rural life-style lends itself more readily to the abundant supply of this type of water. Further, in dealing with physical health, the use of water as a healer should not be overlooked. The healing properties of the body are increased when a hot shower is followed by a cold, thus stimulating the circulation of the blood and toning the system. The use of alternating hot and cold fomentations is of great value in the treatment of colds, fevers and inflammations. A thorough knowledge of all the principles of hydrotherapy greatly enlarges the therapeutic uses of water, reducing the need for the use of drugs, which in some cases have dangerous side effects.

It is not suggested that God's people take a fanatical attitude to the use of medications. Because of our misuse of the principles of healthful living, it not infrequently becomes necessary to use certain medications. For example, anyone who has seen patients in severe heart failure will recognize that no form of hydrotherapy will then change the prognosis of the patient. Such patients in many cases have only minutes to live unless supported by appropriate intravenous medications. To see a patient snatched from certain death by the emergency use of digitalis, a diuretic, a bronchial tube dilator, and even in some cases small doses of morphine, is one of the more satisfying duties of a physician. But even in such situations, simple physical measures are used by the wise physician to supplement the work of powerful medications. The head of the bed is elevated to assist breathing. Tourniquets are often applied to the limbs in order to restrict the flow of blood to the heart and thus reduce its work and assist it to supply blood to the vital internal organs.

Some believe that drugs should not be used under any circumstances. It is quite right that serious warnings be heeded concerning the use of drugs. But it is hardly a sound health principle to withhold drugs when to do so leads to the death of the patient. Many lifesaving interventions are done by surgeons. But does anyone suggest that these men perform their operations without the use of anesthesia? Of course not; yet anesthetic agents are among some of the most potent drugs used by physicians.

In no disease was physical treatment more used in the first half of the twentieth century than in tuberculosis, yet the graves of those who succumbed to this dread disease were numerous. Sanitoriums proliferated. It has to be acknowledged that it was not until the discovery in the 1940s of streptomycin and other drugs, that the mortality rate of this disease dropped to negligible levels and sanitorium after sanitorium closed.

A carefully chosen rural environment is also the greatest guarantee of fresh air. Often an elevated environment is necessary in order to be above the smog zone. The value of fresh air cannot be overestimated. One's vitality depends to a major extent upon the oxygenation of the blood. Unpolluted air permits the maximal transfer of oxygen to the cell tissues of the body. If a large amount of pollutants is constantly breathed into the lungs, poisons such as carbon monoxide become linked with the hemoglobin of the red corpuscles of the blood, thus reducing the amount of oxygen transmitted to the cells. Each day special intakes of fresh air should be planned. This intake can be achieved by regular deep breathing and by vigorous exercise.

The frequent exposure of the skin to sunlight also has a protective influence against disease. The ultraviolet rays of sunlight are a most effective means of destroying bacteria. In warmer weather this protection can be achieved through regular sunbathing. In those climates where for long periods of each year there is much cold weather, similar therapeutic results can be achieved by the use of sun lamps. Sunlight also effectively changes 7-dehydrocholesterol in the skin into vitamin D. There is some evidence that the risk of skin cancer from sunlight can be reduced when the exposure to the sun is combined with a natural diet—especially a low-fat diet where the fats are obtained in their natural state in whole grains and nuts and other vegetable products. Nevertheless wisdom dictates that excessive sunbathing or use of sun lamps should be avoided. A few minutes of exposure to ultraviolet rays per day is sufficient to kill harmful bacteria. This exposure, associated with sun-filled rooms, achieves the advantages of sunshine without overexposure which can be damaging.

Next to diet, exercise has perhaps the most profound influence upon physical health. Regular exercise in the fresh air is important for both physical and mental health. Inactivity on the other hand results in physical weakness and predisposition to disease and mental illness. The best and most beneficial exercise is that which is consistent, moderate and of sufficient duration to elevate the heart and breathing rates significantly over a reasonable period of time. Unquestionably, exercise of noncompetitive nature achieves the best results. The education of youth in competitive sports is of less value than that which has a noncompetitive basis. Competitive sports are largely a residue of the slave mentality of the ancient Greeks, where all useful manual labor was done by slaves and was thought below the dignity of a free man, so that sports were devised as a means of physical exercise for the children of free men. God's provision for man employed useful labor. In the Garden of Eden, the physical needs of men were supplied by work in the garden.

> And the LORD God took the man, and put him into the garden of Eden to dress it and to keep it.   Genesis 2:15

The sons of the prophets in Israel also were regularly engaged in useful labor:

> But as one was felling a beam, the axe head fell into the water: and he cried, and said, Alas, master! for it was borrowed.   2 Kings 6:5

It was the practice of the Jews that every child, no matter what his future occupation might be, was taught a physical trade. Thus it was not unusual that Christ was taught the carpenter's trade, and Paul was trained as a tent maker.

> Is not this the carpenter, the son of Mary, the brother of James, and Joses, and of Juda, and Simon? and are not his sisters here with us? And they were offended at him.   Mark 6:3

> After these things Paul departed from Athens, and came to Corinth; and found a certain Jew named Aquila, born in Pontus, lately come from Italy, with his wife Priscilla; (because that Claudius had commanded all Jews to depart from Rome:) and came unto them. And because he was of the same craft, he abode with them, and wrought: for by their occupation they were tentmakers.   Acts 18:1–3

Competitive sports, although providing physical exercise, also have many harmful side features. Competition is born of conflict, and rather than encouraging the positive grace of cooperation, these sports encourage contest. Further, competition is ordinarily associated with a striving for the mastery over another person or team. The failure of one is necessary for the success of the other—a principle contrary to the kingdom of Christ. Competition also tends to add tension to the exercise, and this tension is known to have severe physical consequences when continued over an extended period of time. There is also a tendency to take competitive activities to excess, often resulting in physical injury. This possibility is greatly accentuated when the sport is of a combative nature as in such activities as football, boxing and wrestling. Finally, competitive sports rarely provide a basis for lifetime exercise habits and are often discontinued, with little replacement except spectator sports, once youth has passed.

Noncompetitive activities such as brisk walking, hiking, noncompetitive cycling, running, and swimming offer a much more balanced basis for the development of physical health. Yet good though these are, perhaps the most productive physical exercise is useful labor. If the labor requires vigorous activity such as in gardening and construction, most of the exercise required for health will be obtained with profitable and money-saving results. Such work in the sunshine and fresh air can have an excellent therapeutic influence upon those who engage in it regularly.

Sound physical labor also has other physical benefits; for example, Solomon declares,

> The sleep of a labouring man is sweet, whether he eat little or much:
> but the abundance of the rich will not suffer him to sleep.
>
> Ecclesiastes 5:12

Thus there is probably more than surface meaning in Solomon's challenge to—

> go to the ant, thou sluggard; consider her ways, and be wise.
>
> Proverbs 6:6

Regularity and soundness of rest are in themselves important criteria of physical and mental health, and also a barometer of emotional contentment. Late and irregular hours of sleeping upset the equilibrium of the body, thrusting stress and strain upon it and upon the mind. Christ recognized the need for rest when He encouraged his disciples to relaxation after a heavy program:

> And he said unto them, Come ye yourselves apart into a desert place,
> and rest a while: for there were many coming and going, and they had
> no leisure so much as to eat.   Mark 6:31

There is also a wonderful rest from daily cares when one's life is fully submitted to Christ. He has promised to give rest to all who come to Him:

> Come unto me, all ye that labour and are heavy laden, and I will give
> you rest.   Matthew 11:28

There are a number of aspects that are to be considered by Christians—the rest that submission to the claims of Christ brings, the evening rest of sleep, the weekly rest of the Sabbath and the rest that comes in a change of occupation and pace during a vacation. All play a significant role.

The rest Christ gives is revitalizing, both physically and emotionally. Perhaps the greatest basis for true rest is that resulting from the knowledge that all our sins are forgiven and that we are secure in Jesus. The regularity of the nightly sleep is also of great importance. Studies indicate that relatively early departure for bed is best combined with an early rising in the morning. It is true that some feel they function better at night than in the early morning, but perseverance will habituate the change to more profitable sleeping habits, just as is accomplished in a week or two when jet lag takes place as a result of rapid time changes. There is also evidence that seven to eight hours sleep per night is the most advantageous. Significantly more or less time than this tends to be associated with shortened life expectancy.

God has also provided for man a weekly rest day—a day that allows him to break the routine of the work week to engage more directly in study of His Word and in fellowship with other Christians. This day was given to man at Creation.

> And on the seventh day God ended his work which he had made; and he rested on the seventh day from all his work which he had made. And God blessed the seventh day, and sanctified it: because that in it he had rested from all his work which God created and made.
>
> Genesis 2:2–3

To His people Israel, God directed that physical preparation should be made for the Sabbath so that only essential work would need to be done that day:

> And he said unto them, This is that which the LORD hath said, To morrow is the rest of the holy sabbath unto the LORD: bake that which ye will bake to day, and seethe that which ye will seethe; and that which remaineth over lay up for you to be kept until the morning.
>
> Exodus 16:23

The fact that most Christians do not preserve God's holy day as a rest day and either completely or partially continue in an everyday routine, must contribute to the many ills of society. It is an area that no earnest Christian can ignore. Jesus Himself said that the Sabbath was made to benefit man.

> And he said to them, The sabbath was made for man, and not man for the sabbath.
>
> Mark 2:27

The rest and rejuvenation resulting from annual vacations should also be clearly evaluated. Activities diverse from one's regular occupation are best suited for maximum results from such vacations. The using of vacations to work around the home is rarely as rewarding as when the vacation is taken in a different locality, although if one is a sedentary worker, such a plan may have some value. Yet if there are children in the family, vacations should be well considered. A vacation, especially in the beauties of nature, may often be achieved for a minimum cost. It is usually more beneficial if the vacation can be taken for an extended period of time. The taking of vacations one day at a time rarely has the rejuvenating effects of a vacation for at least a period of two weeks. The whole purpose of rest is to better fit the recipient for the routine tasks of life. Often jaded nerves and weariness can be eliminated so that the tasks of life can be faced with greater strength and enjoyment.

The eighth physical principle—trust in God—has been discussed extensively elsewhere.[2] It forms the unifying principle underlying all physical and mental health and provides the motivation for a selfless concern to fulfill all of the seven other principles. Intemperance of all kinds is born of selfishness and results in stress, impatience, strife, depression, and acts of passion. Further, intemperance slows down the rate of recovery from illness and in some cases totally jeopardizes the prospects of recovery. Health and happiness are consistent results of temperate living. Each of these health principles is established upon the law that simplicity of life strengthens physical and mental power. Each is also established upon the principles of a balanced life-style allowing for the full beneficial powers of the body, mind and spirit of man to complement the functioning of the other. It is in this sense that mental and spiritual growth are to be dependent to a significant degree upon the development and maintenance of one's best physical health. That which enfeebles the body places considerable strain upon all other human resources. Conversely a careful attention to the principles of physical health is of great benefit to mental health and the stabilization of a well adjusted life-style.

Trust in God results in the development of secure emotional relationships. David acknowledged this truth when he said,

> Blessed is that man that maketh the LORD his trust, and respecteth not
> the proud, nor such as turn aside to lies.   Psalm 40:4

---

2. See chapters 2, 3, 5, 6, 7 entitled "Mental Health and Spiritual Growth," "Mental Health and Character," "Love and Mental Health," "Law and Love," and "The Problem of Guilt."

It is better to trust in the LORD than to put confidence in man.

Psalm 118:8

Great social stability would be experienced if the unsettled of society could find that inner peace that only trust in Christ can bring.

21

The Prenate and the Infant

A childless home is frequently a lonely home and can lead to self-ishness. But on the other hand, parenthood is often undertaken with far too little thought of the responsibilities that devolve upon parents. The mental health of the child begins with the parents. A well adjusted family environment is perhaps the greatest legacy that parents can give to their children in developing sound and secure mental health. Thus responsible parenthood requires that parents have a secure and well adjusted life-style before initiating a new life within the family. This basis is fundamental if parents are not to commence the prenate's life with that which will predispose him to a faulty character.

The responsibility of the mother is particularly important. In the formative prenatal months it is essential that the mother follow a simple life-style not given to frequent bursts of emotionality. There is abundant evidence of the profound influence of the earliest intrauterine experience of the child upon its subsequent emotional, physical and personality characteristics. Strong emotionality leads to sympathetic nervous system reactions, such as the secretion of adrenalin and other substances into the blood stream. Though the placenta is a good filter, these substances enter the bloodstream of the fetus, resulting in its hyperactivity. Frequent emotional outbursts by the mother prior to birth, can lead to emotional behavior patterns in postnatal life. These reactions militate against the development of sound mental health in the infant and child. Often parents of highly emotional infants wrongly conclude that the cause is generic, overlooking the critical role of the prenatal environment. It is not that genetic factors do not have a profound influence on childhood and later adult characteristics; they do. But parents who themselves are calm and happy during the time of pregnancy tend to predetermine, to a marked extent, a similar temperament in the child.

The education of the first child should be approached with special care, for it sets the pattern for parents in their approach to subsequent pregnancies and births. Further, the attitude and the behavior of the first child have a strong educational influence upon all other children born into the home.

We cannot overestimate the role of sound health habits in the life of the expectant mother. There is incontrovertible evidence that alcohol, narcotic drugs and tobacco all have strong detrimental effects upon the developing fetus, and the caring mother will completely disassociate herself from the use of any of these. Each year hundreds of neonates die from drug withdrawal symptoms and thousands of others, though surviving, show very clear evidence of drug withdrawal symptoms because of the heavy drug intake of their mothers. The use of tea, coffee and other drug-containing preparations should also be avoided. A simple, regularized healthful diet is of inestimable value to both expectant mother and fetus.

It is the responsibility of the father to assist the mother in providing a calm and peaceful environment during pregnancy. The husband who is irresponsible and uncaring of his wife, or who is unfaithful, places an enormous burden upon her which she will find difficult to bear, especially during pregnancy when physical resources tend to be lower than normal. It is just as much the expectant father's responsibility as the mother's to structure the most suitable environment for the prenate. Every effort should be made to reduce those burdens which exhaust and weary the expectant mother. The toxins built up by weariness will have an inevitable impact upon the unborn child. It is best if husband and wife can arrange their programs so that the wife does not continue in an outside work program. By this means stressful influences are reduced. On the other hand, a regular, moderate exercise program is helpful. Overworking on the part of the mother can lead to stress and tension which will militate against the healthy development of the baby.

It is probable that there is not much more than 18 months to develop the temperamental patterns of infants, and nine of these are before birth. Because the infant is very impressionable, self-control needs be taught from the earliest time. The Scripture indicates in a number of experiences the need for careful temperate living on the part of an expectant mother so that the child may have the maximal opportunity of healthy growth and development. For example, the wife of Manoah, who was to be the mother of Samson, was warned by the angel of the Lord to abstain from strong drink and to avoid eating any unclean foods.[1] At perhaps no other time is a simple diet more important than during pregnancy. This observance of health principles forms a first basis of right behavior for the child later. It is essential that in both the prenatal period and the early childhood the child be educated in self-denial, for much of his later happiness depends upon this training.

In the early postnatal period, there is the possibility of underestimating how critical is the learning process of the child. Yet this is probably the most dramatic learning period in the experience of life. The neonate appears so helpless that few parents begin to realize the lasting effects of those early experiences. The security established in the first few months will have much to do with the emotional security of the child in later years. It is always best if a careful and regular daily pattern can be developed. The best environment is a rural one in which the mother can provide full-time care for her child. Other factors important to the development of worthwhile tastes in later life should not be overlooked. For example, music will play an important part in his later life, and the frequent exposure to good music in infancy will be of great value in later life when tastes mature.

The infant will soon learn regular feeding habits if the mother will schedule these regularly. This schedule will help, at a very early stage, to avoid anxiety that irregular handling of the child will produce. In almost all cases scheduled feeding is to be preferred to demand feeding. Demand feeding is erratic and frequently can form the habit of demanding self-gratification. The baby learns to cry not only for food but also for anything he wants, and parents will soon discern that such cries are almost always temper cries rather than need cries. Thus will be developed habits which in later life, while sophisticated to meet increased maturity, will nevertheless be established upon egocentric principles. Another important influence upon the child is a happy relationship between parents and other members of the family.

It is wise for the infant to be present at morning and evening family worships on a regular basis. While it is true the infant cannot initially

---

1.　See Judges 13:14.

grasp the spiritual life that is involved in the worship period, nevertheless attitudes are developed at this early stage which will make it much easier later for the child to find the worship period a blessing. Here are taught true reverence and also the joy of fellowship with God, making it much easier for him in later life to show true reverence to God, to the place of worship, to God's Word and to His ministers. The worship period should be suited to the interest of the youngest child, and as soon as possible the children should be involved in singing, in Bible stories, reading and learning Scriptures and in prayer.

The development of wise habits in early infancy will militate against the efforts of Satan to lead the child away from God. The parents must very quickly learn the difference between a cry of pain and a temper cry. Never should a temper cry be reinforced by any form of attention. But the parent should always be ready to respond appropriately to a cry of pain or serious discomfort. Neglect of biological needs greatly inhibits sound emotional growth.

In the earliest postnatal period the child should be taught in a careful, loving way to respond to the commands of the parent. This plan is not simply to train the child in a behavioristic sense, but it is vital in helping the child to form suitable habit patterns which will facilitate, at a later stage, the claims that Christ will make upon his life and service. Long before the child is able to respond verbally, he may be taught many valuable lessons of obedience. As soon as the child is able to understand, however, this understanding should be involved in the education and training of the child. Careful attention to early education can forestall a multitude of problems. Yet the wisest parents will need much of the grace of God and a continual prayer life to successfully educate the children entrusted to them.

The overwhelming principle in the relationship of parents to their children will be tender love. From the earliest years babies sense this love and respond to it. This love will not gratify every selfish desire, but it will provide the warmth and closeness of parental love which does much, under God's blessing, to draw the child to God and to others in the family circle. It also influences the child to warm and satisfying interpersonal relationships with those outside the family.

Some parents today are neglecting the dedication of their children to God. Let this not be overlooked. Jesus' parents set us a sound example in this matter.[2] Nothing is more important than this dedication, if accompanied by a sincere desire and effort on the part of the parents to place God's will first in their responsibilities of parenthood.

---

2   See Luke 2:27–32.

22

Childhood

THE will is the most critical aspect in the development of sound mental health; therefore it is vital to develop the child's will and decision-making processes as quickly and effectively as possible. In the very early stages, the parent will be mind for the child. This relationship provides for the biological needs as well as for the protection of the infant from danger. But step by step, usually at first in regard to danger, the child must be confronted with the cause-effect relationships involved. For example, he needs to know that fires, or creeks, or busy highways are dangerous.[1] Initially the parents will have to think for the infant, but as soon as possible it is important for them to let the child see that there is reason behind their decisions. Thus when giving a response to a request, the parental answer is best linked with the reason. For example, Johnny may ask, "May I play with Billy?" It may be inappropriate for him to play with Billy, but a simple answer such as "No, because we are just about to have supper" indicates that mother has a reason for saying No. To say simply "No" is to evoke the almost inevitable question "Why?" A response such as "Because I told you so" does nothing to deepen the child's understanding of reasoned behavior and often creates the stimulus for negative and angry exchanges between parent and child.

Later the child may be helped to make some decisions for himself in cooperation with parental encouragement and guidance. Special attention should be given to consideration of possible outcomes. For example, the

---

1. When James, the youngest son of one of the authors, was eight months old he crawled out a gate which had been inadvertently left open. The driver of a huge log truck stopped two feet short of him as he crawled across the busy highway, quite oblivious of the danger. This incident not only told much of God's protecting care, but fully illustrates the lack of the perception of danger in early childhood.

parents may help the child to make decisions in terms of such experiences as the purchase of clothing until such time as the child can be trusted with those decisions independent of his parents. There is no specific time when such maturity will be reached, and parents will have to determine wisely how much independence can be allowed to each child, and at what age level each decision can be entrusted to him.

It is best that the child learn to make decisions in nonmoral areas before he is given increasing freedom in the area of right and wrong. Step by step, in simple matters, however, the parents may educate the child even to make decisions in areas of moral consequence. Sometimes the parents must take the risk that the child will make a wrong decision. If it happens, it should not be the signal for panic action, for the parents also make mistakes; but it may be necessary to retreat a little after seeing the child is not yet ready to take full responsibility. Certainly the child should never be allowed to reach the position where he feels that he has no responsibility to mother or father in major decision-making. But the time may come when the child rebels against any intrusion into his decision-making by his parents; yet even this reaction will be unlikely if the parents have wisely guided the child from his earliest years so that a trust relationship between parent and child has been firmly established.

Perhaps the two greatest mistakes parents can make are to overly control the child, or at the other extreme, to permit the child to do just about what he wishes. Both are destructive of the child's decision-making development. In the first case, the will tends to be crushed by the coercive discipline, and when in later life the child is faced with decision-making, he does not have an adequate basis upon which to make those decisions, and tends to behave in a manner consistent with the "natural man," which is inconsistent with a commitment to Christ. On the other hand, the child who has grown in a permissive environment learns to be self-willed and to validate his behavior by hedonistic principles. He, too, finds it difficult to make right decisions when he reaches adolescence, and has a strong tendency to move away from God toward unrestrained behavior patterns. Thus the coercive and the permissive homes both fail to teach adequate principles of decision-making to the child. Both methods can have disastrous effects in adult life. The Scripture places this training in fine balance. The Christian parent will faithfully lead his household.

> One that ruleth well in his own house, having his children in subjection with all gravity
> 1 Timothy 3:4

The parent will not ignore the punishment of continued, willful disobedience.

> He that spareth his rod hateth his son: but he that loveth him chasteneth him betimes.
> Proverbs 13:24

> The rod and reproof give wisdom: but a child left to himself bringeth his mother to shame.
> Proverbs 29:15

However, he will do everything to avoid a negative, destructive, unloving environment which would crush the child and inhibit true positive growth and development.

> And whosoever shall offend one of these little ones that believe in me, it is better for him that a millstone were hanged about his neck, and he were cast into the sea.
> Mark 9:42

> And, ye fathers, provoke not your children to wrath: but bring them up in the nurture and admonition of the Lord.
> Ephesians 6:4

It is most important for the child to learn obedience to his parents, not from fear or from threat, but upon the basis of responsibility that he has toward his parents who stand, especially in his early life, in the place of God to him. If the child is placed under continual criticism and is subjected to much physical or psychological punishment, the character of God will be perverted in the mind of the child, and the child-parent relationship will be ever defective. Self-control is vital to good parenthood.

By learning implicit obedience to parents and other authorities, the child learns obedience to God. Obedience is an integral part of one's relationship with God.

> Elect according to the foreknowledge of God the Father, through sanctification of the Spirit, unto obedience and sprinkling of the blood of Jesus Christ: Grace unto you, and peace, be multiplied. 1 Peter 1:2

It extends even to the thoughts:

> Casting down imaginations, and every high thing that exalteth itself against the knowledge of God, and bringing into captivity every thought to the obedience of Christ
> 2 Corinthians 10:5

However, just as those who are truly obedient to God will be motivated by love, so too, true obedience to parents will be elicited by the emotion of love. It is by witnessing the love and affection of their parents that children learn the true meaning of the fifth commandment.

> Honour thy father and thy mother: that thy days may be long upon the land which the LORD thy God giveth thee.   Exodus 20:12

Only then can a harmonious development be maintained.

There must be suitable rules in the home. These should be simple, necessary rules which are consistently enforced in love. As the child increases in age it is often profitable to allow him to help in the formation of rules. In this way he will be more encouraged to keep them. Obedience should be required consistently, and parents should expect their requests to be responded to the first time they are made. In the ultimate it is far kinder, for the child then understands the predictability of the parent. If the request has to be repeated many times, the child will tend to become confused. The parent will eventually become impatient if not irrational, and may respond violently to the child. Such actions do not foster good family relationships.

The child will need to be reproved from time to time, but all reproof should be given in love, not in anger. Impatient words destroy true family relationships, and harshness leads to bitterness. The strong censure of children leads to insecurity, low self-image, despondency and hopelessness. Resulting negativism may split the family so that irreparable damage results. There is a need to represent the true character of God to the child—His love, His mercy and His long-suffering, which is often best exhibited in handling discipline problems. The positive aspects of the child should be recognized and while flattery should be avoided, commendation, approval and encouragement should be liberally given when appropriate.

Another important factor in the mental health, growth and development of the child is his mental food. Today's artificial life, with the complexity that modern society offers, makes it much more difficult for today's children to grow up in an emotionally secure environment. In an article entitled "Troubled Children—the Quest for help,"[2] it was estimated that at least 1.4 million children in the United States under the age of 18 have emotional problems of sufficient severity to warrant urgent attention, and as many as 10 million more require psychiatric help of some kind if they

---

2. See *Newsweek*, April 8, 1974.

are ever to achieve the potential that medical progress on other fronts had made possible. Some suggest a figure even as high as 30 million, an inordinately large segment of the under-18 population of the United States. This figure is not limited to mild neurotic conditions, but also includes deep psychological problems such as autism, schizophrenia, and hyperkinesis. As one psychiatrist quoted in the article says, "The fortunate child is the one with good heredity, and adequate care provided by two parents who are able to recognize and meet the child's need in early life, and a minimum of chronic overwhelming stress situations as the child grows up." Unfortunately, fewer children today have the privilege of a two-parent home. Nor do they have an environment devoid of stressful situations. It was further pointed out that today's mobile society has almost abolished the extended family concept in which aunts, uncles, grandparents and other relatives formed a further fabric of support for the growing child. Thus the Christian church, if properly organized and alert, must become part of the extended family to the children of its members, and in this sense adults should consider themselves the fathers and mothers of all the children in the church. One psychiatrist quoted in the report indicated that he did not believe that two parents, let alone one, could rear a child entirely alone, and therefore church support is critical.

We face the situation where many young children do not have the privilege of a mother constantly with them during the day. The complexity of society, and the drive for modern conveniences, mean that frequently both parents are working, and yet there are many who would agree with Dr. Salk's opinion: "I'd much rather see people not have children at all than leave infants in a day care center" (Ibid.). There is no question that under almost all circumstances the mother is best able to care for her child in the early formative years, and this God-given responsibility should not, except under only the most pressing circumstances, be placed in the hands of someone else. It is far better to have fewer of the so-called comforts of life than for a child to be without his mother for long periods of the day.

However, the survey went on to pinpoint as one of the great causes of mental breakdown in children the devastating influences of television. "In today's push-button society, children tend to learn about the world around them vicariously by television. Many of our children and young people have been everywhere by ear and eye, and almost nowhere in the realities of their self-initiated experience. Much of what the children see is a vivid depiction of war, violence and social upheaval. Aggression has become one of the most pervasive childhood experiences of all. Children learn abnormal behavior by observing other people" (findings of the Commission on Mental Health of Children, quoted in ibid.).

It is now accepted that television is playing a primary role in the establishment of the value system of society and is significantly affecting attitudes and morals. That the television depicts much which is in contradistinction to biblical morality is a sober warning to parents who have the moral and spiritual well-being of their children at heart. Even advertisements and news bulletins often emphasize that which is immoral or distasteful.

It is thus vital that parents monitor what the children see and what they hear. Not only does this need apply to television but also to reading, to radio, to record players and like devices. Often, because of indulgence or lack of strength on their part, parents have surrendered to the environmental influences, but the responsibility of parenthood in developing an environment that will maximally assist in the spiritual and emotional growth of the child is very critical. Children must be taught that any indulgence which interferes with mental and spiritual growth is not profitable and should be eliminated. Indulgence does not make children happy, but restless and discontented; and although it is natural to crave the sensational and the exciting in entertainment, such have no value for fruitful living. To secure the child's life against evil influences or that which is less than fully rewarding, the child must be surrounded by useful and interesting activities. The development of creative and constructive interests which absorb the child is primarily the responsibility of the father for sons, and of the mother for daughters. However, many activities involving the whole family together, especially in the out-of-doors, do much to cement family ties while also filling the void that the exclusion of sensational entertainment leaves in the life of a child. Such excursions also help to establish worthwhile lifetime patterns.

The Bible is replete with examples of the devastating effects of permissiveness on the part of parents. Perhaps none is more obvious than the experience of Eli, the high priest of Israel, whose sons were not disciplined nor their lives directed in a fruitful way toward God. The indulgence of Eli led to the death of his sons and tragic consequences for himself.[3] Fathers are just as responsible as are mothers for the education of their sons. Parents hold a solemn responsibility to provide the highest quality of environment and direction for the children entrusted to them. Only in such circumstances can children rise up and call their parents blessed. God discerns limitless possibilities in all humans, and to parents is given the sacred task of doing everything to encourage the child to reach the heights that are before him as his life is linked with the infinite power of God.

---

3. See 1 Samuel 4:11–18.

STAGES IN THE DEVELOPMENT OF
THE CHILD'S INDEPENDENCE

BIRTH

COORDINATION OF HAND

CRAWLING

WALKING

TALKING

PRESCHOOL / SCHOOL

DRIVER'S LICENSE

FINANCIAL INDEPENDENCE

LIVING AWAY FROM HOME

MARRIAGE

23

Adolescence and
Independence

OFTEN the most difficult reality for parents of adolescents is the realization that what is happening at the adolescent level is largely the result of past parental training in the child's formative years. Frequently what seemed merely minor idiosyncrasies in early childhood develop into annoying characteristics and even emotional disorders in adolescence, and too late parents attempt to reverse the results of poor home training in earlier years. Conversely, a careful and well-balanced relationship between parents and child in infancy and childhood years is the greatest insurance against the development of serious problems in adolescence. However, the parent who has been less than adequate during his child's earlier years may still reap some benefit by a more responsible relationship with the child in adolescence, though the task is much more difficult and the results often less. There is, however, no reason for not doing everything possible.

All major change periods are especially critical to mental health, and certainly adolescence with its metamorphosis from childhood to adulthood is a most critical time in terms of mental health. It is not uncommon for emotional disorders to become very apparent during the adolescent years. This fact is especially true of such psychotic manifestations as schizophrenia.

Adolescence is a time of frequent vacillation between childish and more mature behavior; thus, as the child seeks to find his own identity and independence, there are many frustrations and many pressures. Especially in sophisticated Western society, adolescence tends to be prolonged. It is often said to commence with a physiological change involving puberty and to end when psychological development characterized by emotional and social maturity has been achieved. It is during this period that youth attempt to break away from the dependency of childhood. To many youth this growing maturity brings many problems and frustrations. The frustrations are frequently related to the tug-of-war between the parental value system and that of the peer group. The adolescent is often placed in a conflict situation, in which to respond to the peer group pressure is to elicit the disapproval of parents. Conversely the response to parental values and wishes often alienates him from the peer group mores. Parents need to exercise much care in helping the child and the adolescent to make wise decisions in the choice of companionship. Companionship affects both the reputation and the character. Habits and motives will grow to resemble those of the companion, although they seemed widely separated at first. Almost inevitably, it is the companion with the poorer character who influences the one whose character was originally more noble.

To a considerable extent, wise parental guidance will have led to the development of independence and decision-making skills prior to adolescence.[1] Parents who have instilled sound bases for decision-making in the child will usually discover that the adolescent will more effectively accomplish the transition into the independence of adulthood with few areas of difficulty. It is usually thought that the beginning of independence comes when the infant is first able to move from one location to another in his crawling stage. This independence is increased with his ability to walk and later to run, and certainly it is greatly increased with the development of more and more sophisticated ways of communication. The ability to run away from the parents or to say No is the initial flexing of the child's independence. This may sometimes be done in play acting, but will eventually form an integral part of the ability to decide independently on various issues. At the time the child leaves home either for nursery, kindergarten or school, this independence increases to some extent although frequently he is placed in another environment where, though not directly responsible to his parents, he is responsible to some other adult. Thus it is usually in adolescence that he obtains his first real opportunity to make total decisions independent of his parents.

---

1. See chapter 22 entitled "Childhood."

There are many factors even in adolescence which tend to increase his independence; for examples, the possession of a car, the ability to earn his own income, and the ability to be with others without supervision. All these factors tend to increase the independence, but they also thrust a very great responsibility on the youth, that hitherto he has not experienced. Unfortunately many young people have not been prepared for such a responsibility, and tend to yield almost unthinkingly to group pressure. It is for this very purpose that strong and early training and education become very critical. This truth was certainly recognized by Solomon:

> Train up a child in the way he should go: and when he is old, he will not depart from it.   Proverbs 22:6

Through Moses, God expressed the same concept when, after the giving of the Ten Commandments, He admonished the children of Israel,

> And thou shalt teach them diligently unto thy children, and shalt talk of them when thou sittest in thine house, and when thou walkest by the way, and when thou liest down, and when thou risest up.
>   Deuteronomy 6:7

Tragically, poor education of infants and children leads to rebellion and insubordination when the opportunity for independence arises.

The right and effective education of children is the safest security against a totally wrong pattern of life when they reach their years of independence. It does not mean that the children of parents who have wisely educated them during their formative years will not still have problems in the adjustment to adolescence. So complex and so difficult are the decisions of youth today that it can be expected that most, even from the best homes, will have difficulties. It must further be asserted, however, that there will be a much greater probability that such young people will eventually adjust adequately and make secure and strong decisions, if the home environment has been secure and consistent during their early life.

It has often been a shock to wise parents to see their children who have been apparently well adjusted in their formative years, suddenly showing signs of inadequacy or even rebellion in their early adolescent lives. However, the same firm but loving management of earlier years, maintained through these difficult years, will usually produce sound and satisfactory results. It is important for parents not to panic, nor to feel that all is lost when their adolescent children make a few poor decisions. On the other hand, the same principles and guiding rules of life should be maintained by parents in an effort to help their youngsters to have security in knowing what is right and what is best. Parents must stand ready to answer the needs of their youth. The adolescent who still feels free to seek his parents' counsel and advice reflects the result of a wise upbringing. Perhaps there is no greater compliment to a parent. Nothing is gained by compromise or by vacillation on the part of parents, and much is lost by parents who, in their inability to cope with the adolescent turmoil, resort to compromise in the hope that somehow they will retain the affection of their children.

It is helpful to reinforce with positive comments the right decisions and actions of adolescents and to help the adolescent to attempt to make decisions consistent with high Christian purposes. It is during the teenage years that most of our value system is developed. Beliefs, attitudes, prejudices, biases, life-styles become more fixed during this period. Much conflict can result when adolescents choose attitudes and beliefs which vary significantly from those of the parents. Considerable emotional conflict may also result in the mind of the adolescent and may lead to rash or irrational forms of behavior. There is frequently greater emotional stability when the life-style chosen by the adolescent is similar to that of the parents, than when it differs markedly. Naturally, in an age when it is more likely than in previous generations for the life-style of the adolescent to be in contrast with that of the parents, it is not surprising that there is much emotional breakdown. Parents should carefully avoid making any issue over differences not of a moral nature. All their wisdom and energies will be needed to meet those situations which might have a moral base.

Another area of concern during the adolescent years is the issue of status symbols. To satisfy their ambitions for adulthood and to avoid child status, teenagers almost universally try to bolster themselves with adult status symbols. Status symbols may involve just about anything characteristic of adult patterns of life. These patterns can involve distinctive dress styles, use of makeup and jewelry (especially for girls), smoking, alcohol drinking, financial independence, cars and girlfriend/boyfriend relationships. While not all status symbols are undesirable, many are opposed to moral and health principles. Basically, the pressure upon teenagers is to conform to patterns of society in general. Thus the increasing maturity of the adolescent should be recognized by parents, teachers, and the church. Greater responsibility in recognition of this maturity allows for suitable status symbols which will aid, rather than dwarf the spiritual, emotional, and physical development of the adolescent. Such responsibility has greatest effect if suited to the interests and needs of the youth. This period provides an unusually good opportunity to educate youth for all branches of church life and activities. It also offers the opportunity to develop a relationship in which the adolescent senses that he is being treated as an adult and in which his contributions are perceived to be appreciated.

Adolescence links the formative years of childhood with the responsible years of adulthood. Soon the youth of today will be required to shoulder the responsibilities of tomorrow. There is evidence in contemporary society that the difficulties and complexities of the modern age have markedly reduced the effectiveness of parental guidance. The success of the family unit, the very fabric of society, is frequently in question. If there is to be a significant reversal of this trend, the role of parents must be more carefully fulfilled. God has promised His wisdom to all who earnestly follow Him. This wisdom is needed as perhaps at no other time in history.

24

Adolescence and
Decision Making

IT is during the adolescent years or just after, that the major decisions of life tend to be made. There are none greater than the decision for Christ, the decision to follow a life calling, and the decision to choose a life partner. It is usually better if these commitments are made in that order. Frequently a premature marriage, or a marriage before a decision to follow Christ has been made, has frustrated the aims of Christ in the life of a young man or woman. It is wholly desirable that both husband and wife have a commitment to follow God's leading, whatever that may be. For one partner to oppose God's leading is to establish a conflict that may never be fully resolvable.

Unquestionably the greatest and most significant decision that humans can make is a decision for Christ. This decision will affect all other decisions and therefore, in the education of young people, primacy should be placed upon it. While it is often true that young children may make decisions to accept Christ, it is more likely that a firm, irrevocable decision will be made during mid-adolescence. Usually youth must face the peer group and biological pressures of adolescence for firm confirmation of decisions to be made. It is not uncommon for parents to become overly concerned if they see that their children are apparently hesitating in making a decision for Christ, and perhaps many try to force their children to do so. But it is impossible to force anyone to Christ. Although parents have a responsibility to place before their child in the most attractive way, the claims that Christ is making upon his life and service, only as he himself makes that decision can any positive consequences for the kingdom of God result. The consistency of the parent, the encouragement of the parent, the example of the parent can all help, but there comes a time when the youth himself must make that decision. However, once again, the special dedication of parents to the upbringing of their child can assist greatly. The special dedication of Samuel by his mother, Hannah, seems to have played a most vital role in the subsequent mission of the prophet. It is a fine example for modern parents.

> And she vowed a vow, and said, O LORD of hosts, if thou wilt indeed look on the affliction of thine handmaid, and remember me, and not forget thine handmaid, but wilt give unto thine handmaid a man child, then I will give him unto the LORD all the days of his life, and there shall no rasor come upon his head.   1 Samuel 1:11

There is no question that emotional conflict and stress can be great in the experience of adolescents who are in a state of indecision concerning their relationship to Christ. This indecision causes not only conflict, but often tense, emotional outbursts and may even lead to apparently inconsistent and irresponsible behavior. Parents should recognize that young people who have yet to make their decisions for Christ will go through a very difficult period. In one sense it is not discouraging, for it means that the child has not rejected the claims of Christ. On the other hand, careful understanding is necessary so that in this difficult period the youth may have the easiest opportunity possible to make a firm commitment to Christ. If in adolescence a decision is not made for Christ, it is much less likely that in a later period such a decision will be made. For this reason Solomon urges,

> Remember now thy Creator in the days of thy youth.
>   Ecclesiastes 12:1

Satan seeks to weave a web of circumstance around those who do not submit their lives to the will of God, making it as difficult as possible for them ever to make that decision in later life. It is essential to realize that there must be a definite decision to serve God. All that is needed to follow Satan is to make no decision at all. Happy is the young person who can say to God,

> Thou art my trust from my youth.   Psalm 71:5

Such a one has followed the counsel of Paul to Timothy to—

> Flee also youthful lusts: but follow righteousness, faith, charity, peace, with them that call on the Lord out of a pure heart. 2 Timothy 2:22

The second great decision is for a life calling. This decision is not easy in our complex age in which there is such a proliferation of opportunities. When in earlier times it was likely that a child would follow in the trade or profession of the father, decisions were simple; but today when it is more likely that the youth will choose an occupation other than that of his parents; and when there is such a wide range of opportunities, indecision can cause deep emotional concern. Parents may reduce the tension level of their children if they have helped them to understand that Christ is leading their lives and that, as they follow His leading, they have nothing to fear. Some time, like Abram, they may be required to step out in faith, for it would seem to work to Satan's advantage for young people to decide to do nothing. Moving forward in faith, allowing the Lord to lead them into the direction most fitted for their unique role in His plans and purposes, will bring the most satisfying results. Such a course can produce, on the one hand, the positive motion of achievement, and on the other, the tranquility that comes from the assurance of following God's leading. The fruitful use of one's talents is essential to the person who claims to be a servant of Christ.[1]

It is easy for parents to fire their youth with unholy ambitions, ambitions related to finance, power, or prestige. In doing this they are minimizing God's claim. Such goals stress self-centered competition rather than selfless service, and often heighten the tension levels in the adolescent. In the restlessness of youth it is easy to shortsightedly underestimate the value of education, but each youth should be encouraged to continue in habits of industry, going as far as he can to fulfill God's purposes in his life.

The third major decision is the choice of a life partner. This decision involves the second-most important vow that humans make, a vow directed to the establishment of a home in which the husband and wife will hold inviolate their relationship one to the other. Obviously this vow is much more effective when the husband and wife have both made a commitment to Christ and when they have established a compatible understanding of God's leading in their lives. Thus young people need godly counsel and guidance concerning the true principles of love and the re-

---

1. See Matthew 25:14–30.

sponsibilities of marriage and parenthood. Hasty decisions can lead to lifelong misery.[2]

Perhaps the most critical positive element of youth is its idealism. How important it is for parents, teachers and church leaders both to recognize the idealism of youth, but also to utilize it and mobilize it! The youth tend to fail to discern barriers, hurdles or encumbrances. They want to move forward. They want to forge ahead to do the things that mature adults often see as impossible. It is vital not to crush this idealism nor to destroy youth's enthusiasm, but to utilize the exuberance in a positive outreach for the work of God. Such a result can be wonderfully achieved when this idealism is linked with true principles of self-sacrifice and service.

With each commitment for Christ, there are concomitant physiological changes for action. Motivation by an idealism unmatched in earlier or later years, youth tend to respond with great personal involvement. As the love of Christ is unfolded to them, not only is their intellect challenged, but there is also considerable concomitant emotional response. No man or woman can experience the love of Christ without reciprocating that love. This emotional response, like all human emotion, is associated with bodily changes mediated by the sympathetic nervous system. These changes stimulate and facilitate behavior by the secretion of adrenalin into the blood supply, increasing heartbeat and breathing rate and improving muscle tone. Thus a general response to the call of Christ brings with it an automatic preparation for action. The soul cries out for something to do to reinforce the commitment.

Frequently those who are older fail to provide for the challenge of this situation. They send away those who have signified their acceptance of Christ without providing any opportunity whereby they may reinforce their decision for fruitful Christian behavior. Soon the youth become confused and equivocate upon the commitment made, and therefore often fall prey to other activities which are unsanctified and unprofitable. Discouragement and emotional inadequacies associated with embarrassment occur, and the end result is often worse than if no challenge had ever been accepted. The appeal for personal surrender has a very real place in the

---

2. See chapters 27, 28 entitled "Preparation for Marriage" and "Marriage and the Family."

life of every youth. But Scripture is replete with examples of the immediate reinforcement of that commitment in action. When calling Peter and Andrew, Christ said,

> Come ye after me, and I will make you to become fishers of men.
>
> Mark 1:17

Later when Christ personally questioned Peter regarding his love for Him, Peter was directly commissioned to feed the lambs and the sheep.

> So when they had dined, Jesus saith unto Simon Peter, Simon, son of Jonas, lovest thou me more than these? He saith unto him, Yea, Lord; thou knowest that I love thee. He saith unto him, Feed my lambs.
>
> He saith unto him again the second time, Simon, son of Jonas, lovest thou me? He saith unto him, Yea, Lord; thou knowest that I love thee. He saith unto him, Feed my sheep.
>
> He saith unto him the third time, Simon, Son of Jonas, lovest thou me? Peter was grieved because he said unto him the third time, Lovest thou me? And he said unto him, Lord, thou knowest all things; thou knowest that I love thee. Jesus saith unto him, Feed my sheep.
>
> John 21:15–17

The last counsel of Christ to Nicodemus was,

> But he that *doeth* truth cometh to the light, that his deeds may be made manifest, that they are wrought in God.
>
> John 3:21—emphasis added.

Similarly the rich young ruler was challenged with a task when he sought the way of salvation:

> If thou wilt be perfect, go and sell that thou hast, and give to the poor, and thou shalt have treasure in heaven: and come and follow me.
>
> Matthew 19:21

The apostle Paul, during his conversion experience, recognized the vital need for action when he inquired,

> Lord, what wilt thou have me to do?   Acts 9:6

Before he spent preparatory time in Arabia, he witnessed to his newly accepted faith in the synagogue. After his eyes were restored, he straightway—

> preached Christ in the synagogues.   Acts 9:20

These last two important decisions hinge upon a decision to surrender the life to Christ. In fact, in almost all pursuits of life, this surrender will have overriding significance.

Unfortunately many young people yearn to follow Christ but do not know how. They have but vague understandings of what to do when Christ calls. Discouragement and despondency take over from their initial enthusiasm. Resistance to the subsequent call by the Holy Spirit follows, and their eternal destiny as well as their earthly happiness is in jeopardy. It is important in the education of our adolescents that each may have the opportunity not only of coming to Christ, but also of knowing how to reinforce that commitment in actions of a positive and profitable nature. In this way, the mental health and the emotional stability are secured, and there is a strengthening of the young person's reserves for the stern duties of life ahead.

25

Morality and Sex

MORALITY deals with the total response of men to the law of God, but today this topic has been focused primarily upon the response to sexual drives. This area has profound influence upon the behavior of adolescents and adults and perhaps, as much as any one factor, has a decided influence upon both happiness and fulfillment. The sex drive of man was clearly part of God's unique plan for the reproduction of the human race.[1] Sexual intercourse was not designed to be a part of man's life-style outside the ordinance of marriage. When God's design for man is altered and when His laws are violated, man pays an inevitable price in misery and discontent. Thus the present permissive age is the result of man's chosen alienation from God, which also is a root cause of much of the misery in the world in general and family life in particular. There is a fatal inevitability about man's quest for the freedom from moral restraint from which he reaps fearful consequences.

> There is a way that seemeth right unto a man, but the end thereof are the ways of death.   Proverbs 16:25

The very solidarity of the home, its cohesiveness and its perpetuation, is dependent upon the highest level of morality. Further, the state of society is dependent upon the quality of home life. Thus it is no surprise that there are frightening cracks in the fabric of society which are irreparable without a return of true morality which is established upon both restraining and emancipating principles of the love of God.

All sexual excesses in and outside marriage have their foundation in self-seeking. Thus when parents themselves exercise the utmost self-control as they submit to the power of Christ in their lives, they are in a

---

1. See Genesis 1:27–28.

position to help their children develop the most important principle of their Christian life—that of self-control. As each child learns to overcome the excesses of self-seeking, he opens the way for that loving concern for others that will preserve him from any activity which will in any way rob another of the joy of a pure life.

Bible morality is in sharp distinction from that of modern Western society. While to many the "new morality" is seen as casting off the inhibitions, puritanism, false values and modesty of a past age, it has in reality served notice of the fact that man has returned to the wickedness of past ages. Scripture compares to the days of Noah, and the days of Sodom and Gomorrha the period immediately preceding the Second Coming of Christ.

> But as the days of Noe were, so shall also the coming of the Son of man be.   Matthew 24:37

> Even as Sodom and Gomorrha, and the cities about them in like manner, giving themselves over to fornication, and going after strange flesh, are set forth for an example, suffering the vengeance of eternal fire   Jude 7

God has promised that in the midst of that age He will have a pure people who have washed their robes and made them white in the blood of the Lamb, and who keep God's commandments.

> And he said to me, These are they which came out of great tribulation, and have washed their robes, and made them white in the blood of the Lamb.   Revelation 7:14

> Blessed are they that do his commandments, that they may have right to the tree of life, and may enter in through the gates into the city.
>   Revelation 22:14

> And the dragon was wroth with the woman, and went to make war with the remnant of her seed, which keep the commandments of God, and have the testimony of Jesus.   Revelation 12:17

> Here is the patience of the saints: here are they that keep the commandments of God, and the faith of Jesus.   Revelation 14:12

It is with these reassuring promises in the mind that Christian parents must seek to educate their youth into a mindset totally distinct from that of society at large.

The Bible unhesitatingly condemns all sexual aberrations, for each is soul-destroying and demeaning to man. Even in marriage, sexual relationships between a Christian husband and wife will be under the control of noble principles and will not cater to lustful passions and sexual excesses. When marriage is seen as giving rather than getting, that which is unnatural will be avoided. Much of divorce, separation and unmarried cohabitation can be attributed to the sexual self-seeking of man. That each of these has been a problem in the Christian church is a sad index of impurity in the church as well as a challenge to reestablish the church's clear testimony against such excesses.

Morality, like immorality, has its origin in the mind. While it is true that the sex drive is biological in nature, and usually achieves overt expression during the years of adolescence, its expression may be held under the controlling influence of the will. Obviously it is impossible for children and youth to totally avoid the mental stimulation suggesting that they allow their sex drives free rein, for in advertisements, radio, music, television, and literature such suggestions are dominant. Further, it is likely that many of their school companions will communicate their own perverted sexual ideas and practices to the youth. Thus parents are confronted with an awesome responsibility to provide the purest possible environment while also recognizing that the knowledge of some of society's perversions cannot be avoided. It is in the area of moral choices that the wisest of counsel should be given sympathetically, understandingly, but always uncompromisingly. Boys must be taught the highest respect for girls, and their duty to do nothing that in any wise might compromise them in a way which will lead to the eroding consequences of guilt. On the other hand, girls must be taught to preserve their bodies inviolate, remembering that their bodies are to be—

the temple of the Holy Ghost which is in you, which ye have of God,
and ye are not your own.   1 Corinthians 6:19

Young women are to control the situation and certainly must avoid acting the role of temptress. Most young women seem scarcely aware that the surrender of her body to a young man does not increase his love for a woman, and may cause the young man to despise her. The Bible has a classic example in the hatred of Amnon, the son of David, for his sister Tamar after he had forced his attentions upon her.

And Amnon said unto Tamar, Bring the meat into the chamber, that I may eat of thine hand. And Tamar took the cakes which she had made, and brought them into the chamber to Amnon her brother. And when she had brought them unto him to eat, he took hold of her, and said unto her, Come lie with me, my sister. And she answered him, Nay, my brother, do not force me; for no such thing ought to be done in Israel: do not thou this folly. And I, whither shall I cause my shame to go? and as for thee, thou shalt be as one of the fools in Israel. Now therefore, I pray thee, speak unto the king; for he will not withhold me from thee. Howbeit, he would not hearken unto her voice: but, being stronger than she, forced her, and lay with her. Then Amnon hated her exceedingly; so that the hatred wherewith he hated her was greater than the love wherewith he had loved her. And Amnon said unto her, Arise, be gone.   2 Samuel 13:10–15

In any case such unrestrained actions by a young man provide a clear indication that he has not developed self-control, that he is motivated by self-centered, lustful passion, and thus is at best a risky prospect for a life partner. The young men and women who have learned self-control through Christ offer a much better prospect for a happy marriage than those who have allowed their sex drives unrestrained satiation. God-controlled restraint before marriage will provide the best guarantee of a truly lifelong, loving relationship after marriage. And such control is the product of pure and holy thoughts.

Even more destructive of moral standards has been the burgeoning incidence of extramarital affairs. Some have argued that if one is honest with his partner, such extramarital affairs are justifiable. Others have reasoned that if both engage in extramarital affairs, then this infidelity is wholly justifiable. Some have even suggested that such behavior adds "spice" to the marriage and increases its fulfillment. This sophistry is the basis of widespread "swinging" clubs in which married couples exchange partners to minister to their sinful and lustful desires. But however the act might be justified, it is built upon a hedonistic and sensual motivation which simply ministers to the basest of human passions—a passion upon which no sound human relationship can be built. Not infrequently the husband has, by various means, coerced his wife into participating in such activities, and the wife, frantic to please her wayward husband, has succumbed to the pressure, often in the vain hope that it will help her to repair her fragile marriage. However, no matter what the pressures may be, the Christian wife must remember that her body is to be kept holy unto the Lord, and no act of lust can possibly restore true love to the marriage. Sexual relationships with another man's wife are explicitly forbidden in Scripture.

> Moreover thou shalt not lie carnally with thy neighbor's wife, to defile thyself with her.   Leviticus 18:20

Promiscuity has its basis in paganism, when city-states such as Sparta encouraged nonmarital relationships with a view to producing a superior race.

The Word of God provides ample warning and counsel upon looseness in sexual matters. Paul faced many such problems in his day, even among the early Christians. Thus in writing both to the Roman and to the Corinthian believers he made it clear that not only do those who engage in moral excesses face tragic human consequences, but that those who continue in such excesses cannot enter the kingdom of heaven. To the Corinthian believers he declares that fornication (premarital sex), adultery and homosexuality are specifically among the sins that will keep men out of the kingdom of heaven.

> Know ye not that the unrighteous shall not inherit the kingdom of God? Be not deceived: neither fornicators, nor idolators, nor adulterers, nor effeminate, nor abusers of themselves with mankind
> 1 Corinthians 6:9

Paul also warned the Romans against unnatural practices of women, as well as homosexuality by men.

> For this cause God gave them up unto vile affections: for even their women did change the natural use into that which is against nature: and likewise also the men, leaving the natural use of the woman, burned in their lust one toward another; men with men working that which is unseemly, and receiving in themselves that recompence of their error which was meet.   Romans 1:26–27

Further in his counsel to the Corinthians, prostitution is thoroughly condemned.

> Know ye not that your bodies are the members of Christ? shall I then take the members of Christ, and make them the members of an harlot? God forbid.   1 Corinthians 6:15

The freedom cry is heard far and wide today calling for liberation from the "repression" of a former age, but such cries are not for true freedom which liberates man from the fear and anxiety which sin engenders, but for a sordid permissiveness which enslaves the mind and emotions of man. Homosexuality and lesbianism are paraded as normal and healthy sexual practices, and many have been encouraged to participate in bi-sexual practices, thus adding a "new dimension" to their already perverted and unrestrained sexual lives. Even some Christian churches have thought to sanctify what God explicitly condemned.

> Thou shalt not lie with mankind, as with womankind: it is abomination.
> Leviticus 18:22

Thus today there are declared homosexuals practicing as ordained ministers in Christian churches.

The Christian must have a sympathetic understanding of the temptations of the homosexual and the lesbian. It is true that the modern one-parent society greatly predisposes young people to seek affection from their own sex. However, except in the rarest of cases, there is no known biological basis for homosexuality. Those who practice it have learned to be oriented to it. Unfortunately this orientation, like many other evils, is learned early in life. It is generally thought to result from an identity crisis in which the child tends to identify himself with the characteristics of the parent of the opposite sex. Thus for example, the son identifies with the mother, modeling his behavior more on hers but more important, identifying emotionally with feminine roles. In adolescence such persons discover that they have only a platonic relationship with a member of the opposite sex while finding much deeper emotional attraction with members of the same sex. Heterosexuals cannot fully conceive of the trauma that such a realization brings to most homosexuals, and there is a tendency for most homosexuals to seek at first to deny this orientation. However, the inevitability of lifelong homosexual tendencies often claimed by practicing homosexuals, is not valid. The fact that homosexuality is learned clearly indicates that it can be unlearned, and there are those who declare they have overcome the problem and are now enjoying normal heterosexual married life. Whether this progress can be true for all homosexuals is uncertain. But certain victory over homosexual *practices* is assured through Christ.

The Christian is aware that Christ has the power to give man victory over all learned as well as innate evil tendencies, and homosexuality, though it is a most deeply entrenched problem, can be certainly overcome. The Christian must realize his responsibility to help sympathetically all homosexuals who are genuinely seeking a reversal of their orientation. It must be recognized that God's love for homosexuals is as great as for heterosexuals, and that His forgiveness is as complete. But love for the homosexual is not the same as acceptance of the sin of homosexuality. It is impossible for the Bible-believing Christian to see the practice of homosexuality in other than the most degrading light, or fail to oppose the widespread efforts to parade it as an acceptable and morally desirable alternative to heterosexual marriage. The very God-given fiber of society as ordained in the home is broken down by these homosexual relations. The sordid excesses of these unnatural love affairs are based upon the same egocentric indulgences that are condemned in heterosexual deviancy. God destroyed the ancient city of Sodom for its homosexual practices, among other sins.

In man's craving for sexual excitement, he has sought other forms of sexual expression. Bestiality—a sexual relationship with animals—is yet another aberration warned against in Scripture.

> Neither shalt thou lie with any beast to defile thyself therewith: neither shall any woman stand before a beast to lie down thereto: it is confusion.   Leviticus 18:23

It is clear that God condemns all forms of sexual expression which are not born of pure love expressed within the marriage relationship. While the Scriptures do not specifically refer to masturbation, the principles of Scripture would warn against this practice. First, it is a sexual deviation, and second, it has all the characteristics of an egocentric act. While it is true that among teenagers masturbation is widespread, often relating to experimentation involved in adolescent development, its strong egocentric basis, like all forms of sexual deviation, links it with emotional problems. The strong claims that masturbation is normal and unharmful, and indeed possibly beneficial, cannot be substantiated either emotionally or spiritually. While adolescent self-control will be extremely difficult and will call forth a total commitment to the life of Christ, such self-control will pay wonderful dividends in subsequent marital life.

In today's permissive society where sexual expressions of all kinds have been condoned and encouraged, it is most difficult for Christians, especially the young, to see sexual excesses in their truly destructive light. This true evaluation is made much more difficult by the manner in which television and other media forms have routinely represented much of this deviance, often in a glamorized and approving way. Further, the lives of many of the "heroes" of society—actors, sportsmen, and other entertainers have been established on self-gratifying principles easily emulated because they cater to the natural depravity of man. Rather than teaching a God-centered morality in which the youth are encouraged and supported in their efforts to grow in moral strength, the entertainment world does everything to facilitate immorality. Parents, having failed to establish with their children those principles of life which will fortify them against yielding to the pressures of premarital sexual indulgence, take an easy way out, simply dispensing contraceptive pills to their daughters. These parents seem in total contradistinction to the compassionate command of Jesus to the woman taken in adultery,

Go, and sin no more.   John 8:11

Society seems to be saying, Go and sin again. Thus parents face an awesome responsibility.

Probably there are few indices of permissiveness of the modern age greater than the attitude to life as expressed by permissive abortion. That substantial segments of the Christian community see fit to support this ruthless assault upon the unborn is of even greater concern. Usually the argument for abortion is built upon the view that it is wrong to bring unwanted children into the world. This fact cannot be denied, yet surely the taking of life is entirely as unacceptable. It is often urged that life is not really life until it is self-supporting; that is, can continue independent of its mother's womb. But this assertion raises issues for which there is no known answer. Modern science has made it possible for very young fetuses to survive when removed from the mother. Surely the only valid definition of human life is that it begins after conception. Abortion generally takes place between the end of the second and the end of the third month. It is probably at least five weeks after conception that pregnancy is tentatively confirmed. By the time abortion usually takes place, the embryo is developed to the extent that many human characteristics are observable. His nervous system is developed to the extent that he can respond to external stimuli. To destroy an embryo is to destroy life. Inconsistently, many who bitterly oppose the execution of the most vile murderer argue in favor of the right of women to abort their innocent unborn children at will.

It is often argued that women should have the right over their own bodies, but a fundamental human-rights principle allows for individual rights only to the extent that those rights do not infringe upon the rights of others. Abortion does so. It is true that many of those who seek abortion are unfit for motherhood, but even this fact does not justify permissive abortion. Many wonderful homes would be available in which to rear these children with the maximal opportunity to develop their God-given faculties.

There is scriptural evidence that God recognizes the human identity of the embryo. The prophet Jeremiah declares that God knows us from the time we are in our mother's womb.

> Before I formed thee in the belly I knew thee; and before thou camest forth out of the womb I sanctified thee, and I ordained thee a prophet unto the nations.   Jeremiah 1:5

Permissive abortion is a most serious sin with frequently severe and long-term psychological consequences. Many girls or young women suffer lifelong guilt subsequent to their abortions. Even if this is not the case, the act is not to be condoned by the Christian, for it is symptomatic of an age where people claim the right to do whatever they like without consideration of the consequences. Yet consequences there are, spiritual and emotional. It is a sad reflection upon our age that in some urban centers of the United States there are annually more legal abortions than live births. Coupled with the wide use of all forms of contraceptive devices, the extent of moral decadence in society is alarming. The very basis of society's structure and human contentment and happiness is seriously undermined.

Only a total reversal of current social patterns can hope to salvage the future of the human race, and such a reversal is not possible outside the context of the ministry of Christ in human life. Strangely, when abortion was conducted in back alleys and when it was a crime punishable by severe penalties, many who now strongly support abortion on demand were horrified by it. But no government legalization can alter a principle of God's law, and Christians must stand steadfastly against this enormity.

When the pure principles of Christianity are practiced by young men and women, the problem of abortion is not even an issue. Christian doctors and hospitals have a grave responsibility to refrain from participation in permissive abortion. However, Christian doctors and medical personnel frequently have the opportunity to assist young people who have been engaging in premarital sex to realize their obligations for marriage. The Bible makes plain that sexual relations bring obligations, and the requirement of Israel was that a couple engaging in premarital sex were obliged to marry.

> And the elders of that city shall take that man and chastise him; and they shall amerce him in an hundred sheckels of silver, and give them unto the father of the damsel, because he hath brought up an evil name upon a virgin of Israel: and she shall be his wife; he may not put her away all his days. Deuteronomy 22:18–19

> And if a man entice a maid that is not betrothed, and lie with her, he shall surely endow her to be his wife. Exodus 22:16

True moral principles are founded in the home. Here the Scripture encourages modesty which will bring a rich reward in later life.[2] The tragedy of the free morality of the present age is that it destroys self-respect and human happiness because it is built on the self-destructive principle of self-indulgence. And further it excludes all who continue this indulgence from participation in the kingdom of Christ.

> Marriage is honourable in all, and the bed undefiled: but whoremongers and adulterers God will judge. Hebrews 13:4

Because sexual excesses are among the most widespread expressions of self-indulgence in modern society, victory here can be a big step forward to victory in other areas of life. Yet it must be recognized that outside of Christ, human beings are not capable of this control. For those who have engaged in sexual excesses or abortion, there is the ever-loving assurance that Christ is able to save to the uttermost all who come to Him in true repentance; ready to allow Him to turn them away from their old ways. None need feel hopeless or helpless. The God who condemns sin sent His Son in the likeness of sinful flesh,

> That the righteousness of the law might be fulfilled in us, who walk not after the flesh, but after the Spirit. Romans 8:4

---

2. See Leviticus 18:6–19.

26

Homosexuality

RECENTLY homosexuality has become a topic of some significance within the Christian church. Christians have always accepted that the practice of homosexuality is a sin. In recent years, however, many are pressing the concept that Scripture condemns only homosexual prostitution and rape and abuse of the young, while remaining silent on the subject of homosexual relations between consenting adults. Such contend that "What began to be clear was that a simplistic English reading of the few scriptural references to homosexual acts would not suffice to determine the Lord's will for homosexual persons today" (*Spectrum*, vol. 12, No. 3, p. 35). In the same article it was asserted "that the Old Testament *by itself* (without counsel of the New Testament and a contemporary theology of sexuality based on the whole testimony of Scripture) is not sufficient to settle the question of morality of homosexual relationships in today's world (ibid.). However, when the New Testament was explored in this article, it was concluded that there was "clear New Testament disapproval of some kinds of sexual acts, both homosexual and heterosexual, even if determining exactly what those acts were is difficult" (ibid., p. 36).

Since these statements were made to a group of practicing homosexuals, they could only be judged to be of encouragement to them in their continuance of that practice. The indulgence in homosexual acts has caused widespread anxiety and distress among those who wish to follow the teachings of Christ. In view of this distress, it is imperative that God's Word be searched in order to know His will in this matter. The Jewish people were left without doubt upon this subject:[1]

> Thou shalt not lie with mankind, as with womankind: it is abomination.   Leviticus 18:22

> If a man also lie with mankind, as he lieth with a woman, both of them have committed an abomination: they shall surely be put to death; their blood shall be upon them.   Leviticus 20:13

Even these plain words are diluted by the view that "theologians, arguing that some of the holiness code rules are moral and some only ceremonial, have justified these divisions of the Levitical admonitions, but that a careful scholar wouldn't divide them in this fashion. If they can be ignored, perhaps none should be considered binding" (*Spectrum*, vol. 12, No. 3, p. 35).

The New Testament, however, confirms God's word in Leviticus:

> Know ye not that the unrighteous shall not inherit the kingdom of God? Be not deceived: neither fornicators, nor idolators, nor adulterers, nor effeminate, nor abusers of themselves with mankind
>   1 Corinthians 6:9

> Knowing this, that the law is not made for a righteous man, but for the lawless and disobedient, for the ungodly and for sinners, for unholy and profane, for murderers of fathers and murderers of mothers, for manslayers, for whoremongers, for them that defile themselves with mankind, for menstealers, for liars, for perjured persons, and if there be any other thing that is contrary to sound doctrine.
>   1 Timothy 1:9–10

Other translations confirm the obvious meanings of these texts. Examples are cited below:

> those who participate in homosexuality (1 Corinthians 6:9—The Amplified Bible)
> homosexuals (1 Corinthians 6:9—The Living New Testament)
> homosexual perversion (1 Corinthians 6:9—RSV)
> homosexual offenders (1 Corinthians 6:9—NIV)

---

1. In the Old Testament the term *sodomites* is used a number of times (see Deuteronomy 23:17; 1 Kings 14:24, 15:12, 22:46; 2 Kings 23:7). This term is consistently translated as *male prostitutes* in the *New English Bible*, therefore these texts are not cited in this chapter.

partakers in homosexuality (1 Corinthians 6:9—Berkeley)

abusers of themselves with men (1 Timothy 1:10—American Standard Version)

homosexuals (1 Timothy 1:10—Living New Testament)

homosexuals (1 Timothy 1:10—The New American Standard)

those who abuse themselves with men (1 Timothy 1:10—The Amplified Bible)

who sin sexually . . . with other men (1 Timothy 1:10—Beck)

Sodomites (1 Timothy 1:10—RSV)

Undeniably, God condemns the sin of homosexuality, and no amount of theological explanation can alter that fact. It is essential that this matter be understood, for to continue indulging the homosexual desire not only causes serious personality disturbances, but even more seriously, also excludes one from God's kingdom.

Many Christian ministers today believe that they are assisting men and women by excusing this particular sin, and assuring them that they will not be excluded from heaven because of their acts. But sin never brings peace of mind nor true mental health. Men who have been ordained to the gospel ministry must never ignore their God-given charge:

> So thou, O son of man, I have set thee a watchman unto the house of Israel; therefore thou shalt hear the word at my mouth, and warn them from me. When I say unto the wicked, O wicked man, thou shalt surely die; if thou dost not speak to warn the wicked from his way, that wicked man shall die in his iniquity, but his blood will I require at thy hand. Nevertheless, if thou warn the wicked of his way to turn from it; if he do not turn from his way, he shall die in his iniquity; but thou hast delivered thy soul. Therefore, O thou son of man, speak unto the house of Israel; Thus ye speak, saying, If our transgressions and our sins be upon us, and we pine away in them, how should we then live? Say unto them, As I live, saith the Lord GOD, I have no pleasure in the death of the wicked; but that the wicked turn from his way and live: turn ye, turn ye from your evil ways; for why will ye die, O house of Israel? Ezekiel 33:7–11

Is there no hope for the homosexual unless he or she becomes reoriented sexually? There is abundant hope. Much of the endeavor to present homosexual practices as consistent with Christian standards arises from a false view of man's nature and a failure to properly delineate the distinction between sin and temptation. Many today believe that the carnal nature[2] is not changed at conversion. Thus those with homosexual orientation are believed not only to continue in this desire, but also to have little power to resist its practices. But Peter summarizes many similar scriptural promises[3] when he assures us:

> Forasmuch then as Christ hath suffered for us in the flesh, arm yourselves likewise with the same mind: for he that hath suffered in the flesh hath ceased from sin; that he no longer should live the rest of his time in the flesh to the lusts of men, but to the will of God.
>
> 1 Peter 4:1–2

Much discussion has taken place concerning whether homosexual tendencies are inherited or acquired. Since God offers power for victory over every inherited and cultivated tendency to evil, such discussions serve little purpose in our understanding of God's promises of victory.

Some have finally accepted that God can give victory, but have interpreted it to mean that they will receive a miraculous "healing," whereby they will cease to have their former tendency and will become oriented to heterosexuality. It is true that this appears to be the experience of a small group, but it is scant comfort for the vast majority. The authors have spent much time with dejected homosexuals who wait and pray, apparently ineffectually, for this "healing." Often their hopes have been raised by reading of those who have succeeded, but their own experience proves to be so different that they become even more depressed by their failure.

It must ever be recognized that homosexuality is not the only overpowering tendency to sin experience by mankind. Every one of us has some great predisposition to sin. Sometimes we tend to set homosexuality apart, as if it were some unique form of sinful tendency. It is not so. Many people have a tendency to an ill-temper. We do not help them by promising them eternal life while they indulge this sin. We do not assist such a one by assuring him that it is his emotional orientation, and that God will certainly understand. It would be ill-considered to hold a special

---

2. The carnal nature should not be confused with the fallen nature. Our carnal nature is expressed in the pursuit and enjoyment of sin without acknowledging its sinfulness. Our fallen nature is such that without God's strength, we are helpless to turn away from acknowledged sin. Both natures are exemplified in Romans 7, verses 7 and 15.
3. See also 1 John 3:9, 5:18; Romans 8:8–10.

meeting for bad-tempered church members in order to assure them that their sin is not specifically condemned by Scripture. We must not overlook the fact that even in a victorious Christian, Satan will continue his attacks upon our weaknesses. Thus those, who through God's power overcome the temptation to follow homosexual life-styles, will nevertheless still be subject to Satan's devices. But never must it be assumed that yielding to temptations is inevitable. Each one has the choice and the power at his or her disposal to live a life of rectitude. Many still feel polluted because of recurring temptation. However, if through the indwelling of the Holy Spirit, they neither cherish the temptation nor act upon it, they are no more trespassing God's law than was Jesus when He was tempted to bow before Satan. Thus James could encourage us with the promise,

> Blessed is the man that endureth temptation: for when he is tried, he shall receive the crown of life, which the Lord hath promised to them that love him.   James 1:12

Manifestly, those with homosexual inclinations have every hope indeed. But those who persist in cherishing the temptations are lost eternally. This situation differs not one whit from those with other sinful inclinations. God's Word to homosexuals, as to all of us with our various weaknesses, is to call upon Him for victory, for He has promised,

> There hath no temptation taken you but such as is common to man: but God is faithful, who will not suffer you to be tempted above that ye are able; but will with the temptation also make a way to escape, that ye may be able to bear it.   1 Corinthians 10:13

Some have rightly pointed out that homosexuals face a particularly severe form of temptation, since to follow God's way deprives them of a family life, unless they become reoriented. One can sympathize with this problem, it is indeed a most difficult cross to bear. But we must ask ourselves, Is Jesus worth this burden? Each Christian has his cross to bear. When we accepted Jesus, He told us,

> Whosoever will come after me, let him deny himself, and take up his cross, and follow me.   Mark 8:34

We should never overlook that many heterosexual Christians have suffered severe sexual privation for their faith. Many have been cast into prison or exile, yet continued in obedience to God's will both in thought and in deed. No doubt temptations continually presented themselves to men such as Joseph, Jeremiah, Paul, John and others. Yet their fidelity to God was maintained. Others have spent years away from their spouses while undertaking military or similar service. While presented with numerous opportunities to desecrate the seventh commandment, some have so trusted God as to remain true and loyal to Him throughout their ordeals.

It may be that many homosexuals, perhaps the majority, will need to forego the hope of a family relationship other than that offered by their brethren and sisters in Christ. This test of devotion to Jesus is severe, but offers everlasting rewards.

We must remember that homosexual relationships never produce children and thus that aspect of family life is always missing. Further, homosexual relationships frequently are tempestuous and fickle. This fact is perfectly understandable, as they cannot be based upon true, unselfish love, for sin is never unselfish. Homosexual relationships are always self-centered, and therefore do not produce contentment and satisfaction. Ministers who give implicit encouragement to the practice of this sin doom the participants to a life of guilt, shame and unhappiness, when God, in holding out victory to all sinners, including homosexuals, thus offers hope, joy and contentment. Those who support the practice of homosexuality need to consider God's Word which severely condemns those who have "strengthened the hands of the wicked, that he should not return from his wicked way, by promising him life" (Ezekiel 13:22). It is not love and concern which promises eternal life to those who continue in sin. This mistaken course condemns the one who accepts the false assurance to eternal loss, and destroys any hope of a life of mental tranquility on this earth. True love and concern always point out sin and lead to Jesus, who offers power to obey.

We can but feel a great depth of sympathy for those who have this inclination. In almost every case, each has gone through terrible mental anguish and struggle as he or she has come face to face with the realization of his or her sexual orientation. Such need our utmost sympathy and support. As we have listened to many recall their experiences, we have found almost always there is one common misunderstanding. Each has felt condemned of God because of the orientation he or she has. Almost all have felt that unless this orientation is reversed they are alienated from God. Each has prayed and anguished over this matter. But God never condemns us for predispositions. It is only as we cherish and/or act upon these wrongful tendencies that sin ensues. It is true that with each victory over temptation, strength to meet the next temptation is gained. It is also true that as we draw nearer to Jesus, those sinful things which once attracted us, lose their power in our lives. Those whom God has empowered to obey Him in this matter are redeemed by Him just as surely as those who, having other sinful predispositions, love Jesus so fully that they accept not only His forgiveness of sin, but also His power to obey.

27

Preparation for Marriage

IN spite of the great uncertainties associated with marriage as revealed in ongoing divorce statistics, there nevertheless seems to be an almost indecent haste for young people to enter into the marital state. Modern society has placed unreasonable pressures upon the immature, thus sowing seeds for problems in later life. Much of this pressure could be traced back to the elementary school where children, totally unable to handle the issues of dating, are almost forced by circumstances into accepting a role designed for much older and more experienced human beings. Frequently, through banquets and other social events, immature youngsters are forced into dating arrangements in such a way that they are led to believe that unless they have a partner of the opposite sex, somehow they are not being accepted. The dangers of early dating and romances cannot be overstressed. Such a course stimulates the sexual drive and leads naturally toward the habituation of promiscuous practices at a time when youngsters are too immature to handle, or even to understand the consequences of their actions.

This situation persists into high-school and academy-age levels, where there is a great intensification of relationships, and long before these young people have the opportunity to fully surrender their lives to Christ, many of them have succumbed to the pressure to premarital sexual relationships, which often haunt them for the rest of their lives. These immature romances do much to frustrate the educational and emotional development of young people, for when they have "fallen in love," they find it very difficult to concentrate upon their study programs. When the immature relationship breaks, they are distressed and there is a concomitant loss of emotional poise and academic achievement. Dating encourages trifling with the affections and emotions of members of the opposite sex and can but have many harmful consequences.

There are suggestions that young people of a given age are more mature today than in former generations, but this assertion may not be borne out if the evaluation is based upon emotional maturity, rather than general knowledge. Certainly the complexity of modern society dictates that it will take a much more mature person today than in previous generations, to forge a successful marriage. Thus in general, wisdom indicates that there should be a slowing down rather than a speeding up of the movement toward marriage.

There is always resistance to any reactionary suggestion, but it does seem that there is a need to return to "the old paths, where is the good way" (Jeremiah 6:16). It is obvious that our forefathers were able to establish more secure and more lasting marital relationships. In an age when fifty percent of all marriages are destined to end in a divorce, there is good reason for the Christian to look back to those situations which helped facilitate the security and endurance of the marriage relationship.

College has often become a time of frantic expectation on the part of many mothers, hoping against hope that their daughters may find a young man to marry. To many young people, it appears that the most important reason for being at college is to find a life partner. While this achievement may be a very excellent spin-off from a college education, nothing should detract from the primary emphasis of the education of young men and women to play their roles in developing the talents that God has entrusted to them. Anything seriously detracting from this purpose, even if it be a romance, ought not to be encouraged. In general, many young people are taking upon themselves inordinate responsibilities during their college life. They find it almost impossible to meet the financial strains upon them. Often at least one of the partners has to drop out of school, sometimes both. And if both do succeed in remaining in school, unless they have a very strong financial support, perhaps from parent, they are likely to establish huge debts by accepting money from loan programs, and therefore are faced with the added strain of financial difficulties for years to come.

It is usually best if young people can complete their academic work and have the security of a steady income before the responsibilities of marriage are accepted. It must be granted that this aim is sometimes difficult to realize, especially in professional areas where in America post-graduate programs are necessary before employment can be obtained (e.g. in medicine, dentistry, law and other professions). However, the longer this step can be postponed, the greater the likelihood of reducing the pressures competing against the balanced development of the young people concerned. Nevertheless, it is most difficult to resist the social pressures placed upon the youth in their early years, and often an early marriage is considered the answer.

One does not here advocate the segregation of the sexes until young people are mature. On the contrary, there is an essential need for young men and young women to fellowship together in an open and relaxed environment. It would be much safer, however, and would lead to more mature relationships later, if young people were allowed to mix in small groups over a considerable period of time without engaging in any specialized relationships. In this way they would get to know each other in more informal relationships, beginning to understand the qualities and the weaknesses of one another and to make firmer evaluation when later they may seek a more intimate, individualized relationship with one of the group. Too often young people who do not know each other and perhaps have hardly met before, date, and before long an emotional relationship and attachment have developed. It is obvious that in these first experiences, each has little concept of the character of the other, and when the true character begins to be revealed, the emotional attachment is often too strong, and the courage too little, for a proper decision to be made. Thus before any specialized dating takes place, it is wise if each already has a firm knowledge of the character of the other, and both are old enough to act in a responsible way.

The concept of dating, widely held in society today, could hardly be consistent with God's pattern for His children. Frequently young people have dated scores of other young people and have cast their affections, often most passionately, upon a wide range of members of the opposite sex. Humans are creatures of habit, and the development of a pattern of intimate relationships with a large number of members of the opposite sex is in itself habit forming, and will militate against holding the marriage inviolate when one is eventually chosen as a life partner. It will be more difficult to break the habit of casting affection on other persons. Thus the seeds of infidelity and marital discord have already been sown.

This practice becomes even more critical if there have been sexual relationships with some of these others. Whereas commonly accepted dictums indicate that premarital relationships are sound, or at least acceptable, preparation for marriage, in reality they are one of the greatest causes of marital breakdown; for there is a direct relationship between the avoidance of promiscuity before marriage and the prospect of a successful marriage. In fact, it would be fair to say that very few marriages, in which there has been much promiscuity by both parties before marriage, are likely to survive inviolate, unless there is a deep later acceptance of Christ in the lives of both partners. Habit patterns are strong, and after a short period of time, the partners will become bored with, and disinterested in the partner they have chosen. There will be the tendency to look for "new fields to conquer." In the promiscuity of youth are sown the seeds of infidelity in marriage.

Neither can we overlook the effect of promiscuousness upon the total emotional development of young people. There are the inevitable feelings of guilt associated with illicit sexual relationships, and this result is especially true in the lives of those who have a Christian background. Often this guilt is hard to live with, and frequently leads to feelings of inadequacy and low self-esteem. Tragically, there is often a vicious circle in which, because of the declining self-esteem, a person accentuates the promiscuous behavior, and that in turn only reinforces the low self-image.

A life of purity and chastity is still a wonderful safeguard against inferiority feelings, and even parents who think that by dispensing the pill to their daughter they have safeguarded her against the possibility of a pregnancy, have in no wise overcome the psychological and spiritual loss that is associated with promiscuousness. Then there is the complication associated with pregnancies contracted outside of marriage. Once again, conflict is thrown into the life of the immature youth. Those who have strong moral convictions will recognize that abortion is certainly not an acceptable solution to their wrong practices—two wrongs do not make a right. And while there are conflicting reports as to the emotional response to abortions, nevertheless, there is a wide spectrum of evidence to indicate that at least a large percentage of women suffer considerable, if not irreparable, emotional damage as a result of abortions. Irrespective of the emotional reactions, there are deep spiritual reasons why a Christian will not want to subject herself to a permissive abortion.[1]

Permissive abortion fits into the hedonistic culture of modern society where men and women are most concerned in avoiding the consequences of wrong acts. But certainly one sin should not be used to efface the consequences of another, and that surely is the basis of permissive abortion.

Unfortunately, in contemporary society, where the goddess of sex has been established just as effectively as among the heathen nations in times past, it has become increasingly popular to allow the counseling of young people to be dominated by discussions of sex as if it were the most essential aspect of a successful marriage. Thus young people are reinforced in the view that sex is the prime purpose of marriage. They come to believe that any problem that might be experienced or that anything less than their ideal of a sexual relationship is grounds for marital dissatisfaction.

There are many vital questions needing to be asked by young people facing marriage, for the quality of courtship influences the later direction of the marriage. The first and most important question is, Will the marriage honor God? The next is, Will the union allow us to better fulfill God's purpose in each of our lives? To come into unity with God is to forge a solid unity with each other in courtship and marriage. Two young people seeking to link their lives together should be convinced that they are one in purpose and one in objectives. This conviction of course does not mean that one must subserve his interest to the other, but that there will be a harmony of direction as each complements and supplements the other in fulfilling the call of Christ. Each needs to understand the other's relationship to God and determination to follow His leading. The character, actions, and habits of the other should be weighed carefully. There is no way in which a Christian can be united in marriage with a non-Christian, and yet honor God. The Bible calls it an unequal yoking together.

> Be ye not unequally yoked together with unbelievers: for what fellowship hath righteousness with unrighteousness? and what communion hath light with darkness? 2 Corinthians 6:14

Neither is it good enough that the planned partner is a professing Christian. True and complete Christian commitment is the only basis for a happy, fulfilling Christian marriage.

---

1. See chapter 25 entitled "Morality and Sex."

Second, each must understand the many responsibilities that marriage brings, and the selfless foundation upon which true marital happiness is established. Both must honestly ask the question, whether they are seeking marriage purely to subserve their own personal interests, or whether there is such a genuine love for the other that their primary purpose in marriage is to seek the fulfillment and happiness of the partner that they are accepting in marriage.

A third important question is, Have we sought wise counsel from spiritual people, especially our parents (if these are committed Christians)? Good parents seek only the happiness and success of their children. And among God's provisions for young people is counsel that they can receive, first from their own parents and then from other Christian adults. Often it will not be completely possible for these persons to fully verbalize their reservations if they have them, but nevertheless the wisdom of age should not be spurned for the impulsiveness of youth. Even in this nuclear society, young people are marrying into a family. And it is of great help to know that the parents of both partners contemplating marriage are in harmony with the decision and are happy to accept the other partner into the family circle. This acceptance certainly reduces the tension and estrangements that can develop when willful marriages are contracted independent of parental advice.

Fourth, Have we known each other long enough and in sufficiently varied circumstances to be sure that God is leading us together? There is no reason for Christian young people to marry with little understanding of each other's character or purposes. Of course, if there has been an opportunity in group situations to get to know each other in the widest sphere, then this will be a great asset when specific courting takes place. Even so, it is essential that young people be objective enough to understand the characteristics of the other, so that they may be able to make their early marital adjustment as simple and as successful as possible.

Fifth, Have we both learned Christ-control as the basis of our relationship? There is no way that marriage can successfully be entered into in a willful or irresponsible way. The control of Christ not only includes the area of sex but also all facets of life in preparation for marriage. This control provides a fine security for married life. Such self-control will be characterized by the avoidance of late nights together, which in themselves produce pitfalls even for the Christian young person.

Sixth, Do we have an understanding of the proper approach to Christian stewardship as a part of true Christian development and home establishment? Finances can produce inordinate difficulties within a marital situation; and the subject of how finances will be handled, and the respective responsibilities of both the wife and the husband in this area, ought to be carefully studied before marriage. The responsibility to God, as well as the careful disbursement of funds ought to be discussed, and compatibility on these matters sought.

Seventh, the relationship to family expectations should be explored, including the attitudes toward children, the number thought desirable, as well as attitudes toward their management and education. Even attitudes to home location, tastes and such matters should be well understood. In fact, the more areas discussed and the more agreements reached, the greater will be the possibility of forging a successful marriage; for in marriage there will be enough unexpected decisions to make without having to be concerned with decisions which could have been faced before marriage. In making these decisions together the couple can establish a strong basis for open communication in marriage.

Then there is the relationship to God. There is importance in learning to pray together, to study God's Word together and to work for Christ together. The courtship ought to be the basis upon which subsequent home values will be established and those areas which will tend toward the happiness of the home ought to be strengthened during this period.

The home ought to be a Christian witnessing unit, and its effective establishment surely starts in the courtship period. The strength of society is derived from strong, secure and stable families of which every member is mentally healthy. A high level of mental disorder in society today must be traced primarily to the instability of the home and the insecurity of the family relationships. Those homes established upon the principles of Christ, secured by Christ in love, are clearly the most effective bulwarks against the collapse of society.

DESIRED ORDER OF LIFE'S GREAT CHOICES

1.   DECISION FOR CHRIST

2.   DECISION FOR A LIFE'S CALLING

3.   DECISION FOR A LIFE PARTNER

4.   DECISION FOR INITIATING NEW LIVES

28

Marriage and
the Family

THERE is no human relationship more sacred than the relationship between a husband and wife. The very first institution established by God after the creation of man and woman was the institution of marriage.

And the LORD God caused a deep sleep to fall upon Adam, and he slept: and he took one of his ribs, and closed up the flesh instead thereof; and the rib, which the LORD God had taken from man, made he a woman, and brought her unto the man. And Adam said, This is now bone of my bones, and flesh of my flesh: she shall be called Woman, because she was taken out of Man. Therefore shall a man leave his father and his mother, and shall cleave unto his wife: and they shall be one flesh. Genesis 2:21–24

It was God's purpose that a husband and wife should live together for eternity; and after sin separated man from God, the purpose was still that husband and wife should live together until the death of one of the partners. The vow that is made to love, honor and cherish "until death do us part" is the second most sacred vow that any human being can make, second only to the vow to love, honor and serve God. The Word of God records many evidences of the sacredness of this vow. Within the Ten Commandments is the injunction,

Thou shalt not commit adultery. Exodus 20:14

And it is God's purpose that no home should be established without a God-given relationship which prevents any consideration of infidelity or separation. Christ Himself on a number of occasions brought to His hearers the importance of the marriage relationship. In the Sermon on the

Mount He extended the commandment even to lustful thoughts, and declared that there is but one ground for divorce, and that is adultery.

> But I say unto you, That whosoever looketh on a woman to lust after her hath committed adultery with her already in his heart.
>
> Matthew 5:28

> It hath been said, Whosoever shall put away his wife, let him give her a writing of divorcement: but I say unto you, That whosoever shall put away his wife, saving for the cause of fornication, causeth her to commit adultery: and whosoever shall marry her that is divorced committeth adultery.   Matthew 5:31–32

Great permissiveness had entered into the society of Israel, and there were those who held that divorce could take place for the most trivial of reasons, but Christ came to uphold God's law and the sacredness of marriage. Much is safeguarded if neither partner entertains the thought that the marriage was a mistake, even when there are problems. Moses had indicated that a woman could be divorced for some uncleanness.

> When a man hath taken a wife, and married her, and it come to pass that she find no favour in his eyes, because he hath found some uncleanness in her: then let him write her a bill of divorcement, and give it in her hand, and send her out of his house. And when she is departed out of his house, she may go and be another man's wife. And if the latter husband hate her, and write her a bill of divorcement, and giveth it in her hand, and sendeth her out of his house; or if the latter husband die, which took her to be his wife; her former husband, which sent her away, may not take her again to be his wife, after that she is defiled; for that is abomination before the LORD: and thou shalt not cause the land to sin, which the LORD thy God giveth thee for an inheritance.   Deuteronomy 24:1–4

The leadership of the Jews had even allowed divorce for the burning of the husband's food. Christ stated that such trivial responses to marriage were never in God's plan for men.

> The Pharisees also came unto him, tempting him, and saying unto him, Is it lawful for man to put away his wife for every cause? And he answered and said unto them, Have ye not read, that he which made them at the beginning made them male and female, and said, For this cause shall a man leave father and mother, and shall cleave to his wife: and they twain shall be one flesh? wherefore they are no more

twain, but one flesh. What therefore God hath joined together, let not man put asunder. They say unto him, Why did Moses then command to give a writing of divorcement, and to put her away? He saith unto them, Moses because of the hardness of your hearts suffered you to put away your wives: but from the beginning it was not so. And I say unto you, Whosoever shall put away his wife, except it be for fornication, and shall marry another, committeth adultery: and whoso marrieth her which is put away doth commit adultery.

Matthew 19:3–9

Marital love draws its strength from Christ's love. It is important that this love be expressed to each member of the family. It should not have to be sought after, but should be freely given. Pleasant relationships, true love and courtesy far surpass the quality of buildings in establishing lasting home relationships. By daily continuing to behold the love of Jesus, husband and wife will strengthen these ties and be secure. John expresses the secret of love when he states,

God is love; and he that dwelleth in love dwelleth in God, and God in him. 1 John 4:16

Each partner in the marriage relationship can share the joy of constantly ministering to the other partner the love that God provided.

There is no question that at the base of every marriage breakup is spiritual declension. This decline does not necessarily involve both partners. It is far too simplistic to say that there are faults on both sides. While it is true that no human relationship is perfect, it is still very possible for a marriage to falter on the self-indulgent and egocentric behavior of one member of the partnership. Often, especially when one has lost his relationship with God, it becomes even more likely that he will seek fellowship and relationship outside of his marriage than if both partners lose their relationship together. The life of the converted partner is often a rebuke to the unfaithful spouse. There is frequently a tendency to harass the partner who is seeking to live a life in conformity to God, and to establish guilt feelings of failure and inadequacy. Thus many outsiders may fail to recognize that the faithful partner has often gone to inordinate lengths to do everything to retain the viability of the marriage. In reality in such circumstances, the only one who can reestablish the marital relationship is the wayward partner.

Marriage is an eternal triangle—not the eternal triangle of the classical novel in which a third party intrudes into the marriage relationship, but an eternal triangle involving God, a husband and a wife. If both husband and wife are linked to Christ by indestructible bonds of love, then the marriage is invincible. If, on the other hand, one partner allows the relationship with God to falter, then there is always the possibility of marital strife, disharmony and even failure. This possibility does not mean that lack of harmony will always be the result, but that the only marriage which is totally secure is the one in which both partners have a close fellowship with Christ. Of course, not every committed Christian can make a suitable partner for another Christian. But those who are committed to Christ will have taken into account the highest Christian values and will not have impulsively nor irresponsibly contracted the marriage relationship. In seeking God's guidance they will have established a basis upon which a happy and holy marriage can be founded. Such a marriage will never be defiled by cruelty, harshness, coarseness, indifference or sensual or blasphemous talk. God has directed that the husband be the head of the family. He must take his leadership responsibilities seriously, while also safeguarding against being overbearing and dictatorial. The wife and family should never be neglected for other responsibilities. It is his responsibility, whenever possible, to lead out in the spiritual exercises of the family. While being the leader of the household, he will preserve the individuality of his wife as the two lives blend together in a unified direction. While head of the house, the husband in his leadership must be motivated by love for his wife and family.

Perhaps the most critical situation in any marriage occurs when one partner has violated his marriage vows by sexual infidelity. This act is a divine base for the faithful partner to divorce the unfaithful one. However even here, should the fallen partner seek forgiveness and be responsive to reconciliation, in love and forgiveness surely it is the faithful partner's God-given responsibility to take back the erring one, just as Christ has extended His matchless love to all those who have been estranged from Him. However, after the very best and fullest efforts have not achieved reconciliation, the innocent one is free to divorce. Under no circumstances does the Scripture give license for the unfaithful partner to remarry, and those who do enter into a new marriage, have entered into an adulterous relationship forbidden by the seventh commandment. Some partners, usually wives, do have to face most trying situations, involving intense cruelty and even a threat to life. These problems may also involve the children of the marriage. Only when all else fails and the danger becomes too intense should a wife see fit to leave her husband, but Scripture gives no permission to divorce unless the husband has committed adultery. When a Christian is married to a non-Christian, the Christian spouse has a great responsibility to do everything possible to live in Christian love. Paul states that in itself the lack of Christian commitment is not a valid basis for separation or divorce.

> But to the rest speak I, not the Lord: If any brother hath a wife that believeth not, and she be pleased to dwell with him, let him not put her away. And the woman which hath a husband that believeth not, and if he be pleased to dwell with her, let her not leave him. For the unbelieving husband is sanctified by the wife, and the unbelieving wife is sanctified by the husband: else were your children unclean; but now they are holy. But if the unbelieving depart, let him depart. A brother or a sister is not under bondage in such cases: but God hath called us to peace. For what knowest thou, O wife, whether thou shalt save thy husband? or how knowest thou, O man, whether thou shalt save they wife?   1 Corinthians 7:12–16

One of the most solemn responsibilities that faces a married couple is parenthood. The responsibilities of bringing a new life into the world must be considered carefully and prayerfully. It is total irresponsibility to decide to bring children into the world when the marriage itself is not stable. Some believe that in doing so they will stabilize the marriage, but it is unfair to bring a little baby into the world in such circumstances. What can he do to mend the emotional disharmony in the home? Indeed, the birth of a child adds further tensions to such a marriage relationship. The child in turn is most likely to become the victim of the parents' instability.

Parents should carefully evaluate the number of children that they can satisfactorily support, recognizing that the cost of education and other commitments to children is very high. Wise Christian planning will not permit the family to grow beyond that for which the parents can provide responsible care.

Just as the spiritual life is important in the preparation for marriage, so it is central to the success of the marriage relationship itself. As previously mentioned, almost inevitably in any marriage breakdown there has been a prior breakdown in the spiritual life of the home, at least on the part of one partner, if not both. It is important to true Christian marriage that the family altar be established within the framework of a loving spiritual relationship; an unhurried period morning and evening when the family worships together. This goal will often mean an evaluation of priorities. But properly handled, with a time set that does not force, rush or offer mere tokenism, family worship can be a period for binding together the whole family in Christian love. Also, as the family works for God together, there can be developed great cohesiveness. This closeness should involve not only the husband and wife but also the children, especially as they grow older. It is an exciting opportunity for young people to be part of a family outreach in helping men and women to know Christ and to follow in His footsteps. They too, in their own way, become part of the spiritual outreach of the home.

The sexual relationship between husband and wife also provides an important facet of the marriage relationship. Too frequently marriage is considered to be a license for lust, and deviant forms of sexual behavior are practiced. Such practices bring a degrading influence into the home, and the relationship which all too frequently develops directs away from true Christianity. The sacredness of the marriage is lost to the satisfaction of sensual desires.[1] The sexual life built upon true love and concern for one another can offer a most intimate relationship and a firm basis for spiritual growth. But that which is built upon carnal desires results in a diminution of spirituality and of true Christian commitment. As in every facet of temperate living, there needs to be control and rational decision-making, and each action needs to be validated by the challenge of the purity of Christ, our ultimate Example. However, some have mistakenly felt that sexual relationships within marriage are evil and have caused terrible pressures to be felt within the marriage relationship by adopting this unreasoned opinion. The unilateral decision of one of the marriage partners to withdraw from the conjugal relationship promotes an un-Christlike atmosphere between husband and wife. Many great evils have been generated by such a decision. Often this decision, while being made ostensibly for spiritual reasons, is in fact based upon a selfish lack of love for the spouse.

---

1. See chapter 25 entitled "Morality and Sex."

There is perhaps nothing more beautiful in this world than a true marriage and home environment, and it is the privilege of every Christian, with the power of Christ and under His guidance, to establish such homes in which our children and youth will have the advantage of Christian examples and strong Christian education.

The parents need wisdom in choosing the education of their children, the responsibility for which always rests with them:

> And thou shalt teach them diligently unto thy children, and shalt talk of them when thou sittest in thine house, and when thou walkest by the way, and when thou liest down, and when thou risest up.
>
> Deuteronomy 6:7

Never can this responsibility be given completely to another. But when the choice of a school and a teacher is made, it needs to be made with the realization that the parents are still the guardians of the child, and they are delegating to a professional educator, responsibility that they still retain. It is essential then that only a committed Christian have this responsibility, and therefore the choice of school and teachers becomes a very sobering God-given responsibility, for as the home and the school combine, there should be harmony and consistency in the program of development for the child. There is much wisdom in allowing the child to remain at home until he is mature enough to gain maximally from the school environment. A good family, where the wife does not work, is usually the best educating agency until the child is at least eight years of age. In some countries legal considerations prevent the attainment of this ideal.

In the difficult era in which we live it is important that every factor possible be directed toward the spiritual growth, development and commitment of the child. This family responsibility is never lost. It would be far better for children to be sent to a Christian school, though it may cost more, than to have the luxuries often considered essential in homes; such as rugs on the floor or lounge room furniture. Once again, the priorities of the parent will determine to what extent not only the child's physical and intellectual development will take place but also how important his eternal destiny is to the parent. The wise choices of parents are at the very heart of spiritual, emotional and physical development of the citizens of tomorrow and of the candidates for heaven.

29

Conclusion

MANY religions and cultures teach that life is bitter, merely a struggle to exist between life's two dominant events—birth and death. And truly when we observe the lives of millions of people, the evidence for this belief is plain to see. But God offers us contentment, peace, fulfillment and true love in this life: He offers us mental health.

Yet spurning or misunderstanding this offer, the vast majority of earth's inhabitants find themselves neglecting it, and seeking a satisfactory life based on human goals. Wealth, power, prestige, and other symbols of worldly success have proved consistent failures in defining such a life. There is no human solution to an existence devoid of real meaning. Without God in the life, its only purpose would be to continue the species.

In 1969 died the great British mathematician, philosopher and pacifist, Bertrand Russell. A direct descendant in the line of the dukes of Bedford, and himself a peer of the realm (an earl), Earl Bertrand Russell was a grandson of Lord John Russell, one of Britain's most distinguished prime ministers of the nineteenth century. Lord John Russell, a devout Anglican, introduced to the House of Commons the first reform bill of 1832. This bill led to the eventual provision of universal suffrage in the United Kingdom (the right of every adult to vote in elections). But Lord John Russell's son, the father of Bertrand Russell, was an atheist.

At the time of Bertrand Russell's death, a film tribute to his life was presented. This film included an interview with him three years prior to his death at well over ninety years of age. In this interview, Bertrand Russell recalled the death of his father seventy years earlier. His father had called his three sons to his death bed. There was no hope, no peace, no surety, as he said to his sons, "Goodbye, goodbye forever." Even the recollection of that moment, seven decades gone by, brought a tremor to Bertrand Russell's voice and a tear to his eye. And then, confirming his own atheistic convictions, Bertrand Russell said, "It will be the same when I die." Such is the "hope" of those who, however distinguished, lose sight of Jesus and His love. This book has been written from deep conviction. There is nothing, outside of Jesus, productive of sound mental health. We uphold our Savior before each reader, for it is He who promised,

> I am come that they might have life, and that they might have it more abundantly.   John 10:10

Appendix A

The Nature of Man

AS late as the early part of the twentieth century, it was confidently predicted by many philosophers and educators that universal education could solve the major social problems of the world, such as poverty, crime and insanity. It had been observed that these social ills seemed to find expression much more in the poorly educated classes than in the middle and upper classes. Perhaps nothing did more to stimulate the thrust for universal education than the hope that these evils would be eliminated as man continued his upward "evolutionary" climb. But sober evaluation of the world during the latter part of the twentieth century indicates that in the western world, where now there is virtually universal education, there has been an intensification of each of these social problems.

The universal-education solution in fact has its origin in Greek philosophy. Socrates established his questioning techniques upon the fundamental belief that through education man could achieve that which is good. This assumption was based upon the premise of an immortal soul preexisting the body, a soul that is good. Thus man could be corrupted only by an unfavorable environment. He viewed man as fundamentally good, and thus all that was needed was to protect the inherently good person from the evils of society, that he might become aware of that goodness. Socrates questioned the youth of Greece on the assumption that "to know is to do." He believed that should the youth discover through his questioning what indeed was good and what was truth, they would automatically live the "good life."

Unwittingly, not a few Christians have accepted this pagan philosophy. Some have felt that their children would make better decisions if they themselves did not exert an influence at too early an age upon their choices. Believing that, given "freedom of expression," children would usually make right decisions because of their inborn goodness, these parents have adopted that course. In our experience, the results have been disastrous. This outcome is not surprising, since undoubtedly Satan does not wait for children to grow up before bringing his artful temptations into their lives. Habits which militate against children making commitments to Christ are easily established in these critical formative years.

Socrates' disciple Plato basically upheld this view, and much of his philosophic energy was directed toward establishing the perfect society wherein could be developed the universally "good man."

With the rediscovery of Hellenistic culture at the time of the Renaissance, there was a resurgence of this concept of man, and even among some Christian theologians there was a tendency to accept this philosophy. Perhaps the outstanding proponent of this theory in the eighteenth century was Jean Jacques Rousseau. The goodness-of-man concept is much in evidence in his classic work, *Emile*. The book is the story of a lad brought up in a good environment, so as to preserve his innate goodness. While one cannot argue with Rousseau on the desirability of a good environment, yet one cannot be a student of the Scriptures without strongly questioning the concept that man is innately good.

The twentieth century has seen a shift from the nativist approaches of Socrates, Plato and Rousseau to the empiricist, or *tabula rasa* view (man is totally the product of his environmental influences). While this concept is not new to the twentieth century, having been spearheaded in the seventeenth and eighteenth centuries by the British empiricists such as John Locke, Bishop George Berkeley, David Hume and David Hartley, nevertheless it has broken out of its philosophic origins into the practicalities of psychological techniques and practice in the twentieth century. The empiricist movement has received great impetus from evolutionary theory, with its emphasis upon the ability to adapt to environment and its failure to recognize God as First Cause.

Closely associated with the evolutionary impact has been the scientific impact. When toward the latter part of the nineteenth century, science was achieving predominant respectability in academic circles, the old philosophic bases for most disciplines were eagerly shed to allow the fostering of the more prestigious scientific approach. Thus when Wilhelm

Wundt established what was perhaps the first psychological laboratory in Leipzig in 1879, the foundation of modern scientific psychology had been laid. By this time the deterministic principles[1] of natural science had been firmly established and these of course were compatible with the empiricist view of man—that man is simply the pawn of his environment; he is born with no moral predispositions. Therefore the resultant man is the sum total of the environmental influences that he has experienced from conception.

In modern psychology, the two views—that of man as innately good, a nativist philosophy; and that of man born with no moral predisposition, an empiricist philosophy—underpin the vast majority of psychological theories and counseling techniques. Perhaps these are best exemplified in the work of Carl Rogers and B. F. Skinner, respectively. That resident within man is a knowledge of how to handle his own problems, is implied within the nondirective therapy of Rogers. It cannot be denied that there are times when, by careful questioning as in the case of Socrates of old, or of Rogers of modern times, men and women can be brought to verbalize and act upon solutions that they have not previously acknowledged. However, to assume that inherent within all are the best answers to every problem, is to assume that man himself is capable of handling every issue and every need. Such a view of man leads to the belief that he is the total master of his destiny; and trust in God, his only real source of strength, is lost. That Rogers for the last decade has enthusiastically embraced the encounter group psychology,[2] again evidences his view that man, in the encounter environment, can indeed be enabled to view himself in a way which will allow for right and best decisions as to appropriate behavior.

On the other hand, most behaviorists from Watson and Thorndike, through Hull and Spence, to B. F. Skinner, have acknowledged that knowledge does not necessarily result in good behavior. Thus the Socratic concept, "to know is to do," could not longer be considered tenable, in the light of the overwhelming evidence that very frequently right knowledge does not lead to good behavior. Therefore, within the framework of empiricism, it was easy to establish a concept in which there was a direct

---

1.   This concept states that man has no real control over his own actions. He is in reality, according to this view, merely a robot doing that which his heredity and environmental experiences dictate. He cannot make a true choice.

2.   See chapter 10 entitled "Encounter and Sensitivity Groups and Christianity."

attempt to change the behavior itself. It was possible, by the process of conditioning,[3] to habituate behavior patterns, and in this way it was hoped to develop the "good man." Thus the behavior modification technique, as employed by B. F. Skinner and others, has received wide acclaim as the most effective technique in changing the behavior of children, of the mentally ill, and of delinquents, to that behavior which is acceptable and desirable in society.

Implied by behavior modification theory is a view of man, holding that good behavior can be equated with the goodness of man. In spite of the fact that the Rogerian approach is nativist in direction and Skinner's is empiricist in origin, they have much in common in terms of their prediction for education and child training. The nativist, assuming that man is innately good, postulates the need for a "good environment" as the only necessary prerequisite to retraining or maintaining that goodness. Likewise the empiricist, assuming that man is the pawn of his environment, that he is what he is because of the sum total of environmental stimuli upon his life, hypothesizes that if a "good" environment can be maintained, then the child will grow up to be a good man. Thus both theories are totally dependent upon the quality of the environment for the development of the "good" man and ultimately the development of the "good" society. But neither view is consistent with the Christian Bible-centered approach.

Contrary to the innate-goodness philosophy, is the biblical alternative nativist view that man is born to sin:

> Behold, I was shapen in iniquity; and in sin did my mother conceive me.   Psalm 51:5

The Bible teaches that man's innate moral tendencies lead to the establishment of a character and behavior which is self-centered and sinful. Such a view of man does not deny the advantage of a good environment, but it cannot assume that a good environment is all that is needed to maintain the "good" life, for then there could have been no possibility of the fall of Adam and Eve, since they had been placed in a perfect environment. Nor could Lucifer and a third of the angels have rebelled against God.

---

3. This procedure rewards good acts and punishes bad acts so that the individual will shun evil and do good as a consequence.

How art thou fallen from heaven, O Lucifer, son of the morning! how
art thou cut down to the ground, which didst weaken the nations! For
thou hast said in thine heart, I will ascend into heaven, I will exalt my
throne above the stars of God: I will sit also upon the mount of the
congregation, in the sides of the north.   Isaiah 14:12–14

The empiricist view as exemplified in behavior modification is also untenable, for it assumes, as previously stated, that right behavior means
right morality; that somehow of ourselves we can become good. The Scripture states that this hope is false.

The carnal mind is enmity against God: for it is not subject to the law
of God, neither indeed can be.   Romans 8:7

The biblical view is that man, after his fall, is caught in the toils of sin and
is unable to escape in his own strength. The good news is that Jesus has
provided for us to be forgiven for past sins; to be given new hearts (wills)
to choose the good way; and to place the Holy Spirit within us to give us
when needed the strength to resist falling back into our previous state.

There is apparent a distinct difference between behavior modification
and the Christian concept of behavior change. Accepting that man's natural predispositions are contrary to the perfect nature of God, the issue is
not behavior modification but character transformation, as Jesus most
beautifully expressed in confrontation with Nicodemus.[4] The real issue
was defined as a need for the new-birth experience. Behavior modification does not say anything about the motives and intents of the heart, and
as such has inherent within it the worst of legalism. That right behavior
alone is not a basis upon which salvation can be expected or achieved, is
clearly shown in the words of Jesus:

Many will say to me in that day, Lord, Lord, have we not prophesied
in thy name? and in thy name have cast out devils? and in thy name
done many wonderful works? And then will I profess unto them, I
never knew you: depart from me, ye that work iniquity.
                    Matthew 7:22–23

Here the issue is not right behavior, for these workers of iniquity have
performed good acts, by human definition. The problem has been in the
motives, in the intents of the heart. Their behavior may be consistent with
Christian practice, but their hearts have not been transformed by the power

---

4. See John, chapter 3.

of Christ. Christ further emphasized this truth in His confrontation with the Pharisees.

> For ye pay tithe of mint and anise and cummin, and have omitted the weightier matters of the law, judgment, mercy, and faith: these ought ye to have done, and not to leave the other undone. Matthew 23:23

Jesus emphasized that the paying of a faithful tithe is right behavior, but it has no significance unless it is the result of the love that flows from a transformed heart.

It is logical to expect that hypotheses of man built upon wrong premises will lead also to wrong conclusions, theories and practices. There certainly are dangers in both behavior modification and nondirective therapy. The behavior modification therapist plays God as it were, to his counselee. He determines what is good behavior, and he administers those conditioning techniques which are likely to bring about the behavior which he himself determines is desirable. The nondirective therapist, on the other hand, allows the counselee to play the role of God, believing that inherent within him are the sure answers to the problems that have produced depression, emotional instability and neurosis. But the Christian therapist has the opportunity to point to the God in heaven who does have the answer.

Careful evaluation of all three views of man is a hopeful one. We face the reality of a world where the vast majority of its inhabitants have a poor environment in which to live. As both the innate goodness and the empiricist views of man depend on a good environment for the retaining or developing of the good man, the vast majority would be hopeless and helpless both in this world and also in the world to come. The Christian concept, however, views no one as hopeless. While acknowledging the advantage of a favorable environment, Christianity asserts that the power of Christ "is able also to save them to the uttermost that come unto God by him" (Hebrews 7:25).

The transforming power of Christ offers hope to all, irrespective of environmental limitations.

There is no question that Christian psychologists need to dig deeply into the Word of God to discover what these answers are, for the same God who through the Scriptures has shown a deep concern for the spiritual and physical well-being of His people, is just as critically interested in their emotional and mental stability. It is only reasonable to assume that God's Word also provides for us principles and bases for mental health in the same way it provides those bases for spiritual and physical health. For without emotional stability, there is little hope that a man or woman can fully reach the potentiality that God has for him or her, nor to participate as fully as possible in the ministry and missions of God's church.

BASIC CONCEPTS OF THE NATURE OF MAN

POSITION	SUPPORTERS	MORAL PREDISPOSITION	RELATIONSHIP TO ENVIRONMENT	PROSPECTS
Innate Goodness	Socrates Plato Rousseau Many Purposivists	Man has a predisposition to goodness.	All that is needed is a "good" environment to protect the "good" inherent within man for the "good" man to be developed.	Man's prospects depend upon a good or a bad environment.
Innate Evil Tendencies	Most Christians	Man has a predisposition to develop patterns of evil.	While acknowledging the advantages of a good environment, holds that the "good" man is developed only by the indwelling Christ.	Man's prospects depend upon a relationship with God irrespective of the environment.
No Innate Tendencies (*tabula rasa*)	British Empiricists Behaviorists Determinists	Man is conceived as neutral, having no inherent moral predispositions.	The environment determines the totality of behavioral responses.	Man's prospects depend upon a good or a bad environment.

Appendix B

Choice and the Will

THE concept of choice is as old as the universe. It is evident that the angelic hosts were given freedom of choice. The prophet Isaiah indicates that Lucifer, the covering cherub, made many choices.

> How art thou fallen from heaven, O Lucifer, son of the morning! how art thou cut down to the ground, which didst weaken the nations! For *thou hast said* in thine heart, *I will ascend* into heaven, *I will exalt* my throne above the stars of God: *I will sit* also upon the mount of the congregation, in the sides of the north: *I will ascend* above the heights of the clouds; *I will be like* the most High.
>
> Isaiah 14:12–14, emphasis supplied

It is also clear that when man was created, he was given choice; otherwise the direction and warnings of God would have been meaningless.

> And the LORD God commanded the man, saying, Of every tree of the garden thou mayest freely eat: but of the tree of the knowledge of good and evil, thou shalt not eat of it: for in the day that thou eatest thereof thou shalt surely die.
>
> Genesis 2:16–17

Thus from the beginning, both the angels and the parents of the human race were created with a predisposition to do those things which were good; but after man had chosen to disobey the direct and explicit command of God, he no longer naturally sought to follow in pathways of righteousness. There was now a natural inclination to move in pathways that alienate from God. David was thus constrained to declare,

> Behold, I was shapen in iniquity; and in sin did my mother conceive me.
>
> Psalm 51:5

In spite of the clearest indications from Holy Writ as to the nature of man and his ability to choose, yet there have been those who, from the dawn of history, have accepted a deterministic approach to life. Determinism, which is closely allied to the empiricism discussed in the previous chapter, has its roots in ancient paganism, and can still be found in modern mysticism. The concept of the influence of the macrocosm of the starry heavens, upon the microcosm of the human organism, is as old as astrology. Determinism has woven its way into many Eastern religions and can also be seen within a number of forms of Christianity. The question of free will versus determinism is relevant today, not only in the realm of theology, but also in literature, history, sociology, psychology and philosophy. However it is perhaps in the science of human behavior that the determinism / free will controversy has its greatest significance to the Christian believer. While it is unfair to confine the meaning of either determinism or purposivism within the framework of any single set of postulates, there must necessarily be some specifying and limiting of definitions. Therefore the following guidelines represent the arena within which the issues of free will and determinism will be discovered.

1. **Determinism:** the view that behavior is best described in terms of all the environmental influences upon a person, past and present, together with the observable behavior of that person in response to influences.

It is suggested that knowing all the causal events, one can accurately predict the behavioral response to those events. There is no reaction or choice of the person which in any way modifies, adapts or intervenes between the direct relationship of these influences and the behavioral responses. Thus all reference to brain processes or mental factors such as "choice," "decision," and "will" are denied. The person does what he does because he cannot do anything else. He is completely dependent upon his environment for the development of characteristic behavior and personality traits.

2. **Purposivism:** the suggestion that the person actively mediates between the environmental stimuli and his behavioral reactions.

This is to say that by decision or choice or other brain processes, the subject relates his reactions to the situation presenting itself. It is usual to assume that neurological processes and central nervous system mechanisms are the basic structures mediating these decisions. Thus behavior cannot be defined simply in terms of the stimulus and the response. Account must be taken of the person's mental events and his own decisions.

In the scientific realm it is not possible to choose dogmatically between purposivism and determinism on experimental grounds alone. And neither is there universal agreement among Christians concerning the two positions of predestination and free will. This is not to conclude that predestination concepts can be directly equated with determinism, or that free will is synonymous with the psychological position of purposivism. However, there are a number of basic similarities which allow fairly satisfactory investigations of each in terms of the other.

1. **Predestination:** While predestinarians concern themselves little with the relationship of environmental stimulation to bodily reaction, they hold that salvation is independent of man's choices and decision; that God preordains the eternal destiny of each human being.

2. **Free Will:** The proponents of free will, like the purposivists, place considerable emphasis upon the role of mental processes in human behavior. It is contended that everyone makes decisions and choices, both in respect of day-to-day existence and eternal destiny, and that salvation ultimately depends upon acceptance or rejection of Christ.

In the study of human behavior, the determinism / purposivism controversy becomes critical to an understanding of psychological and sociological principles. While it achieved its academic independence about 100 years ago, psychology has been investigated by man for centuries under the connotation of mental philosophy. The deterministic / purposivistic controversy was not so intense in former years as it is today. But there is little doubt that purposivism was more readily accepted by the majority in past times, possibly because of the strong Christian bases from which most philosophers worked.

Richard Ruble seeks to summarize and define the controversy largely within the framework of Christian theology. He assembled basic arguments in favor of the free will position:

    1. Without free will man would not be responsible for his behavior.

    2. Man has free will because of the subjective experience felt in deciding.

    3. God has decreed that men have free will.

4. The gospel assumes that men have free will.

5. Man conducts his affairs as though he believes in free will.

6. Free will is the only rational position that can be taken by a Christian.

He summarizes his arguments in favor of determinism as follows:

1. Determinism is more consistent with the nature of God. If God is omnipotent and omniscient, determinism naturally follows.

2. Scientific views must be deterministic.

3. Determinism is more humanistic than is Free Will.

4. The determinist view accounts for unconscious motivation.

5. Determinism is more in harmony with God's election, sovereignty, foreordaining and foreknowledge.

6. Determinism enables man to accept whatever happens as being in God's will and therefore ultimately good. (Richard Ruble, "Determinism versus Free Will," *Journal of American Affiliation*, June 1976, vol. 28, No. 2, pp. 70–76)

The majority of Christians—Roman Catholics, Orthodox Christians and many Protestants—support the free will doctrine; however, there is a large segment of reformation Christians who hold to the Augustinian view of predestination as expressed by Calvin and Luther. While it is not germane to this book to discuss the variations between high and low Calvinism, it is fair to say that high Calvinists especially hold strongly to the predestinarian doctrine. Their view is that it is a miracle of the grace of God that anyone should be saved. Thus it is not for erring man to question divine justice in preordination. It seems altogether unreasonable, however, to accept as fact that God could have allowed man to make choices while also having preknowledge of the choice that he would make. Some have argued that the very fact that God knows what will take place absolutely preordains that event. It would be more reasonable, surely, to assume God knows, not because He has ordained the event, but because He is aware of the choices that man will make.

Of course, this dilemma raises the issue of sin. Could not God have created beings in both heaven and in earth who would have chosen always to follow in perfect obedience to His will? This is an exceptionally speculative field of inquiry in which the Word of God has given us little direction, and thus possibly is outside the scope of profitable debate or discussion.

The authors accept the view that man's eternal destiny is contingent upon his choice to accept or reject the gift of God made accessible to men by Christ's propitiation for his sins. The Bible is replete with assurances of the crucial nature of man's choice in his salvation. In the Old Testament Joshua made a great plea for the children of Israel to choose to serve either the Lord or heathen gods:

> And if it seem evil unto you to serve the LORD, choose you this day whom ye will serve; whether the gods which your fathers served that were on the other side of the flood, or the gods of the Amorites, in whose land ye dwell: but as for me and my house, we will serve the LORD.   Joshua 24:15

Elijah made a similar appeal on Mt. Carmel, asking those present to choose to yield allegiance either to God or to Baal.

> And Elijah came unto all the people and said, How long halt ye between two opinions? if the LORD be God, follow him: but if Baal, then follow him. And the people answered him not a word.
> 1 Kings 18:21

THE VIEWS OF MAN IN RELATIONSHIP TO MAN'S DESTINY

VIEW OF MAN	BASIC PRINCIPLE	THE DETERMINANT OF MAN'S DESTINY
Determinism	Man is the sum total of all his environmental influences from conception to death.	Environment
Predestinarianism	Man's eternal destiny is preordained by God and thus is external to him.	God
Purposivism	Man modifies, mediates, makes choices and decisions in response to his environment.	Man himself
	Man may choose to accept or reject Christ's provision of salvation.	Man through the power of the indwelling Christ

Appendix C

Mental Health and Creation

THE last two decades of the nineteenth century saw the emergence of modern psychology, and with this emergence came a determined effort to break with its philosophic origins and develop as science. It was this direction toward science which foreshadowed the growth in popularity of determinism as the most effective method for psychological study. There have always been those who have clung to a purposivistic explanation of behavior, but these have tended to be in the minority. The extensive acceptance of determinism seems to have been motivated by four basic considerations.

1. The major sciences, such as physics and chemistry, were strongly deterministic in direction about the turn of the century, and psychologists were anxious to follow the lead of these better-established sciences.

2. Determinism as a method offered greater prospects than did purposivism for the establishment of general principles and laws governing behavior. It is easier to obtain an understanding of stimulus conditions when these are independent of the so-called metaphysical notions of the mind. It has been held that no universal law could be deduced while holding to a purposivistic explanation of behavior.

3. Determinism offered a satisfactory vehicle for the incorporation of the evolutionary doctrine by assuming that differences between human and animal behavior were quantitative, not qualitative.

4. Assuming the tenability of the quantitative hypothesis, scientists found it possible to examine human behavior through animal investigation.

The use of animals offered not only a broader scope for the investigation, but also the possibility of examining behavior devoid of many of the complexities associated with human performance. In the last forty years or so there has been a partial revival of the purposivistic position headed by such theorists as Krechevesky, Tolman and Woodworth, but most psychologists still favor the deterministic approach.

The tenability of a Christian position favoring free will must be examined in the light of the four reasons cited above, which provide the rationale for the acceptance of determinism by most behavioral scientists.

1. The deterministic nature of the major sciences

While the deterministic postulate was universally accepted by physicians seventy years ago, such acceptance could not be said to be the case today. Rather, advances in subatomic physics have directed the thinking toward indeterminacy. This fact was pointed out in an article attributed to Sir Marcus Oliphant. "The smug Victorian idea of certainty of science has been replaced by uncertainty and indeterminism. . . . The scientists no longer expect to find a final answer to any question. . . . At the end of the past century the march of science had intoxicated mankind, and in the physical sciences the great success of [applying] mathematical reasoning to experimental observations had bred a certainty that the ultimate knowledge of matter was close at hand." He said, "This conception of an arrogant and immoral science, rapidly enmeshing mankind in a web of materialism to satisfy its enormous ego, still persists among very many today. . . . As knowledge has increased it has been found necessary to modify progressively almost all the cherished laws of classical physics. . . . causality has been redefined and determinism has given way to uncertainty" (Sir Marcus Oliphant, *Adelaide Advertiser*, May 18, 1959).

This very forthright statement of the current trends in physics ably demonstrates that one of the basic considerations in the original moves toward determinism in psychology is no longer as tenable as it might have seemed at the turn of the century.

Perhaps one of the most famous theories bearing upon Oliphant's contention is the Heisenberg Uncertainty Principle. Basically, the principle states that having located the position of an electron one cannot determine a precise calculation of its momentum but can only approximate it within certain limits and, conversely, having calculated the momentum of an electron, one cannot determine the precise position it occupies in space.

While the same shift of the major sciences opens the door to the re-analysis of the deterministic method in psychology, the implications would go even further for the reductionists who hold that higher-order processes are best explained in terms of lower-order processes. Taken to their logical finality, the psychological processes require an explanation in terms of physical data, and the physical data in terms of subatomic physics. Thus we have an explanation of the more complex by the less complex, psychology by physiology, physiology by physics, and physics by subatomic physics. If indeterminism and uncertainty apply to subatomic physics, should not these also apply to the physical and thence the physiological and consequently the psychological? If not, at what level of understanding does indeterminism give way to determinism?

Unless a purposive or deterministic position is postulated for all levels of understanding, a reductionist position becomes untenable. It may be suggested that at the microscopic levels of physics, where Newtonian laws hold, the deterministic method is applicable. If this be so, then subatomic physics cannot successfully explain macroscopic physics and a link is broken in the reductionist chain.

2. Determinism's value to law establishment

It was suggested a hundred years ago that determinism offered a more promising approach to law establishment than did purposivism. This suggestion does not preclude the possibility that purposivism offers the more *accurate* explanation of behavior. That even early theorists thought this might finally be the case can be seen in the following statement by William James: "In the last chapter we handed the question of free will over to 'metaphysics.' It would indeed have been hasty to settle the question absolutely inside the limits of psychology. Let psychology frankly admit that for her scientific purposes determinism may be claimed, and no one can find fault. If then, it turns out later that the claim has only a relative purpose and may be crossed by counter claims, the readjustment can be made" (William James, *Psychology's Briefer Course*, p. 461).

Almost a century has passed since James made this statement, yet it cannot be claimed today that any absolute progress has been made toward the establishment of a firm foundation in determinism. In fact, Cattell sums up the situation in two separate statements published in 1950: "Whatever the degree of theoretical determinism we are prepared to admit in regard to human behavior, it is certain that in practice, no matter how good our measuring instrument and our understanding of the processes at work, the accuracy of our predictions is limited" (Cattell, R. B., *Personality*, London; New York: Hutchinson's University Library, 1950, 1st Ed. p. 662). "At present our predictive equations in regard to personality or to memorizing and learning, willing and deciding, have certainly not reached such a pitch of dependability that any psychologist can claim that there is no room for the unpredictable freewill. As scientists, we have kept an open mind concerning what we shall find about mechanistic operation as we penetrate further. And it may be that we shall find a necessity for unforeseen ways of thinking and conceiving that will make both determinism and free will equally correct in their proper contexts" (Cattell, R. B., *An Introduction to Personality Study*, New York, McGraw Hill, 1950, p. 25).

In spite of the high hopes held for determinism at the turn of the century, these have not been realized. The student is often asked to accept the view that this failure is due to the lack of present knowledge and refinement of techniques; and sometime in the unforeseeable future, a complete understanding of behavioral cause and effect will be achieved. Perhaps a better explanation lies in Cattell's unpredictable free will.

3. Determinism and Evolution

The relationship of determinism to evolution is given by two quite opposite views written about the turn of the century. Haeckel says, "The superstition of freewill, together with belief in the two other 'buttresses of mysticism,' God and immortality, has been shattered by the doctrine of evolution" (E. N. Haeckel, *Riddle of the Universe*, p. 210).

While Haeckel claims evolutionary theorizing completely disproves the free will postulate, Smith argued that if the determinism / evolutionary link is tenable, then evolutionary theorizing must be denied. Smith's conclusions are much more acceptable to conservative Christians.

There seems little doubt that it is easier to substantiate a "free will" postulate in the examination of many aspects of behavior than the evolutionary postulate. While evolutionists often suggest that Christians make untenable assumptions, there are certainly even more made by evolutionists, some of which follow:

a. The preexistence of matter, or at least of energy is inexplicable in finite terms.

b. The transition from the mineral to the vegetative to the animate has never been adequately explained or demonstrated.

c. If there is no qualitative difference between man and animal, then logically there can be no qualitative difference between the animate and the vegetative or the vegetative and the mineral.

This last problem has been discussed at length by F. W. Headley in his discussion of consciousness. "Either consciousness is present in the lowest forms of life, or else it was introduced at a higher stage of development. The latter principle is abhorrent to the very principles of evolution. We are driven then to believe that even the microorganisms, whether animal or vegetable, have some consciousness, however dim" (Headley, F. W., *Problems in Evolution*, London: Duckworth, 1900, p. 210).

Perhaps Headley could have taken this conclusion a step further and suggested the presence of consciousness in the lifeless minerals which the evolutionist claims to be the logical precursor of the microorganisms in evolutionary theorizing. To make this assumption is, of course, absurd. Yet the evolutionist is hardly logical if he does not do so.

4. The value of Animal Investigations to the Understanding of Human Behavior

Understanding of the behavior of animals is more readily achieved than that of human subjects, partially because of ethical considerations. However, it may be questioned that human behavior is explicable in the same terms as that of animals, hence there are considerable limitations to the usefulness or applicability of such experiments.

Perhaps one barrier to the development of the psychological understanding of human behavior has been the obsession with parsimony. This barrier has led theorists to resist any explanation that suggests the great complexity of human behavior or any theory that involves a pluralistic interpretation. Even today when there has been a resurgence of dualistic interpretations, monism is still strongly supported. Where dualistic notions have been put forward, few have seriously suggested a dualism of determinism / purposivism. Such an explanation is inherent in Betterman's dual-process hypothesis of discrimination learning,[1] and can be sensed in

---

1. (J. Wodinsky, M. A. Varley, M. E. Bitterman, "Situational determinants of the relative difficulty of simultaneous successive discrimination," *Journal of Comparative Physiology & Psychology*, vol. 47, 1954, pp. 337–340)

Cattell's statement that both "determinism and free will may prove to be equally correct in their proper contexts." However, no careful formulation of such a duality has been made.

There seems little doubt that many simple reflexes are of a deterministic nature, and it might be hypothesized that all that behavior falls within this category, which is mediated by spinal and lower brain areas of the medulla, pons, midbrain and cerebellum. Here we would place the knee-jerk reflex, eye-blink reflex, pupillary reflex and the like. However, most behavior involving the cortical areas of the cerebrum might well be categorized as purposivistic, particularly behavior mediated by the association areas of the frontal lobe. There are one or two problems for such an hypothesis, notably the Babinski reflex[2] which is mediated by cortical processes. However, this hypothesis might form the general basis for such a dualistic explanation of behavior. It would follow from such a dual approach that many lower forms of animal life and all vegetative life could not exhibit purposivistic behavior.

Christianity, based upon what has become known as freedom of the will, does not suggest that all behavior results from choice. The basic choice comes in the acceptance or rejection of God's call to salvation. This fundamental choice forms the cornerstone to one's decision-making in everyday experience. The making of such decisions consistently over a period of time leads to the development of habit structures which, when finally developed, act similarly to reflex-type behavior. This development is consistent with the biblical teaching that early training is of vital importance to subsequent spiritual growth.

> Train up a child in the way he should go: and when he is old, he will not depart from it.   Proverbs 22:6

The Christian also, by prayer and supplication, invites divine aid to assist in his daily life, whether it be spiritual or physical. Thus it is accepted that all things work to the final good of the consecrated follower of Christ.

---

2.   Normally when the sole of the foot is stroked the great toe bends downward. When there is damage to certain areas of the cortex of the brain as in a stroke, the response of stroking the sole of the foot is that the great toe bends upward. This latter effect is known as a positive Babinski reflex.

And we know that all things work together for good to them that love God, to them who are the called according to his purpose.

Romans 8:28

Once one has decided to serve God, and while he continues to do so, the divine agencies are present to direct and minister to him. Thus consecration to God and the choice of the Christian way of life foreshadow special divine ministration to his needs, which precludes an exclusively purposivistic explanation of behavior by the Christian, as every day of the life is submitted to the will of God. However, he is always free to reverse his decision for Christ.

Appendix D

Theories of Personality and
Individual Differences

T HERE have been many attempts to categorize personalities. The
ancient Greeks identified four types of personality, each of which
was said to be related to a different fluid in the body. The *san-
guine* personality was said to result from a rich flow of blood, enabling
the possessor to be happy, outgoing and optimistic. The *choleric* personality was said to have an excess of yellow bile, and thus to be bad tem-
pered and rather negatively aggressive. The *melancholic* personality, on
the other hand, was said to have an excess of black bile, which accounted
for frequent changes in mood involving many periods of depression. The
phlegmatic personality was thought to have an excess of phlegm, resulting in listlessness and docility. But obviously such a description of personality is too simplistic, and certainly there are many reasons why such
unfounded concepts have been rejected by modern psychology.

However, there have been many recent attempts to define personality.
Freud, through his psychoanalytic theory, attempted to define it in terms
of psychosexual dominance. Others have attempted trait descriptions of
personalities. Carl Jung chose typologies of introversion and extroversion, where the introvert was defined as the withdrawn, unsociable personality and the extrovert, the outgoing, warm sociable personality. Subsequently others have seen introversion and extroversion as a continuum
in which the average personality is referred to as ambiversion. Some, in
their attempt to define personality, have looked for physiological types to
be concomitant with personality characteristics. For example, Kretschmer
described three kinds of body build—the asthenic, tall and thin; the pyknic,
short and rotund; and the athletic, muscular. Kretschmer related the introvert to the asthenic; the outgoing, sociable personality to the pyknic build;

and the somewhat in-between ambivert to the athletic build. On the other hand, Sheldon, believing that Kretschmer's typology was too rigid, substituted a system of body typing known as somatotypes. In these each person is classified according to a seven-point scale on each of three basic somatotypes—endomorphy, the degree of predominance of fatty tissue over muscular and bone tissue; mesomorphy, the degree of predominance of muscular tissue over adipose or bone tissue; and ectomorphy, the predominance of bone and skin tissue over muscular or adipose tissue. From this scale Sheldon defined a large number of somatotypes which he in general related to personality characteristics. The predominantly endomorphic person is seen as extroverted, sociable, generally aggressive, and conventional. The predominantly mesomorphic person is thought to be aggressive, with leadership characteristics and a generally ambivert personality. Ectomorphic persons are seen as introverted, with a predominance of interest in intellectual pursuits, often shy, withdrawn and unsociable. However, none of these theories fully explain the true uniqueness of every personality and, while there may be some value in attempting to classify personalities, nevertheless, every single human being is unique, having a distinctive heredity, environment, and relationship to God. No two persons have ever had or ever will have identical heredity, environment, intelligence, interests, aptitudes, physical characteristics, beliefs, biases, and attitudes.

Scriptural Index

Genesis

1:27–28	169n
2:2–3	142
2:7–8, 15	125
2:15	140
2:16–17	211
2:21–24	194
3:1–19	119n
3:9–10	56
3:15	23
4:3–8	55n
4:17	126
12:1–4	61n, 99n
16:1–4	57n
19:26	100n

Exodus

3:10–17	98n
14:10	62n
16:23	142
20:7	45
20:12	153
20:14	194
22:16	178
32:19	54

Leviticus

2:1	126n
6:4	45
18:6–19	178n
18:20	173
18:22	174, 180
18:23	175
20:13	180

Numbers

6:26	87
ch22, ch23	61n

Deuteronomy

4:4–9	117
4:10	112
6:7	160, 200
14:23	112n
21:20	126
22:18–19	178
23:17	180n
24:1–4	195
30:15	49, 84
31:12	112n

Joshua

1:8	93
4:5–8	100n
24:15	97, 215

Judges

13:4, 7	132
13:14	147n
16:20	99
16:28	99

1 Samuel

1:11	164
3:10	95
4:11–18	156
8:7	93
18:6–11	55n

2 Samuel

13:10–15	172
24:12	64n

1 Kings

8:56	101
14:24	180n
15:12	180n
18:21	97, 215
18:39	97
19:1–4	94n
22:46	180n

2 Kings

6:5	140
23:7	180n

1 Chronicles

22:10	101

Job

13:15	17, 95

Psalms

19:14	106, 115
29:11	48, 87
34:14	115
37:3	115
37:27	116
40:4	78, 143
51:5	31, 206, 211
51:10	106
71:5	164
87:6	28
103:3	137
103:12	45n
103:14	28
118:8	78, 144
119:11	104
119:37	120
119:165	48
141:4	113

Proverbs

4:19	113
4:23	114
6:6	141
12:5	106
13:15	96
13:24	152
15:1	55
15:26	105
16:25	169
16:32	72
20:1	132
22:6	114, 160, 222
23:7	103, 114
23:21	126
23:29–32	132
29:15	152
31:4–5	132

Ecclesiastes

3:8	53
5:12	141
12:1	164

The Song of Solomon

2:15	111

Isaiah

1:17	115
6:8	95
14:12–14	207, 211
26:3	48, 108
26:9	115
28:7	133
32:17	87
53:7	55
58:6–8	136
59:2	50
64:6	47

Jeremiah

1:5	177
6:16	186
12:16	115
13:23	116
17:5	78
17:9	105
24:7	107
31:33	107
38:2	64n

Ezekiel

13:22	184
33:7–11	85, 181
36:26	25, 107

Daniel

4:30	92

Hosea

4:11	132

Joel

2:12	106

Amos

2:12	132

Jonah

4:1–3	94n

Micah

7:19	45n

Habakkuk

2:4	66n

Zechariah

3:1–4	49

Malachi

4:2	12

Matthew

5:8	108
5:22	55
5:23–24	48
5:28	107, 195
5:31–32	195
5:44	54
7:12	24
7:22–23	207
10:22	98
11:28–29	57
11:28	18, 141
12:34	114
14:26–31	92n
15:7–8	108
15:19	105
16:24	35
19:3–9	196
19:16–22	61, 80n
19:21	167
21:12–13	53
22:37–40	39
22:39	32
23:23	40, 208
24:37	170
25:14–30	28n, 97n, 165
25:21	28
26:39	24
26:42	62

Mark

1:17	167
2:27	142
4:37–41	56n
6:3	140
6:31	141
8:34	183
9:24	56
9:42	152
15:23	131
16:15	82

Luke

1:15	132
2:27–32	149n
6:35–38	116
19:1–10	110
21:1–4	102n
22:3–4	55
23:39–43	110

John

3	207n
3:1–21	80n
3:3–6	21, 104n
3:3	111
3:21	167
8:11	42, 176
10:10	202
13:34	24
14: 21	65n
14:15	38
14:27	48
15:5	47
16:33	87
18:29–30	21n
21:15–17	167

Acts

8:3	27
9: 27	27
9:1–2	27
9:1–6	110
9:6	24, 95, 167
9:20	167
16:23–25	56n
18:1–3	140
20:35	34
24:16	22

Romans

1:17	17, 66n
1:26–27	173
3:10	47
3:23	47
5:20	39
7: 15	182n
7:14–24	87n
7:24	104
7:25	105
8:1	46
8:4	178
8:5–6	118
8:6–14	113n
8:7–8	105
8:7	113, 207
8:8–10	182n
8:11	106
8:16–17	35
8:28	57, 92, 223

(continues)

Scriptural Index

Romans (continued)

8:35	98
8:37–39	99
10:17	84
12:1	137
12:2	20, 97
13:9	32
14:23	40, 56

1 Corinthians

2:14	122
2:16	16
6:9	173, 180, 181
6:15	173
6:19	171
7:12–16	198
8:7	22
10:13	16, 64, 183
10:31	124
12:7–12	29
12:31	53
13:1–3	30
13:8	92
13:13	23
15:31	34

2 Corinthians

3:6	38
3:18	119
5:17	104, 111
6:14	190
9:7	102
10:5	106, 152

Galatians

2:20	93
3:11	66n
5:6	35
5:14	32
5:22–23	30
6:7–9	111

Ephesians

4:11–13	29
4:12–13	30
4:13–14	100
4:15	112n
4:26	53
6:4	114, 152

Philippians

2:3–4	35
2:5	20, 79, 106
3:14	100
4:7	12
4:8	119

Colossians

1:27	93
2:10	18

1 Timothy

1:5	22, 42, 108
1:9–10	180
1:10	181
3:4	152
3:9	22
4:2	22
6:20	12

2 Timothy

1:7	40, 46, 86
1:12	18
2:15	95
2:22	164
4:7	98
4:10	96

Titus

1:7	132

Hebrews

7:25	48, 208
10:25	73
10:38	66n
11:8–9	57n
11:8–10	99n
11:24–26	96
11:24–27	61n
11:29	66
11:32–33	67
13:4	178

James

1:5–6	78
1:6	67
1:12	183
2:8	32
2:10	45
4:4	53
4:7	114

1 Peter

1:2	152
2:2	112
2:11	124
3:11	54, 115
4:1–2	182
4:10	29
5:7	67

2 Peter

2:10–15	113
3:18	112n

1 John

1:9	45
3:1	36
3:4	40
3:9	182n
3:14	43
3:15	107
3:15	55
4:10	36
4:16	196
4:16	66
4:18	40
4:21	42
5:4	67
5:18	182n

Jude

7	170
24	64

Revelation

7:14	170
12:17	170
13:10	67
14:12	67, 170
22:14	170

General Index

abortion, 176, 190
air, 139
alcohol, 130
anger, 54
attitude toward sexual deviants, 174
behaviorism, 109, 205
caffeine, 135
character growth, ch. 3
competitive sports, 139, 140
conflicts, types, 60-62
conscience, 22
dating, 186-189
dedication of children, 148, 164
dependence, psychological, 10, 11, 18, 75
depression, 33, 54, 56, 168, 224
determinism, 9, 205, 212, 217–223
diet, ch. 18, 147
drugs, 11, 128, 138
empiricism, 205
Encounter groups, ch. 10, 205
eight laws of health, 137
emotionality, 51
evolution, 220
exercise, 139
existentialism, 65
food, ch. 18
free will, 9, 213
frustration, 33
guilt, overcoming, 17, ch. 7, 90

hypnosis, ch. 11
individuality, ch. 4
L.A.W., 10, 88
legalism, 206
love, ch. 5
marriage outside the faith, 190
nakedness, 69, 71
nativist, 205
nutrition,
paranoia, 32
pastoral counseling, 49
predestination, 213
promiscuity, 188
purposivism, 212, 217
remarriage, 197
reputation, 21–22
rest, 141
schizophrenia, 32, 158
self-image, 34, 47, 189
situationism, 65
sunshine, 139
talents, 28, 187
temperance, 143
treatment, psychological
    conflicts with Christian methods, 20–21,
    44, 72–73, 86, 206–208
trust in God, 143
vacations, 142–143
water, 137

Books by Colin and Russell Standish

Antichrist Is Here, The   10.95

A newly updated, second edition! Colin & Russell Standish look carefully at the Scriptural identification of the antichrist.This is a "must-read" for those who are interested in Biblical prophecy and its outworking in contemporary history.

Big Bang Exploded, The   11.95

The Big Bang hypothesis has held sway as the dominant explanation of the origin of the universe. The authors boldly present evidence which they assert supports, far more closely, the fiat creation concept than the evolutionary model. This is another of the increasing challenges which evolutionary scientists must address if their credibility is not to be seriously undermined.

Education for Excellence   11.95

In the ministry of the apostle Paul, the culture, philosophy and education of paganism was confronted by the principles of God-given education."For the wisdom of this world is foolishness to God. For it is written, He taketh the wise in their own craftiness."(1 Cor. 3:19) It goes directly to the word of God for the educational principles for the sons and daughters of the King of the Universe.

Entertainment Syndrome, The   8.95

Never in our history has there been such a systematic attempt to destroy the minds of a generation. In graphic detail, the authors portray what can be the outcome of even the simplest forms of what many might consider to be "innocent" entertainment. With alternative activities.

Evangelical Dilemma, The   10.95

Rarely has a book in modern times so thoroughly examined the teachings of Evangelical Protestantism as does the Evangelical Dilemma. The authors leave no stone unturned not only to expose the dilemma of modern-day Evangelicalism, but also to offer clear biblical solutions to the dilemma. This is a must book for evangelical clergy and laity.

Georgia Sits on Grandpa's Knee   7.95

Pastor Russell Standish, an Australian physician who specialized in internal medicine, spent many years in Southeast Asia as a medical missionary. Russell's grandaughter Georgia loved to sit on her grandpa's knee and hear stories of "the old times" when her daddy was a little boy in the mission field, and had such exciting times. Of course, it is Russell's delight to relate to children of all ages these tales of a family era now past, sharing the joys of life together as a family.

God's Solution for Depression, Guilt and Mental Illness
9.95

The authors believe that true biblical principles have the most complete answer to the escalating emotional and social issues confronting society today, that true mental health is dependent upon a right relationship with God. You will find the insights of this book to be of inestimable value to their Christian experience.

Grandpa's Back   available soon

Holy Relics or Revelation   14.95

For the devout Christian, faith is in the revealed Word. When Biblical archaeology confirms the Scripture, it stirs the heart. Yet mostly within a single decade, Ron Wyatt had sought out and claimed the most amazing Biblical sites and relics. In this book, the Standish Brothers examine the Wyatt claims in depth, going beyond his videotaped claims.

Liberty in the Balance   12.95

The blood-stained pathway to religious and civil liberty faces its greatest test in 200 years. The United States "Bill of Rights" lifted the concept of liberty far beyond the realm of toleration to an inalienable right for all citizens. This book from the Standish Brothers traces the courageous battle for freedom, a battle made glorious by the lives of many martyrs.

Lord's Day, The

The Lord's Day is a term used only once in Scripture. In his famous encyclical *Dies Domini*, Pope John Paul II commenced with these words, "The Lord's Day–as Sunday was called from apostolic times." To many Protestants, this was an unexpected and much approved declaration from the pontiff of the Roman Catholic Church. In preparing this book, the authors thoroughly researched the claims made in favor of the apostolic roots of the Lord's Day, Sunday.

Modern Bible Translations Unmasked   10.95

This is a fascinating book that will challenge the reader to consider two very serious problems with modern Bible translations: first, the use of corrupted Greek manuscripts; and second, translational bias. This is a must read for anyone interested the veracity and accuracy of the Word of God.

Mystery of Death, The   8.95

Most people hold life precious, yet all know that death is inevitable. But what then? Pagan or Christian, the opinions vary widely. In this book, the history of these various concepts is reviewed and the words of Scripture are investigated for a definitive and unchallengeable answer.

Perils of Ecumenism

The march of ecumenism seems almost unstoppable. It would seem that only a handful of small church groups has continued to resist the power of this movement. The authors see this movement as very clearly identified in Holy Scriptures, one devised by the arch-deceiver to beguile the inhabitants of the world. This book is too important to be treated lightly by those who are the architects of the ecumenical movement or by professed Christians inclined to support them in their objectives.

Pope's Letter and the Sunday Law   7.95

Unquestionably the most trenchant critical evaluation of the recent papal Apostolic Letter. Examines the Biblical foundations upon which the pope seeks to buttress his cleverly crafted letter. John's illumination of end times in Rev. Chapter 13 reveals a unity of two superpowers which will unite together to fearfully persecute those who will yield their will only to Christ and His truth.

Sacrificial Priest, The   15.95

Moses, Paul and John all witnessed the splendor and majesty of the heavenly sanctuary. But beyond the sanctuary itself, Paul and John testified to the two thousand year ministry of the risen Saviour in this sanctuary. The authors provide a fascinating Biblical explanation of this little-studied ministry of Christ. They offer irrefutable evidence of the first and second apartment ministry of Jesus. As the sun sets on this world's history, they present an impelling reason for the study of this fascinating theme.

Second Coming, The   7.95

The Apostle Paul refers to the Second Coming of Jesus as the blessed hope (Titus 2:12). As you study the New Testament you will find a central theme of hope in the return of Jesus Christ. In this newly updated work, Colin & Russell Standish present a "wake-up call" for every complacent Christian, despite what their belief is concerning man's state in death.

Two Beasts, 3 Deadly Wounds & 14 Popes   16.95

The Book of Revelation has been characterized as a mystery. Yet the book describes itself as the "Revelation of Jesus Christ" (Rev. 1:1). A revelation is the opposite of a mystery. In this book, Russell & Colin Standish, using Scripture as its own interpreter, unravel aspects of the "mystery" and unveil a portion of the revelation.

Youth Do You Dare   6.95

If you are a young person looking for workable answers to the many issues that confront you today, this book is meant for you. Set out in short, relevant chapters, this book addresses questions concerning the meaning of life, and how to handle the myriad temptations that Satan places before young people today.

Other HP Publications

Christ and Antichrist   24.95

First published in 1846 by a well-known Presbyterian minister, who calls this book "not sectarian, but a Christian & Protestant work." He hoped that the removal of obstacles might result in a more rapid spread of the Gospel. He saw one of these obstacles as "Anti-christianity," by which term he described the Papal system.

Distinctive Vegetarian Cuisine   14.95

100% vegan cooking, with no animal products–no meat, milk, eggs, cheese, or even honey. Even more healthful . . . no irritating spices or condiments are used. Most of the ingredients can be found at your local market. Additional nutritional information and helpful hints. Make your dinner table appealing to the appetite!

Food for Thought   10.95

Where does the energy which food creates come from? What kinds of foods are the most conductive to robust health and well being in all dimensions of our life? What is a balanced diet? Written by a healthcare professional, this book examines the food we prepare for our table within a setting which provides "food for thought."

Heroes of the Reformation   14.95

This volume brings together a comprehensive picture of the leaders of the Reformation who arose all over Europe. The authors of this volume have made a sincere endeavor to bring the men of Protestantism alive in the hearts of this generation.

History of the Gunpowder Plot   13.95

Originally published on the 300th anniversary of the November 5th, 1605, plot aimed at the destruction of the English Realm, Philip Sydney's account of one of the most audacious conspiracies ever known to the ancient or modern world is filled with royal intrigue of the court of James the First, Rome-backed Jesuit infiltrators and an aristocratic little band of traitors. The failed plot became part of English popular culture.

History of the Reformation of the Sixteenth Century
19.95

In history and in prophecy, the Word of God portrays the long continued conflict between truth and error. Today we see an alarming lack of understanding in the Protestant Church concerning the cause and effect of the Reformation. This reprinted masterpiece pulls back the curtain of history and divine providence to reveal the true catalyst for the Reformation—God's Word and His Holy Spirit.

History of the Reformation in the Time of Calvin
(Merle d'Aubigne, 4 volumes)   129.95

Originally an 8 volume work, is reprinted in these 4 volumes. The renovation of the individual, of the Church, and of the human race, is the theme. If the Holy Ghost kindles the lamp of truth in man, it is (according to Calvin) to the end that the entire man should be transformed. In the Kingdom of Christ, he says, it is only the new man that flourishes and has any vigor, and whom we ought to take into account. This renovation is, at the same time, an enfranchisement; and we might assign, as a motto to the Reformation accomplished by Calvin, as well as to apostolical Christianity itself, these words of Jesus Christ: The truth shall make you free (John 8:32).

History of the Waldenses   12.95

During the long centuries of papal supremacy, the Waldenses defied the crushing power of Rome and rejected its false doctrines and human traditions. This stalwart people cherished and preserved the pure Word of God. It is fitting that this edition of their history should be reprinted to keep alive the spirit and knowledge of this ancient people. May it rekindle in the heart of all God's people the love of the truth and an unflinching courage to stand, whatever the cost.

Law and the Sabbath, The   9.95

If Christians are under grace and not the law, how can the Sabbath be relevant today? A fierce controversy is swirling around the role the Ten Commandments should play in the church of the 21st Century. With a foreword by the late Elder Joe Crews, here is a book that dares to examine the Bible's own answers—with unfailing scriptural logic and a profound appreciation for the doctrine of righteousness by faith.

Method of Grace, The   14.95

In this faithful reprint, John Flavel thoroughly outlines the work of God's Spirit in applying the redemptive work of Christ to the believer. Readers will search their hearts and find their faith challenged and enriched. In the true Puritan tradition, a clearly defined theology is delivered with evangelistic fervor, by an author urgently concerned about the eternal destiny of the human soul.

The Reformation in Spain   13.95

The boldness with which Luther attacked the abuses and the authority of the Church in Rome in the 16th Century attracted attention throughout Christendom. Luther's writings, along with the earlier ones of Erasmus, gained a foothold with a Spanish people hungry for the truth. Thomas M'Crie makes a case for a Spain free of the religious errors and corruptions that ultimately dried up the resources and poisoned the fountains of a great empire.

Romanism and the Reformation   12.95

The Reformation of the Sixteenth Century, which gave birth to Protestantism, was based on Scripture. It gave back to the world the Bible. Such Reformation work needs to be done again. The duty of diffusing information on the true character and history of "Romanism and the Reformation" is one which presses on God's faithful people in these days.

Truth Triumphant
14.95

The prominence given to the "Church in the Wilderness" in the Scriptures establishes without argument its existence and emphasizes its importance. The doctrines of the primitive Christian church spread to Ireland, Scotland and Wales. The same challenges exist today with the Remnant Church in its final controversy against the powers of evil to show the holy, unchanging message of the Bible.

Strange Fire
11.95

The Olympic games are almost universally accepted as a great international festival of peace, sportsmanship, and friendly competition. Yet the games are riddled with conflict, cheating, and objectionable competitiveness. Discover the disturbing truth about the modern Olympics and the role of Christianity in the rise of this neo-pagan religion.

Who Are These Three Angels?
6.95

Millions believe angels exist and thousands have encountered them in the last few years, but few truly understand the nature and purpose of these heavenly beings. The messages of three holy angels unfold for us events that are soon to take place in rapid succession. Their warning is not to be taken lightly, as they tell of political and religious movements that signal the soon return of Jesus.

About Hartland Publications

Office hours: 9:00 a.m. to 5:00 p.m. Mon.—Thurs.,
9:00 a.m. to 12:00 p.m. Fri. - Eastern time
You may order by telephone, fax, mail, email or on the website.
Payments in $US by check, money order, most credit cards.
Order line: 1-800-774-3566   FAX 1-540-672-3568
Website: www.hartlandpublications.com or
www.hartlandpublications.org
Email: sales@hartlandpublications.org